The Magical Empath

Book I
Healing & Evolution

By Lyra Adams

Copyright © 2020 Lyra Adams
All rights reserved.
This edition: 978-0-578-65536-9
First Edition

Book reviewers, booksellers and librarians may quote brief passages (75 words or less) and post cover image in a printed, online or broadcast review of book without permission from the publisher. Otherwise, no part of this publication may be reproduced physically or digitally, stored in a retrieval system, or transmitted in any form or by any means (including electronic, mechanical, photocopying, recording or otherwise) without prior written permission from the publisher.

Cover Design was divinely inspired
Cover Creator: Sam Smith
Photographer: Miroslav Halama
On The Cover: Natural Labradorite Photo Used With Permission

Media info available at www.lyraadams.com

Life Garden Publishing Inc.
P.O. Box 333
Borden, IN 47106

Table of Contents

About The Author 1
Introduction 3
An Army of Us 9
Are Empaths Real? 15
Myths About Empaths 25
Empaths in Culture & History 31
Glimpses & Goals 37
Science & The Woo Woo 47
Self Care & Regulation 53
Working With Energy 65
Chakras 87
Filtering & Protection 107
Luck Energy 117
The Flow of Money 123
Receiving Energy 129
Managing Energies 135
Walking Backward 151
Selflessness = Less Self 155

Building Trust	171
Acts of Transformation	193
Blessing or Curse	201
Balance	211
Patterns	215
Inner Child	221
Creativity	231
Fear of Conflict	237
Alone or Lonely?	249
Victim or Victor	259
Anxiety & Depression	265
Control vs. Allowing	279
Wealth	283
Attracting Synchronicity	289
Geo-Politics	305
Appendix	309
Bibliography	319

Dedication

*This book is dedicated to
all who desire a magical life*

Acknowledgement

*Many thanks to my current loyal followers and those
in the future! I would like to acknowledge my
extreme gratitude to God/Goddess/All That Is for life,
inspiration, wisdom and revelations.*

About The Author

Some say she is a dreamer ... and that is true. Lyra is a dreaming empath, but so much more. She is an advocate and champion for those that have been victimized. She is a mentor to those who want to level up on their spiritual path. Lyra is affectionately known as the Queen of Synchronicity because she often experiences events way beyond coincidence. She states her "life is an extraordinary mixture of extreme blessings, divine intervention, and tragedies that often turn to triumph."

To date, her writings have focused on self-help within the holistic healing spectrum. She has been working steadily on an alternative history fantasy series.

Lyra hosts the Podcast, *Breaking Free ~ Healing the Emotional Effects of Sexual Abuse* available on numerous platforms. She is an advocate for males and females who are victims, survivors and eventually SUR-THRIVERS!

Areas of lifelong interest are astrology, divination, channeling, meditation, herbs, flower essences, psychology and holistic healing. Lyra views many of these topics as tools for tapping into her favorite subject of all ~ consciousness.

Join Lyra at her website or any of her social media accounts. She loves to hear from you!

Website: https://www.lyraadams.com
Email: hello@lyraadams.com

Twitter: @lyraadams
Pinterest: lyraadamsauthor
Facebook: @authorlyraadams
Instagram: @booksbylyra
Goodreads: goodreads.com/lyraadamsauthor

Other Media By Lyra Adams

Books:

Dreaming Synchronicity: Journey of an Empath
BLOOM ~ Holistic Healing Methods For Sexual Abuse
Real Love ~ Finding "The One" Lasting Relationship
The Magical Empath Book II ~ Rebirth & Manifestation

Journals:

Dreams & Synchronicities: A Recordkeeping Journal

Podcast:

Breaking Free ~ Healing The Emotional Effects of Sexual Abuse

Introduction

Dear Fellow Empath,

I always ask myself when working on a piece of writing the 'why' of doing the task. Do we really need another book about empaths? Yes, we do. Now that so many have discovered their true nature, it is time to bring ourselves into a new paradigm. A new world of thought and emotions where we utilize our gifts in a way that brings relief from personal suffering. This rise in our evolution levels us up for the consciousness shifts people are moving toward.

At some point in life, almost everyone wants to reach out and scoop up an invisible force often referred to as magic. Fantasy literature and movies featuring magical powers are extremely popular. Humans are attracted to finding a way to level the playing fields of their lives. Often, they feel the only way this leveling can be achieved is through something which only requires the wave of a wand along with reciting words. Those who have grown up watching many of the children's movies know that the concept of magic was presented often. Deep in our psyche, we suspect it exists. At times, we have seen or touched this elusive force in our own life. Yet, our logical rational mind tells us to snap out of this thinking and back to 'reality'.

Magic is a concept that we would love to harness. We want it to make our lives easier and bring us the results we desire. What humans often fail to see is that it's real and exists all around us. It could be that the word 'magic' does not fully express the miraculous energy that is ever present. Physics plays with trying to define and capture its essence but always describes it with scientific terms that somehow fall flat and take out the very magic they are attempting to reduce down to a process. Religions strive to use its existence to prove their specific faiths, but the emphasis is on someone or something else containing the magic or miracles, not you. Paranormal researchers study its components in hope of proving the invisible to be visible.

Real magic is in everyday life. It appears moment by moment if we only open ourselves to its existence. All things that science can explain in detailed processes are indeed magical when viewed through a different life lens. And it is with that attitude that we attract more of the same magic. We are geared to attract more of what we focus upon. When it comes to empathic individuals, they have the capacity to affect or enact magic … if they choose to. Many empaths do not realize this about themselves yet. They are caught in a tight web of being different and not knowing how to live more free. No matter how much they desire that freedom of being, it often eludes them due to misunderstandings about their role and human conditions they find themselves in.

This book has been forming over a couple of years. It began with scribbles on paper and then a rough outline which evolved into typed chapters. Birthed over time, I saw many empaths struggling, and sometimes absolutely suffering, with how to deal with people and situations in their life. While I felt books available by other authors were doing a great job of defining what an empath is and how they experience life in this third dimensional reality, only some were giving tools for assisting an empath in navigating their high energy absorption and educating on what to avoid. This book series focuses on some of those same subjects, but the greater purpose is to show empaths how to create an absolutely magical life. And magical empathic lives do come true.

This does not mean that some beam of light comes down, shines upon you and turns everything understandable and wonderful. Although, it sounds simple if it could happen. Rather, what we explore in *The Magical Empath* are all the little nuances that are holding us back from utilizing our gifts into the next decade and beyond.

While we look at practical, real world tools for conquering many of the hurdles empaths feel daily, we will also employ metaphysical concepts that greatly assist in allowing empaths to leap forward. These tools provide a path to make this paradigm shift with grace and ease. Likewise, for those who prefer a slower pace, that choice is possible as well. Come as you are, where you are.

Yet, there is something pushing us. Don't you feel it? It nags at us to do something now. Time itself is speeding up and some of the old rules of physics are being washed away. It is time for us, as empaths, to level up our game — to grow in maturity and leadership. The only way we can do that is to work on ourselves.

Like any solid role playing game, we must possess the tools to wield our way through a maze of confusion and fears, seizing the right fortunate opportunities when they arise. While this game we are engaged in is completely an illusion, when we are playing it, the game feels very real. And that is what we do as empaths -- feel.

However, here is the dichotomy: part of being magical is never feeling hurried. Rather, we must feel encapsulated in an ethereal bubble floating toward our purpose and eventually home. What a delicate balance to achieve when faced with all the emotions that pour into the empath's field of knowing. Together, we can achieve this more of the time.

The Magical Empath is designed to be jumped into at any particular point you want. Each chapter is geared to equip you in moving forward toward clarity as an empath and fulfillment of your purpose. My hope is that you will read it in an intuitive fashion, allowing your own inner guidance to highlight what you want to accomplish each time you read, no matter which chapter you open up to. For convenience, many techniques within chapters are included in the Appendix, making it easy to find and review them when desired.

Another point I want to make in this introduction is that, often, the words or information just came to me. Subjects I needed to address were often presented as life lessons I was still experiencing some version of. I needed those events to happen to relay it to my empathic sisters and brothers. One event, in particular, seemed to come out of nowhere in the early morning hours. It raised my vibration significantly and gave thought impressions that, as far as I know, have not been openly taught before. Yet, I will admit that my own training is limited to my life experiences with others. I have been fortunate to have some of the most unique mentors with incredible gifts. Most of my exposure to those individuals began around the 1980's and extended for about fifteen years.

I then entered a different period, a healing time I needed to clear away serious debris from the past. This was coupled with earthly matters such as making career changes and financial gains for awhile. Later, I went through a dark night of the soul time for a decade that transformed me to the person you would meet right now.

During your reading of this book, I want to implore you to take notice of what topics or sections provide the most resistance for you. Any area that you feel an instant rejection of or any part that you avoid even listening to is showing you something. Some may read these areas and say, "Yes, I relate to that. I have been there, done that. Hope I don't do it again, but it could happen. Except this time, I will catch myself from falling into that behavior." This is because that empath now has the tools to do so. Find the parts that you want to avoid or regurgitate and embrace them if you can. It is there that your growth is calling you to master the next step and level up your game in this lifetime.

If something does not resonate with you at all, put it on a shelf. Perhaps you will come back to it later or maybe not at all.

I do not present myself as an ultimate expert, but only a teacher and idea generator. As a teacher, my goal is to inspire, offer solutions, and facilitate growth. Yet, I am keenly aware that as I take that role, often I grow more than the student. There is no doubt I am an empath. Assuming you are as well, we share that in common.

While writing this book, I dreamed I acquired a narrow wooden boat. Small in size, it could accommodate two adults. For the purpose of lying down within it, only one person would fit. In the dream, I fell asleep with my boat high up on a sandy beach. The location was warm and tropical and as I awoke in my boat, I found it had now gone to sea while I slept within it. Arising to a sitting position with my boat floating in the water, I was initially worried that I could have drowned while asleep, but I didn't.

Around me in the water were many others in their wooden boats. We laughed together as we floated on this beautiful day. We were shouting things in a friendly manner back and forth to each other. There were broad smiles and intense happiness.

Sensing I had work to do, I thought about getting my boat back to the shore. No sooner than the idea occurred, the boat was now on the sand. Without ores, thought alone moved me where I wanted to be. I waved goodbye from the sand and I saw others were also beginning to appear in their wooden boats alongside me on the beach. Many were coming into shore to join me.

While my dream time extended beyond where I ended it above, I began analyzing it as I awoke. I realized that the water my vessel was floating in represented the spiritual and the earth's sand represented the physical. My work, my mission I felt calling me was drawing me into the shoreline. I saw my fellow empaths in the spiritual waters alongside me and we were having a joyful time in the light of the sun. Yet, it was time to come into shore and get to work. While our tasks may not always be as euphoric in the physical as they are in spiritual waters, I hope you will join me in your vessel on this journey. Together, we each change reality as we usher in earth's paradigm shift.

Lyra

Author's Note: Throughout this series, I use the term God, Goddess, All That Is, God Source, Creator Source, to refer to the one ultimate Creator God Being

An Army of Us

"There's something magical about putting yourself into life. You've got to stand up and take responsibility for your own life and you cannot abandon that." ~ Bill Kurtis

Our galaxy is moving its position in space. Other galaxies are moving toward our current position. There is constant motion within the cosmos propelled by energy we do not fully understand yet. All of this motion creates change on all levels. On our planet, this includes changes in the plant and animal kingdoms. It also affects the waterways and land. Humans are also feeling the effects mentally, physically and spiritually. I believe you chose to come here now to assist in these changes. Empaths are helpers of the highest order and your kind is needed as we move from third density reality to the fourth "heart centered" density. We feel and know with our hearts. I believe we volunteered for this assignment and it is not easy.

You will hear some speak of moving into the fifth dimension. I have no quarrel with that statement. My studies taught me about specific densities which are separate from dimensions — yet similar in one sense. Ultimately, the numeral does not matter as much as the knowledge that this occurrence is happening now.

It has been said that, as we move from third to fourth density, a paradigm split will occur. This will consist of some humans staying in a world that may destroy itself, while others move into a beautiful new experience — a golden time spoke of as the true age of Aquarius. I learned of these two reality creation worlds in the early 1990's. Although no specific date was given, I wondered how such a thing could occur and have watched for the increasing signs of it over the years.

Around 2011 or 2012, the intensity of this move began to pick up steam. As truth continues to contract against matrix constructed realities, the birthing pains of splitting these two fraternal twins is evident. History and esoteric teachings that were pushed underground have told of this time for thousands of years. With this shift in mind, this first book in *The Magical Empath* series is produced with a distinct focus: to amplify and continue clearing away old residue so that we can land in the favored paradigm world.

Our position and where we land is a choice. The choice is made daily, moment by moment, in our hearts. It is questionable that we will gain admission if we have not leveled up and performed the inner work to get there. Our spirit will arrive where we resonate. Built upon the Universal Law of Correspondence, it is just that natural and simple.

How does the empath fit into this plan? It is common to feel very alone with the person you are inside. You know … the one you have been hiding or trying to tamp down. Yes, that one. The fact is, at this time in our world, there is an army of us. We are here for a reason. It is up to us to help usher in a world that is more transparent, feeling, and ultimately beautifully grounded in truths.

Most of the time when you go to a job, you have the skill set inside of you to walk in and perform the tasks. No one is going to tell you <u>not</u> to do your job. This is not the case with empaths. First, the skill set we were born with does get watered down as parents tell us those people we are seeing or hearing are just "our imagination". We are told we are 'too sensitive' and to let things roll off our back.

For some reason, many of us endured traumas severe enough to incite and elicit more extrasensory skills from us. It is common for empaths to come from families in which there are deeply organized religious beliefs that will never entirely mesh with the real us. So, there are many factors that stymie an empath to perform their work, much less live an extremely empowered, magical life.

Even as you try to come out of your tightly held empathic closet, you are afraid of what everyone will think.

How will they receive you? Will you be ridiculed or labeled crazy? Unfortunately, this can and does happen too frequently. Perhaps you have already experienced this.

Your early religious background may give rise to fears and preconceptions that interfere with you at times. It's like having your vehicle's antennae interrupted by power lines that are stationary in position along the road. You get that fuzzy feedback on the radio as you drive by and you have to learn to navigate past this while keeping yourself in your true space. Those power lines creating the static on your radio are background programming you learned. It is actually something that is indoctrinated in fear.

People often seek you out that steal your time, energy and other resources. Most do this unconsciously. Some do it deliberately. These different 'other selves' reflect back to you everything you need to learn to step into your power. They show you where you lack sufficient limits and how you may not fully love yourself. So there is an entire chest full of items that can interfere with the job you came here to do.

To move from where you are into a state of empowerment is critical to perform your mission and give your soul the satisfaction it is looking for. You have been driven since an early age that you are here to do something. What if that something begins with you finally knowing and being the real you on a very deep level? A true sense of accomplishment and freedom would come from stepping into a place of mastery over your emotions, utilizing them for the highest good of all.

Learning to care about how you feel and making that the absolute main priority will propel you toward the strong empathic person you can be. You have been told many times that your feelings do not count or that you need to put them aside and just ignore them. Yet, this is exactly what empaths must not do. Likewise, if you wallow in the negative, never identifying the root causes of your feelings, it is likely you could shut down and thwart your growth. You could completely crush your ability to do what you came here to do.

It is a delicate tight rope that you walk as an empath. You must actively learn to cultivate feelings of love, yet honor the darker shadowy thoughts as well. You must reach for and place yourself into an invisible world where you feel best. As situations, people and things appear that make you feel otherwise, you become strong enough to quickly identify what that is. This ability to cure it within your own field truly is the definition of rising above it.

The Magical Empath series is designed to show you the more eloquent moves to make on the chessboard of life. Empowerment through regulation and discernment, plus reaching a full understanding of who you are will propel you into your own magical destiny.

I feel an incredible sense of grace bestowed upon me in being an empath. It is a gratefulness that, at its center, contains a spinning ball of joy. I also feel a great sense of responsibility to do my best in this role.

Being an empath is whined about often. You will see in this writing the reasons why and what can be done to eliminate that distress. It is time to celebrate this personality type from a true sense of heart centered gratitude. This comes from having a real knowing that being an empath is an advantageous personality trait. The work of healing and progressing forward in this book will assist you in moving from any misery you experience at times to miracles. You are lucky -- incredibly fortunate!

In this book, you will master:

How to get past the uncomfortable feelings, such as anxiety, and on to the big magic that exists for advanced empaths.

How to consistently attract synchronicities into your life that blow your mind and confirm you are on the right track.

How to be soft, yet a formidable force for good.

How to live in a balanced way with increased sensitivity, creativity and joy.

How to magically erect a filter that allows into your field the feelings of others you want to take on or examine. Likewise, you will learn how to <u>not</u> be affected by those emotions coming in that you do not want.

You will gain considerable knowledge about energy — the essence of all — including how to protect, manage it, attract it and receive more of the good energy you desire.

And much more ….

If you feel ready to move ahead and go another few levels up in this game of life, please read on. The world could use our help, but we must first be adept and ready. Let's get started!

Notes - Thoughts - Ideas -
   Affirmations - Dreams

Are Empaths Real?

"That's the thing with magic. You've got to know it's still here, all around us, or it just stays invisible for you."
~ Charles de Lint

As of the time of this writing, the word 'empath' is still not fully recognized in many modern dictionaries. Software spell checkers will red flag it as being wrong. Auto-suggest will offer the word 'empathy'. Merriam-Webster did include the word with two meanings. Here is one of them:

"one who experiences the emotions of others; a person who has empathy for others"

The Oxford English dictionary offers this interesting definition:

"Empath: (chiefly in science fiction) a person with the paranormal ability to apprehend the mental or emotional state of another individual."

This may be due to the fact that the word empath was first used in the 1950's in a science fiction novel by J.T. McIntosh. In the story, the government is utilizing individuals who have certain paranormal skills. But notice the word 'chiefly'. I take this to mean primarily and added to the definition to negate people from affirming anything paranormal exists. And what does the word paranormal really mean? It means beyond the scope of normal scientific understanding. Yet, I would argue that many in the science community are well aware of what we term paranormal. They have utilized individuals who have these abilities in the past and I am sure they use them now as well. This is well documented in many different government programs in China, Russia and the United States.

Some psychologists and psychiatrists do not yet recognize the empath personality, although this is changing. The field of psychology is still young and mutable. Its classifications of personalities and maladies have made advancements, but it is still in discovery.

Today's student or worker in the field of psychology may describe an empath solely as someone who has been a victim of trauma or abuse and is at risk of continuing to experience trauma at the hands of others. Those "others" are often people who suffer from mental conditions such as narcissistic personality disorder (NPD); anti-social personality disorder; and psychopaths. Yet the one thing those who believe in empaths often say is that we absorb emotions. Certainly, we know that, but it is more than that. Empaths feel energy.

Notice I said energy, not emotions. While empaths certainly pick up on the emotions of others, they first primarily sense the energy of a person, group or place. This energy is often decoded to them via feelings they pick up within their own mind/body/spirit complex. This nuance allows us to further see how an empath experiences people and life. It also explains how empaths and people with personality disorders attract each other; something I go into much more detail about later.

Emotions are a type of fuel for the energy. They assist in spreading what energy is present. They are also a decoding of information, almost like a language of the energy. If an empath is attuned and chooses to, they can pick up the energy of persons, places and things. Think of someone you meet for the first time. All outward behavioral clues being projected by them says they are an outgoing, happy individual. The empath may pick up on subtle energy from that person that projects otherwise. They sense there is something that does not match what is going on. This is an example of what I am speaking of when it comes to reading energy.

Much of the time it feels to an empath as if the emotional aspects hit them first, especially if someone is in distress. Emotional challenges that other people are going through strike the empath with intensity. This does not mean that an empath is always sympathetic with what the other person is directly feeling. Yet, often they are. It means that an empath has their feelers out there and can sense what others are projecting. This is done on a voluntary and involuntary basis. As an empath grows in their skill, they can learn to embrace what they want to pick up or let go of.

Energy is being projected from another person whether they realize it or not. On a more subtle level, the true energy or vibration that person is resonating at is perceptible to the empath. To be fair, this is not one sense picking up on everything. An empath is using all of their senses.

Visual cues are coming in, such as someone's posture or stance. It could be the way they just keep fiddling with their hair when speaking. Auditory cues arrive in the tone and pitch of the other person's voice. We could notice where they stutter or hesitate to answer. Smell may not play a huge part, but who knows? This could also be unknowingly received. Many animals and insects give off certain scents or pheromone signals when in various forms of mating or distress.

Could taste be involved? Have you ever heard someone say, "that person just leaves a bad taste in my mouth"? Yes, it could be. Our physical response to someone may have our saliva flowing more than normal or leave our mouth dry.

Have you ever hugged someone and they seemed limp, distant or cold? Perhaps you felt they were hugging you very hard or too long. All senses can be involved in this unseen knowing about others. All humans have the ability to pick up on these cues.

Yet, empaths go a step further. We see this when an empath speaks of walking into an empty room where something does not feel right and you find out a major fight or argument occurred in the room thirty minutes earlier. In a situation like this, there are no humans present to send visual, auditory or other cues. The lingering vibration is present because everything around us – absolutely all matter is made up of vibration or energy. High emotional situations are fueled and they leave an imprint. So, if you have an argument in the kitchen with someone, don't forget to "clear the air" before leaving.

Empaths often receive messages while asleep in a dream. I am a dreaming empath. They may notice little strange coincidences that happen close together – things where the probable odds are incredibly slim. As they pay attention and look for the meaning in these synchronicities, they are often able to avert disaster; assist people from some type of danger; or even just have a knowing that they need to take another route to work that day due to traffic without using an app for such a thing.

Empaths are receiving information constantly that would make no sense to persons who are not empathic. And we do not need to share that with those who do not believe in the unseen in order to convince them. A common example could happen when you and your non-empath friend meet someone new. This person strikes you as disingenuous and not to be trusted. Your friend is quite taken with them but can detect, from your possible silence or body language, you are not. You can simply tell your friend there is something about that person that makes you uneasy without going into a long speech about being an empath. You are here to help and sometimes your discernment level is very high. Yet, you also have times when you are tricked and it is very low. However, most of the time, you know.

Crowds can be exhausting to an empath. First, they feel their best when in non crowded spaces. More importantly, they are often unconsciously bombarded with the moods and emotions of those around them. Even at a joyful event such as a crowded sporting event or concert, an empath may love the energy they are feeling. However, they may be drained at a certain point and need seclusion afterward. Again, it is about all the varied energies going on.

It is common for empaths to feel the physical pain or discomfort of another person they are close to. For instance, a person with a normal level of empathy may feel great sadness or sympathy for someone they see physically hurt. Some empaths actually have the capacity to feel the other person's pain within their own body. This happens involuntarily and is most common with persons the empath is close to.

Looking at the two most polarized opinions the general public has of empaths, we see those who do not believe they exist at all. They proclaim empaths do not exist! There are probably many empaths throughout history who have been locked up in asylums, perhaps given drugs to control what others deemed was their mania. For certain, there are those who were said to be witches, in league with the devil, and then stoned, drowned or burned at the stake.

Recently, some people believe that empaths are born and often come into families or life situations voluntarily on a soul level to experience certain challenges or lessons that further develop their empathic abilities. We often find that empathic personalities come from a lineage of others who held these same skills but perhaps did not speak of it … or did. I often wish I had been born into a situation where it was nurtured. Even today, if I mention to some relatives that I had a precognitive dream or I have a 'knowing' about something, they will fall silent and then change the subject. Somehow, the conversation is uncomfortable for them so I often do not speak of it unless it directly impacts them. If so, I will not worry about them being uneasy with the information. It may help them in some way.

In between these two ideas are a myriad of explanations as to whether or not empaths are real. As the author, I do not believe it is my position to tell you what to think on this subject. I am an empath. So, this entire book is really for empaths by an empath. Therefore, criticism of it by non-empaths is irrelevant to me.

What about those defining themselves as highly sensitive? There is an ongoing debate regarding this and I trend toward including them in the class of empath personalities. Perhaps they are on one part of the scale of empaths and there are varying degrees of this personality trait.

What about indigo and crystal children? There are many who classify their personalities as star children, lightworkers, starseeds, rainbow warriors and more. Wait! This book is for empaths by an empath. You are getting out of the flow here.

The fact is many empaths share or overlap into these other categories in varying degrees. So, if you felt drawn to read this book, you probably fall somewhere on the empathic spectrum and will benefit from the information contained herein, whether you label yourself as an empath or not. You can be a rainbow warrior and an empath. Your soul group as an indigo or crystal child does not preclude you from also being an empath.

Empaths acutely feel energy vibrations around them whether they are emanating from other people, the collective vibratory current, or positive/negative charges in a space. The empath's ability to interpret this energy is dependent upon their individual advancement and knowledge they have acquired. While a strong intuition is inherent with empaths, they may find that the dissemination of the information they are receiving can be challenging at times. Empaths may have difficulty separating what is their own internal energy and something that is coming from another source because they are often in an absorbing mode of vibration around them.

Highly sensitive personalities still fall under the umbrella of those who are more attuned to these vibrations. However, they could lack broader abilities that we credit to existing more in the sixth sensory arena. This does not mean they could not develop those abilities and broaden into a more traditional empath personality. I have known people who were instantly given clairvoyant or clairaudient abilities. Sometimes they experienced it after waking from a long sleep. Some obtained their psychic abilities after an accident – usually where there was head trauma involved. It was as if something opened up for them and they were able to receive information they could not access before. Hopefully, no one has to be injured or hit their head to access or develop these abilities.

An important, notable difference is that highly sensitive people do not need to be empaths – but empaths must also be highly sensitive. It is possible there could be an evolution wherein the highly sensitive person may spend the majority of their time processing the information they are receiving in a more analytical way and the empath is processing the information they receive as feelings, images and a very sure knowing.

Like the empath, highly sensitive people can feel a need to be alone for time periods and withdraw from others so they may recharge. This is true even if they seem like a very outgoing dynamic person. In that case, it is often more so that they need this time of renewal and reflection. If they are in occupations that put them in front of people where they feel they have to be "on", this is very emotionally draining. Thus, it also can manifest physical stress responses such as anxiety and depression.

Contrary to what many think, there are numerous empaths who are able to carry on in extroverted ways. This can range from professional speakers, performers, sales positions, designers, artists and more. No matter the profession, one thing all have in common is the need to get away and be alone afterward. For some, an alone period might be needed just prior to a performance. The empath's need to have alone time does not mean they do not like being more public. Rather, it indicates they can only be good at it for a limited period of time.

Artists of any type usually share this and every creative artist could easily be highly sensitive, if not an empath. At a book signing, art show or concert, they are putting themselves out there. Because the empath tends to give so freely of their energy at these types of events, the duration can be challenging for them. They will likely feel the need to get away and escape at the end, retreating back to where they feel the most comfort. This is the point where they can begin to recharge.

There is also the possibility that some empaths and highly sensitive people have sensory processing issues wherein certain sounds, sights, smells or touch bother them to one degree or another. The senses coming in could make them feel overly excited or anxious. Although I am very close to two individuals who have sensory processing sensitivities, I cannot say with certainty this is part of the empathic spectrum. Nor can I say it is not. There is not enough research or information to make a clear statement on this.

Certainly, we can agree that all of these things are made of energy or vibration — sound, light, scent, and touch. These are energies the individual is picking up, and for reasons not fully known, are overwhelming to them in some manner. Let us trust there is a reason for this and like many things, it could remain hidden to us at this time. Let us bless all abilities even when we do not understand them.

Further development of psychic abilities can offer a lightening quick answer or knowing for the empath. When an empath is operating in this state, they are doing so at an enhanced level in tune with certain vibratory frequencies that give impressions into what is true or not. To put it in computer speak, they are correctly analyzing the ones and zeros as they are presented in the information field surrounding them. All forms of life (vibration) are made up of this information taking form of some type.

Empaths internalize feelings in their quest to deal with them. At times, it can appear as overly concerned responses at the expense of the empath's own well being. This can lead to a downhill motion over time in which the empath becomes resentful, and eventually angry. At this point, the empath is often surmising that people are not intuiting their needs and reciprocating all the care they have offered to others around them.

Empaths have a knack for attracting those who want to feed off their good nature. They almost always lack sufficient boundaries to protect themselves from such individuals. This behavior is because they do not want to make waves or be perceived as angry. They need considerable skills and tools to deal with such individuals in order to live the wonder filled life empaths deserve.

Are empaths also telepathic? Some definitely have a heightened sense of telepathy. Feeling energy, however, and knowing someone's thoughts are two different things. An empath senses what someone else is feeling through the energy they are putting off. A telepath sees/hears/feels the other person's thoughts or actions that are normally not perceived. It is important to note that people can have high psychic skills and not be empaths.

In parapsychology today, it is recognized that an empath has sensory attributes that allow them to have some sort of psi abilities. Of course, this has always been a given about telepaths. For the psychic empath, often the two merge. They can sense your feelings and also hear your thoughts. A medium may also be an empath, but not all empaths are mediums.

Overall, I feel like we need a new word. Something that goes beyond just feeling empathy for others and brings out the supernormal aspects. If we could break it down, there are those that are empathic and those that are super-empathic. It is within that concept we move toward becoming the magical empath.

The cure for everything in our world is for a certain number of us to push things over the edge with the love we can generate together. We have often heard "physician heal thyself". I am calling for empaths to heal themselves. We need to make a consistent goal to look at what is presented to us, what we need to let go of and what is not working. This is the first step, along with meditation and building skills that will greatly enhance each empath and our world collectively.

Myths About Empaths

"Real magic is not about gaining power over others: it is about gaining power over yourself." ~ Rosemary Ellen Guiley

Information abounds today on the subject of empaths and highly sensitive people. Truly, we are in a period of discovery on this topic. We are also further defining what an empath is or is not. Internet searches will bring up books, blog posts, e-zine articles and videos on empaths. Much of it is relevant. Some of it is redundant or misleading, often being composed primarily as click bait. I found items that are absolute myths or misstatements about how empaths operate and wanted to address these to clear up misunderstandings that could occur.

One statement I came across is that empaths look at the world with wonder and curiosity and they do this from a young age all the way through their later years. The reason given for this is that empaths are, by nature, learners. They ask questions, without judgment, in order to learn and feel the experiences of others. I felt this could definitely be true but it was based upon an unstated weak premise: that other people do not approach the world in the same manner.

The truth is that both empaths and non-empaths can look at the world with wonder and curiosity. Some empaths spend a good portion of their lives not asking questions of people. This could be to avoid taking on more of their feelings as they express their answers. They were already picking up on the feelings the person was knowingly or unknowingly projecting. Often overwhelmed by this, they purposely do not delve further. The exception to this would be either:

1) An empath with good boundary mechanisms in place that seeks to understand more; or

2) An empath in a codependent phase wanting to draw the other person out and fix them.

Another myth is that empaths always act on their intuition. Again, this depends upon the empath's development and self-knowing. An empath who has fully integrated all the parts of themselves will know when their intuition is speaking (instead of fear) and act accordingly. Other empaths still integrating may stay in a state of indecision, waiting for other validations, before going with that gut feeling.

A third myth is that empaths manage their environment by carefully choosing who they allow into their circle. Again, only a very advanced empath will do these things consistently. This is a learning process. Empaths, especially when they are in a codependency mode, will often be the ones to <u>not</u> be able to say "no" and set appropriate boundaries for their environment. Further, some toxic personality types are very attracted to hanging around the empath and sucking the life out of them in various ways. Sadly, most empaths are very susceptible to psychic vampirism.

I came across a myth that empaths can and will engage only in certain vocations. For instance, it was suggested that you would not find empaths in sales. Empaths are employed in a wide variety of occupations. I will agree that those occupations may not always be best suited for them. However, many thrive financially in occupations you would not expect.

Whether they are selling automobiles, widgets or homes, many empaths do well at this occupation. They often have the advantage of knowing what their customers want and clients are feeling. Generally, people purchase items driven by their emotions and only use their logic to back up their decision. Empaths are capable of giving over the top service because of their caring nature. Working closely with the public like this does take a toll on them emotionally each day. If they have a home life where they can unwind and recharge, it makes it easier for them to show up and do their job the next day.

Many musicians, actors, and artists are required to engage with their customers — the buying public. While many of them are more introverted by nature, they know this is part of the gig. Often, performers get energy high from their audience. While they give back everything they have to that audience, there is a reciprocal energy transference going on. This can initially have the performer feeling overly excited after the show. Empaths have a sensitive nervous system. They drain from all the excitement quickly and feel they need time alone. Often, they will need to recharge within a certain period of time after the performance has ended. Many also report they need time alone before going on stage. I, myself, have experienced this feeling of needing to hole up and be alone for a bit when I used to be in a band. I really wanted some space between me and my mates while I gathered my thoughts and energies prior to us beginning the show. The response of the audience definitely had the ability to feed me with great joy and pleasure. In turn, I continued to feed that back to them.

Typically, empaths shy away from crowds. This is certainly true and not a myth at all. Again, in the idea of performance, the crowd is separated by a staging area. The empath is able to put some distance between the audience and their performance so that they do not feel as clustered. Also, they are there for a different purpose — to entertain, to give energy and hopefully receive good reciprocal feelings in the process.

Another mythical idea that has been purported is that empaths are always fully present. Just like all people, they can find themselves caught up in thoughts of the past or the future. Their feelings are not always grounded in what is happening currently, but could be stemming from the past. The empath's feelings could be emanating from the future, either in real possible events or just plain old worries.

There is also the idea that empaths are these shining people who are always inspiring others. Empaths have the capacity to do this, but it is not always true. Young empaths are often on overload with their emotions and still sorting out if the feelings they are experiencing are coming from them or someone else. They are highly affected by things going on in the world — even if they do not cognitively know about them. For instance, an earthquake or other disaster that happens somewhere else in the world may have some feeling anxious for a couple of days before it happens. They do not know what it is or where the anxiety is coming from.

Young or immature empaths may suffer from an overwhelm of emotions and even physical ailments. They are usually picking this up from others, possibly people they do not even know. Until they reach a point of grounding more effectively and not taking on the energy of others so easily, they can suffer from many different feelings of anxiety they don't know what to do with. Anytime empaths are dealing with energies they do not know what to do with, they are not going to be fountains of inspiration. Instead, you may find them withdrawn, anxious, depressed or just "off". During these moments, they often cannot put their finger on what or why.

Empaths are healers. This statement is true. However, healing is a skill that you build. You may have been born with a propensity to understand and compose music but it is only by doing so that you build that skill. It is no different with healing.

Empaths are psychic. This is true for many. Each empath I know of has some heightened sixth sensory abilities. Whether they are born with them or they are developed through challenging childhood experiences is debatable. Just like the skill of healing, sixth sensory abilities and intuition can be expanded and built through practice. This would be true of all humans, not just empaths. But for the most part, empaths are what we currently term psychic in some way. Much of this is because the first way they read their world is through vibrations being emitted around them.

Empaths are comprised mostly of females is a myth. There are an enormous amount of male empaths. This was a discovery I made on my own from being in empath groups within social media. I was also surprised at how many male empaths signed up for my mail list and read my books.

Here is something that is definitely true. Empaths are unlimited. They are evolving like all humans right now. They play a critical role in moving all life forward in a new positive direction.

Notes – Thoughts – Ideas – Affirmations – Dreams

Empaths in Culture & History

"I am sure there is magic in everything, only we have not sense enough to get hold of it and make it do things for us."
~ Frances Hodgson Burnett, *The Secret Garden*

Empaths have existed as long as humans have been in physical form. Early tribal cultures, of which some still exist today, often chose a shaman for the group. A more appropriate way of this choosing would be that the shaman emerged. As others recognized the difference of this individual, they were asked to serve in this capacity. Some ways a tribe would witness that a person born among them is different would be from viewing certain skills they held. This could be assisting in healing, soothing, calming, prophesying, and even magically transmuting certain situations the tribal members had a need for.

It is suggested by some that shamans exist in a more ethereal form in other dimensions as well. They walk in two or more worlds. They see that this dimension is made up of illusion and respect higher and lower dimensions for the knowledge they contain. They will travel to those lower and higher areas to help those in this dimension become more whole or even to accompany them to the other side at death of the human body.

From earth's past, we have accounts of ruler queens and priestess cultures wherein the feminine aspects were celebrated. These yin qualities were held in great reverence by both genders. It is interesting to note that during the goddess cultures in Neolithic times, there was never warfare. I believe this is all making a comeback from the dominating practices of the past few centuries. These aspects include making females feel inferior to males; evil or crazy for their empathic yin qualities; dark for their powers of seduction; weak because they experience emotions; and even a denial of nature in some respects as linear thinking and progress took precedence over same.

In today's world, there are theories put forth that empaths have chosen, with Creator Source, to utilize their free will to incarnate here now. They see earth's dilemmas in moving forward. They see the greater purpose. Empaths are also here to grow in their own understanding by experiencing the harsher contrasts that three dimensional reality offers.

To illustrate how empaths can present so distinctively in the world, I am going to use characters from books and movies to show you these contrasts. Empaths can be meek, mild, almost mousy individuals. They can also exhibit great power in good and bad ways. Empaths can be the people who are the most helpful and hold together the fabric of a family, tribe or community. In your mind, you can think of your own favorite empath and use them as an archetype to boost your own skills. This is a great tool to use to foster growth on your journey.

In *The Lord of the Rings: The Fellowship of the Ring* (1), we encounter several empaths. There is Gandalf and his nemesis Saruman, who turned toward the dark forces. There is the beautiful Elven female warrior and healer, Arwen, who assists in helping Frodo Baggins, giving him her own energy and bravely transporting him to Rivendell. All of these scenes, whether in the books or movies, give us a variety of different empath personalities. One of the most striking is the Lady of the Wood.

Once healed by Arwen and after convalescing in Rivendell, Frodo encounters what some describe as a sorceress or elf witch by the name of Galadriel. As the ring of companions travel into the outlying woods of this domain called the Realm of the Lady of the Wood, Frodo begins hearing her thoughts telepathically. This is happening before he has met her. Once led inside her realm, Galadriel mesmerizes all with her light which is quite visible in the movie. The Lady of the Wood reads, not only their minds, but their hearts as well. From this, she is able to surmise that there is hope that the mission of returning the ring to the mountain of doom and destroying it has some chance of success.

She speaks again telepathically to Frodo and tells them all to get rest which she knows they will need desperately for the journey ahead. In fact, she imparts thoughts of hope into the minds of several in the ring, yet they struggle to feel it or know the way toward it. So, in this respect, she is instilling inspiration inside them.

During night, Frodo hears her telepathic calling from his slumber. He arises to meet her again and she initially asks him if he is willing to look into the mirror. As he wonders what he will see, she imparts that no wise person can tell him that. She tells him the mirror can show him things of the past, present and future. I saw this scene metaphorically as a way she was testing Frodo. She wanted to know if he had what it took to handle the situation with the ring. She also was allowing him to look deep inside himself – losing himself in the possibilities of his shadow side and that of others in his companionship.

Examining the dark within us is a necessary thing for all of us to do in order to shine our light at its brightest strength. She wanted him to see all of his fears, his trauma since he began carrying the burden of the ring, and the tragedy that may come in the future. As he views these things, she utilizes her empathic skills to meld herself with him and she views or intuits what he sees in his reflection. She admits to him that she is engaging in this sort of psychic voyeurism. She tells him that what is in his mind is in hers also. The Lady of the Wood warns that the horrors he has envisioned will come to pass should he fail in the proper wielding and destruction of the ring. She also warns Frodo that the friends he has will fall into disarray as, one by one, they try to take control of the ring.

He offers her the burden of the ring and she is honest, saying she does not dismiss her desire for it, and even walks toward him like she might take it. But, she knows she will not. She transforms herself into something quite frightening and dark, showing Frodo what a mistake it would be to allow her to have the powerful ring and how incredibly destructive she would become.

This scene is quite visual and it shakes the Lady of the Wood to her core as she transforms into this darker being of light that is so malevolent in nature. The ring is not only a test for Frodo, but her as well. She acknowledges that she has passed it and goes back to being herself again. Frodo insists that he cannot bear this task on his own. She frankly tells him that he is a "ring bearer and to bear a ring of power is to be alone".

Often, we feel much like that as empaths. As we take on that which we don't want to feel or see, it can be very lonely. No one can bear this for you. You must find the way to embrace all of it, not just persevering, but overcoming all the adversity thrown into your path.

You see, the value of being an empath lies in the journey you are on. It is not an eventual place of just being. It is the ups and downs, the course corrections, the fun and the sadness. All of it is shaping you for something much greater. It is molding you into the magical empath.

I do not suggest you put yourself in harm's way with other people or situations. You are not here to be a martyr or endure things unfairly. This would not be the way of the magical empath. I believe all empaths will come across a fate of some sort they cannot escape the duty of, but as they learn to be creative and navigate that fate in a different way, they absolutely change their own destiny and it effects those around them. Trust the journey and process of your growth.

Disney/Pixar's hit movie, *Frozen* (2013), revolved around Elsa who has special abilities that she is unable to control or handle. I, along with many empaths, related deeply with this fictional character. In Elsa, we see that she is told to hide this part of herself. As it emerges on its own, she finds that she unintentionally hurts others with it.

Elsa had always been conditioned to hide her ability. Due to the fact that it happened when she did not even expect it, she felt the need to escape and not cause any further sensationalism, criticism of the family, or shame. To keep this from happening and due to the disdain surrounding it all, she scurries away to a lonely mountain of her own. Yet, her sister bravely endures hardship to bring her back, accepting her as she is. We see a real heart centered connection at the end of the movie.

Mention must also be made of Rey from *Star Wars: Episode VIII - The Last Jedi* (2017). While empathic and psi experiences occur throughout the entire series, this particular episode did a great job of showing that no matter which side of the "force" you are on, those abilities can be utilized for positive or negative. There are several representations in the movie where we see the empathic Rey dive deep into the shadow side of herself. This is represented by her actually falling into a watery abyss. She and Ben (a/k/a Kylo Ren) have communications on what appears to be a causal or astral plane. He plays upon her weaknesses. As an empathic type individual, she has hope for him to change and make another choice toward good. Rey has a vision or dream that this is a possible outcome for Ben. The movie is powerful and worth watching with empathic eyes.

Looking at historical empaths, no individual has displayed more magical empathy than Jesus Christ. His example is so high in vibration that we surely feel we cannot come close to that type of light and love energy. Feeling unattainable, remember he told us that we will do greater things than him. It is hard to fathom or believe, but he was telling us that we also have that same source of power he tapped into.

There are many more examples throughout mythology, history and today in our current world. What empath from stories or real life do you identify with now? Is there an empath you would like to fashion yourself into? This is something to ponder and it sets up a dynamic, even though these are fictional characters.

May you be blessed, fellow empath, as you find your avatar and walk this path that is truly strewn with thorns that prick our feet at times. May you be blessed as you reach revelation states of consciousness that expand you — expand us all — toward the heart centered love and light density we desire.

Glimpses & Goals

"The appearance of things change according to the emotions, and thus we see magic and beauty in them, while the magic and beauty are really in ourselves." ~ Kahlil Gibran

The idea of the magical empath can be an enigma to us. At times, we see small glimpses of it. We have experienced certain aspects of it. What if we could have more of that all the time? At times, I have known and experienced mentoring by a few empowered, magical empaths. But, that did not make me a magical empath. It only advanced my knowledge. Perhaps I picked up a few things by osmosis. The only way I can be supercharged as an empath is to do the work required to get there. It is not easy as it requires looking at one's self very carefully. This is a constant thing that needs to be accomplished, almost on a maintenance schedule. Checking in with one's self and looking at our feelings, thoughts and the quality of same.

While you will read these chapters using your left hemisphere primarily, the logical brain, try for more. Attempt to engage the artful side of yourself, the right brain hemisphere. Even more so, engage your heart. The heart is entwined with the empath experience.

I am not consistently an empowered, magical empath, but I am trying. In fact, I can say I have only felt that maybe I was for brief periods of time. In my haphazardness, I am becoming. You may already be there. Or, you may have just awakened to the fact that you are an empath. No matter what stage you are at, I hope you find the following description of the magical empath something you desire to live. The depiction arises from thoughts, images and words given to me. Some traits are ones I have admired in empaths I have known. The vision of the magical empath could expand as we progress on our paths.

The Magical Empath

Surrounded by a society still operating within scientific skepticism, the magical empath is extremely adept at ignoring this and moving forward. They know they would not be here on the planet if it were not the right time for them to share their insights and gifts. Many of them are a part of a blending between science and the esoteric disciplines. They view any divisions between science and spirituality as just a matter of focus, definition and open mindedness.

The magical empath is well connected to their Source stream and consistently experiences intuitive knowing, along with synchronicities. They use the information they gleam, combined with their desires, to co-create consistently with divine Source. They understand that their emotions are the strongest indicators of their guidance system.

The empowerment they feel is best defined as being fueled inside and passionate about existence. The magical empath understands that energy or power management is essential skills they must work at and monitor. By consistently working on this area, they are able to fulfill their purpose and help others. Making time for things that matter to them, self discipline is evident. They indulge in activities that build their line or connection to Source such as meditation. They have regular practices in place to not only guard their energy, but to increase it exponentially.

Magical empaths do not see their traits as a liability or something they must deal with. Instead, they truly embrace the gifts they have and seek to utilize them for the highest good of all. They do not spend time lamenting about negative things that come to them from others. Those are seen as windows into things they need to resolve within themselves. In other words, they recognize that another person, group or situation is mirroring to them something they need to work on. Conversely, it is showing them what they do not want in their life experience and asking them to set intentions. Additionally, it is asking them to follow through with actions when led and appropriate.

The magical empath welcomes all feelings they encounter, even if reluctantly at times. They do this because they know this shows them things to cure and heal. They understand that one cannot just put on a happy, positive face. This would be fake and untrue to their being and those around them. They strive to be authentic, but not get their stuff all over everyone. They know all answers lie within when they connect to Source. To complain to others is only to seek some type of validation when they already know the answer. At times ... especially in their past, magical empaths have learned from pain. Instead of resisting it, they figure out what needs to be done to alleviate it and then move forward with a plan of action.

These attitudes or ways of being allow the magical empath to navigate their journey in a fearless way. The courage invoked within the individual allows them to transcend things that once jolted them and now they find small in nature. They soar above the situation like an eagle or hawk and can view a larger vista of how and why things are the way they are.

Forgiveness is more natural to them as they soar above, looking down on the current stage, rather than being stuck inside situations. This allows them to hold more love for others. Operating at this higher frequency, they become adept at affecting situations through sending intense feelings of love, forgiveness and coming up with creative solutions at times. They know how to hold love and intense emotions and have them on call when needed. They keep this love reserve alive within them because they practice healthy self love consistently. The empowered magical empath understands the power of saying yes — to themselves. Having an understanding on a deep level of their immediate tendencies to forgo self for others, they recognize this pattern quickly and take action.

The empowered empath is a constant creator. They understand that everything around their experience is part of what is being co-created on a continual basis. By adjusting their attitudes and focusing on what they do want with high emotion, they attract more of the good stuff into their lives. When things are not going as they want, they figure out what they need to do to make adjustments. They do not stay in feelings of self-pity for long or perhaps at all. They know that martyrdom is a sure route to ego based identity. When feeling overwhelmed, they surrender to it and ask to be shown the next step to progress past it.

The intense love the empath gathers creates a true joy inside that attracts even more incredible experiences to them. They walk their journey hoping to affect others with this higher frequency, but not judging others when it does not happen. By living in a state of increased vibrational frequency, things that do not match up are quickly and easily released. At times, they are transmuted. Yet, the empowered empath fully knows there will always be items showing up they do not want or like. This is part of the sorting order. It resembles a game at times. They step back, looking at it from a higher level. This allows them to plan their next move on the board to get back to their "normal" operating stance. This is often accomplished by simply asking, "Why is this showing up for me now?" and following clues that lead them to answers.

The magical empath hardly ever says "I can't". You may hear them be more honest and say, "I won't." The magical empath says life affirming things that reveal their inner strength they have spent much time feeding and building. These statements often begin with:

I AM
I CHOOSE
I WILL
I CAN

Ironically, being a magical empath means not knowing you are one most of the time. There is no ego payoff. The moment there is, the empath slips back into mental imprisonment. In these dramas, old ideas of less than/better than are played out. Those thought patterns can manifest in a multitude of ways.

Notice, all of this work is being done on the inside of the empath. They are not blaming others. To do so would be to give up their inner power. The magical empath takes responsibility for all matters in their life. They have a true understanding that being responsible means their ability to respond ... to others, themselves and situations. As long as they retain that and do not play the blame game, their inner power grows in maturity and effectiveness.

Our Goals

The ultimate goal for the magical empath is to be able to control the way we feel no matter what is going on around us. To be able to reach spaces of peace, love, and union with the divine, no matter what is happening. This would be held as a goal in everyday life. No matter the negative news; what people you live with are doing or not doing; or who attacks us verbally, the goal is to be able to maintain solace within ourselves. This is a lofty goal. It is something that would require years of training for most humans and a tremendous desire to obtain this state. How would life change for the empath if they were able to achieve this ideal only part of the time? It would shift in a remarkable way. It would require a deep dive into practices that enhance our abilities. One of those main practices is meditation.

The reason you would even entertain having this high goal is because your emotions are everything. Your feelings dictate your world in such an incredible way that you do not even realize it from moment to moment; day to day. Once we can learn to invoke these beautiful, incredible feelings and connect to Source regularly, things are smoother. We are more tolerant, patient and loving. This is the point where you have more "aha" moments. You are going to be able to navigate life much easier. So, it is incredibly important that we realize on what kind of level we are constantly creating our reality. It is more than we realize. It is bigger than we can imagine. And while there seems to be a heavy responsibility around that, one we often want to avoid, it is the way forward. It is actually freeing once we land there.

You may arrive at this emotional state only at moments. That is the way it is for me currently. I have not been able to stay there all the time. I wish I could. It seems I am constantly realigning myself. I spend time metaphorically navigating my airplane and finding the coordinates I need to land in my happy spot. When we are trying to navigate our plane, attempting to be in alignment with where we want to be, the way we know we are off is just by checking in with ourselves. Looking at and feeling our emotions, instead of living in denial.

We cannot adopt a Pollyanna attitude, telling ourselves that we feel better when we do not. Rather, this is about actually getting there — truly reaching an internal positive emotional state. This point is actualized from clearing away anything that is inside of us that needs to be gone. Our goal is to find the obstructions on our path and remove them by releasing and letting go of things. These are practices that must be done continually throughout life.

When we finally realize that everything that is going on around us is within our control to respond to in a way that is higher and better, it is smoother sailing. This is a difficult point to get to. It seems that even when we reach a certain plateau, we may be challenged with something more devastating or negative. Even within that, we can appreciate that the event is pushing us higher and higher — challenging us to go deeper into love.

A Glimpse of Your Future Empathic Self

In your past, you recognized that you have experienced leakages of your own juice or power contained within you. Sometimes, you did this to yourself with your own thoughts, fears and worries. This was often related to relationships that you engaged in. You found that in order to be all you could be, it required you to develop a fierce trust inside that you could set game rules for those you engage with on a regular and even infrequent basis. Part of your inner power is the ability to speak your truths accurately and kindly, allowing other people to know who you are in a loving way and where you begin and they end.

You have the ability to take on so much from other people as an empath. You found that by developing appropriate boundaries, this solved so many problems for you, It allowed you to live in a free, authentic and true way. You have forged ahead fearlessly to do this. It meant that you had to drop all your concerns about what other people think about you. This was difficult, but you achieved it.

As an empath, your spirit is one that wants to be liked. However, you realized that you cannot allow others to validate you with their definitions of what you are. Rather, you know that in order to be a strong individual who has the capacity to make a difference in the world, you absolutely had to drop the idea that what other people think matters. This was not done in a cold or callous way as you would never seek to insult others. Nor would you display back-biting or vicious behavior. It was accomplished simply by realizing on a deep level that others cannot define who or what you are with their opinions. This allowed you to strengthen your inner power.

You employ many disciplines or practices to keep you on track. You are human and if it were not for this monitoring of yourself, you could easily falter. Some of the ways you move forward and craft or direct your life is through meditation, creative visualization, and written goal setting/tracking. You also utilize various forms of artistic expression. Most, if not all, of these methods allow you to stay connected to your Source. They also increase your awareness and intuition.

You pay attention to the unconscious signals that come to you in various forms. You know when a dream feels important and you should pay attention to it. You honor that sometimes a set of words or an image pops in your mind and you do not consider it irrelevant. You know that nature speaks to you in subtle, but beautiful ways and you learn from it.

You take time for yourself and practice good self care. You have your down periods and when they occur, you know it is time to tend to yourself. By doing this and regularly refilling your well, you have more to offer others where appropriate.

And, you have learned that always giving to some individuals or situations is not healthy, especially if it has turned into codependency and enabling. Sometimes, the best way you can help someone is by letting them figure out ways on their own so they can fulfill their path.

You also use your empathic abilities to send out positivity to other people or situations in order to hopefully balance a negatively charged situation. For instance, if a person is sending out anger, you erect thoughts like:

"I know you are not at your best now. I hear you but refuse to take on any of your anger in this manner."

By doing this, you are not manipulating what they feel, but rather you set up a positive boundary without speaking to what you are doing. If appropriate, you sometimes respond verbally in this manner. Your ability to send feelings and impressions of good to the other person often makes a difference in diffusing the situation. You reserve judgment and choose to respond in a way that is hopefully for the highest good of all. You do not take their words, thoughts, feelings or actions personally. By retaining an air of detachment, you view the situation more as an onlooker which assists you in objectivity.

The magical empath in you has developed a high level of discernment. After having navigated many circumstances, you are able to walk forward with wisdom and trust your instincts in an implicit way. You know the best way to respond in tense encounters that may come around from time to time.

You know you lack perfection and will never achieve it. That is not really the goal in this game of life. Rather, you desire to move about in life feeling as if you are fulfilling the purposes and tasks you came here to accomplish. During that time, you know there will be tough days. You realize you may fall back into lesser desired or unproductive behaviors and thoughts. When this happens, you enact course correction.

You have low periods and recognize this as part of the tidal flow of life itself. To always perform at high tide means not being able to fully examine the sandy beach right under your feet. You know that, without low tides, you will not uncover the hidden gems that lie there, waiting to show or teach you more. You realize self development is an ongoing discovery without end.

This possible view of the future empathic you is a remarkable, magical way to move through life. Some reading this are already living in this manner now. Perhaps it is something you have mastered only parts of. And others are waking up and saying, "I want to live that way." Whatever you do not possess but want with intensity, you can get. Whatever you have lost, you can rebuild.

Science & The Woo Woo

"Magic's just science that we don't understand yet."
-- Arthur C. Clarke

Our brains work as receivers just like you have in a radio or other device that picks up signals whether they are digital or analog. The signals we are picking up are made up of vibration – just like the audio or video signals traveling through the air that our televisions, radios or Wi-Fi connect with. To pick up these vibratory signals, your radio or other device uses an array of hardware to receive, translate and regurgitate the signal into sound, images or both.

The human brain utilizes neurons to interpret information it is receiving from another source. That is a fact. Some purport that mirror neurons, located in only certain sections of the brain, have been found to allow us to feel empathy. In the opinion of some, these mirror neurons are extremely active, almost too much so with empaths. However, some are challenging this hypothesis. What is known for certain is that mirror neurons allow animals and humans to mimic behavior. This is important research to continue following as it may lead to many discoveries about numerous conditions, not just empathy.

Science is always trying to use measures of its own design and control to find the explanations for many things. It is just our way of trying to understand our world. The mirror neuron theory has been challenged. This hypothesis could be an idea that searched to explain empathy, but might ultimately fall short.

In our bodies, we have more than one area that contains neurons. Our human heart contains over 40,000 which communicate constantly with the brain and also receive responses from it. The heart is the first organ to form within an embryo. Once thought of only as a pump, the heart has an electromagnetic field sixty times larger in amplitude, and five thousand times more intense than that of the brain. Perhaps, the heart really could hold more clues about empathy than the brain. Some have asked, is our heart the brain of our soul?

Are human empaths an anomaly in nature? Probably not. Perhaps an empath is somehow closer to a more primitive human state. Others may argue that an empathic human is in a more evolved human state. Regardless, being an empath is not considered a psychological disorder, but more in the category of a personality type.

When we look at the flora and fauna of the world, we can see many empathic traits therein. Bees have a group mind that exists around the hive and queen. Although each exists individually, if I kill one hornet, many of them come to the rescue at distress signals sent from the one that met its demise. Ants also have a complex set of communication skills. We can look at birds and migration and know these are examples of creatures moving together or for each other in some type of coherence.

There are so many examples to be viewed and they are usually revealed by patterns and communication levels. Ultimately, the experience an empath has of absorbing the feelings of another thing, animal or person is the same. So perhaps, being empathic is a primitive skill that has been around for a long time.

As you will see later, much of what we do or have the capacity of is not based upon magic, but science. Science is discovering that large portions of ancient wisdom, regarding what we refer to now as metaphysical or even paranormal, is measurable and scientific. Many of those findings have been achieved through closed, secret government research and quantum mechanics in physics. I predict that, within this century, science will have dropped much of its dogma and will blend with what many now consider magic or myth. This will truly bring about a golden renaissance age for humankind.

I began my metaphysical studies in the 1970's as a dabbler. I had an interest because I had already experienced many things that were either unusual or what some term paranormal. My dabbling included a wide variety of material including astrology, ufology, mythology, and the writings of Plato. The 1980's found me more fully involved with utilizing metaphysical concepts, not just for curiosity, but for self-healing and inner growth. During that decade, I learned to meditate and utilize creative visualization. Slowly, things really did begin to shift for me personally. Living in an area of the world where there were many preconceived notions and judgments about such, I kept all of my studies fairly secret. One of the thoughts I remember having is that science would never accept any of this as real. Over the years, I have seen signs of this changing and that gives me hope.

I do know that living the dream of being a magical empath is easier now because we are beginning to gain a fuller understanding on an intellectual and spiritual level about the concept of energy. The works of many in physics, brain research, psi and consciousness studies are opening up the possibility of science coming around to acknowledge the valid results of a multitude of experiments that lend authenticity and credence to the unseen. Still, many of the diehard academics and those who are positioned as scientific authorities have not accepted this as reality. It appears that most of this is based on fear. They are afraid of how they would need to roll back the curtains and change scientific conclusions that form the basis of everyday education and reason. Instead of viewing this as opportunity, they only see the initial chaos. Change occurs from chaos. Further, they fear the personal power this would open up to the masses who have been indoctrinated to believe something quite the opposite.

An excellent resource on the struggle between the light and dark forces of psi (magic) research is very well detailed in Dr. Dean Radin's book, *Real Magic: Ancient Wisdom, Modern Science, And A Guide To The Secret Power of the Universe* (Dean Radin, 2018), Dr. Radin has spent at least four decades in this field of study and is involved in many endeavors to crack the code on consciousness. While portions of this book can be heavy on the technical side, it is packed with tidbits and giant morsels of information on just what magic is and how it works.

In his book, *Power vs. Force* (David R. Hawkins, 2014), Dr. Hawkins attempted to provide proof that our emotional states not only affect our physical health, but they hold the key to early death and disease of the organism. Conversely, overall feeling states can set up a condition where we live in an enhanced state of Nirvana. Hawkins determined that low level energy can cause cell death. On the opposite end when measuring the human electromagnetic field, he found that organism health increased with positive emotions.

I have seen a visual chart floating around the Internet, with rainbow colors, claiming that our emotions can be measured in hertz. I could find no solid research to back this up. To date, there are no peer reviewed articles on the aspect of measuring the frequency of emotions that I was able to find. However, we know that everything does emit energy. Hertz is used to measure the frequency of anything that has alternating or periodic variations. Specifically, as related to physics, hertz measures waves of frequency. The scientific unproven claim is that when measured in hertz, emotions that rate very low on the scale are feelings like shame, greed, hatred and a myriad of other negative emotions. Whereas positive emotions such as caring, compassion, love, peace and enlightenment scored very high in hertz frequencies.

Certainly, for myself and probably you, we can feel differences in our energy levels when we experience emotions.

When we are feeling exceptionally good, our level of physical energy does feel higher. When we are sad or grieving loss, it can be hard to even move physically. On a daily basis for the magical empath, we should strive to have a constant monitoring of our emotions. Bringing it back to our feelings and being in touch with them is key, along with regulation.

I have hope that science and spirituality will make the merge. I predict it is happening now and the intensity of it will increase as new methods are discovered for testing and measurements of results.

Notes – Thoughts – Ideas – Affirmations – Dreams

Self Care & Regulation

"A great attitude does much more than turn on the lights in our world; it seems to magically connect us to all sorts of serendipitous opportunities that were somehow absent before the change." ~ Earl Nightingale

All empaths have very sensitive nervous systems. When I was a child, fear and anxiety could trigger my vagus nerve, causing me to faint on demand. Through regulation of the emotions producing the anxiety, I evolved and no longer do that — thank goodness. But this shows us how incredibly powerful we are. If we do not want to deal with something, we have the capacity to shut down the entire system.

One day, my husband asked me why people keep talking about self care. With a bewildered look he said, "doesn't everyone just do that?" I explained to him that it is a current term being used in psychological and healing circles for doing something nice or nurturing for one's self. Our discussion ended, but when I thought about it, there are situations where a person could be so burned out they are not taking care of their normal functions as they regularly would. Each person's idea of self care is really different and it could even be dictated by financial circumstances.

Later, I explained to him in more detail that self care is not just grooming, exercising, or taking a bubble bath, though all are worthy endeavors. It is a result of self love and looking out for one's care consistently. Many people encouraged to practice self care have found themselves spending too much time doing for others and ignoring their own needs.

Self care means that you begin to let others pick up the pieces of their own lives instead of jumping to their rescue and ignoring your life. And it can mean spending more time taking care of our physical bodies. Even if you cannot spend money on a day at a full service spa, you can do things to create one for yourself at home. Lighting candles, playing soft relaxing music, taking a leisurely bath, giving yourself a manicure, enjoying an extra long hot shower or anything else you find pampering to your body and spirit.

You can read or listen to things that are uplifting and motivational to you. Eating the freshest food you can purchase and preparing it is an act of self care. Going for a walk in nature can be rejuvenating to your soul along with journaling. All of these things show you care about yourself and they raise your vibration. Just imagine how different you could be by employing many of these items in your life!

If we are living our lives out of balance, it becomes increasingly difficult to manage energies which we will cover extensively later. People today are pulled in many directions mentally and physically. If they are also trying to take care of others, guess who often gets left out? They do!

Often, we do not think about what may be missing in our diets that could assist us in having more balance. Clinical psychologist, Abdul Saad (Vital Mind Psychology), spends considerable time working with empaths. He states that whenever he begins work with an empath, the first thing he does is address their physical state in relation to their nervous system. He stresses this is important because we can do a lot of work on a psychological and spiritual level, but it may not be as effective because we have not addressed physical issues lying underneath. I totally agree with this.

Our physical health affects our ability to move into more heightened states of living and personal awareness. Since empathic individuals can easily feel overloaded emotionally, nutritional considerations are not just important, they could be critical to our well being.

Stress to the nervous system requires calming, especially when the stress is chronic such as financial problems or being stuck in an abusive relationship. Under this type of stress, the body overproduces cortisol, a steroid hormone produced by the adrenal glands. However, the hypothalamus and pituitary gland in our brains are also involved in the actual signals to release cortisol. Whenever we are in fight, flight or freeze mode, cortisol is pumping into our system. Under normal conditions, cortisol is beneficial. As the receptors on our cells drink in this steroid hormone, it assists in regulating glucose levels in the blood; balancing metabolism; adjusting the salt and water ratio which affects blood pressure; and even has critical components for women and developing fetuses (What is Cortisol?, 2018).

With too much cortisol, an inflammatory pattern is set up that depletes our health. It can cause rapid weight gain, skin changes, higher blood pressure, plus anxiety or depression. Abdul Saad uses various supplements and lifestyle changes to get the empath normalized again so that treatment can continue with more success. He also has made a series of videos that are extremely helpful dealing with empaths and toxic relationships, namely the narcissist.

As many empaths are already aware, magnesium is an essential nutrient we often do not get enough of through our diets. For much of the planet, it has become diminished or depleted from the soil. Epsom salt baths and even foot baths with this element can help as our skin is our largest living organ. It will allow the magnesium to pass through the skin's surface to our inside. If you live near the ocean, daily swims in the water will help also.

During a heavy working period, I began forgetting to take some of my supplements. That was remedied by putting an alarm on my phone to remind me each day. I am trying to consume less coffee as it results in flushing many good nutrients from our system.

Female empaths, especially, can feel out of sorts from hormonal fluctuations. It never hurts to ask your physician to order a hormone panel to see where you stand in relation to percentages. Often, there are many other metabolic tests run on this same profile. Some will show if you have an adequate level of Vitamin D. If you choose to use hormone replacement of any type, just know they are very powerful. Just a tad can change your thinking and behavior. I would consider plant based bio-identical hormones over what big pharma has to offer.

As always, consult a qualified physician before embarking upon supplementation of any kind. This is important because many substances can have adverse reactions with either your system or interact with other drugs or supplements you take. Each of us is unique.

Another caution I like to share is that it is safer to introduce one supplement at a time. Take that for a few days to make sure your body is doing well with it. If you are not, you can immediately know what the source is and eliminate it.

I once began a supplement that had me falling into a deep depression. I am really glad it was the only thing I had added to my usual supplemental intake. Otherwise, it would have been really hard to know what was going on. I researched the supplement and the severe depression I was experiencing was not a possible side effect. I then began looking at myself deeply in all ways but nothing was bothering me to make me feel depressed. Looking at the ingredient panel on the supplement, I noticed it included an ingredient for better absorption called Bioperine. Basically, this is a brand extract that is 95% piperine (from black pepper). The strange thing is that I often use fresh ground black pepper on my food. In fact, I love it and have no ill effects. But this very concentrated form is shown to have rare side effects for some people including severe depression. I stopped taking it immediately and was myself again within a day.

Sleep Patterns

Some people believe that spiritual energies are running higher in frequency from dusk to dawn, when the skies darken and the world becomes quieter -- at least in some locales. I have no opinion on this but to say it is something I am observing. Certainly, we know that our circadian rhythm is affected by low to no light cycles.

Many empaths have difficulty with their sleep cycles. Staying asleep, rather than falling into it, seems to be the main challenge. But any continuing disturbance in sleep is something to raise concern for all humans. Proper sleep is necessary within the human body for homeostasis on a cellular level. There are numerous studies on sleep cycles, but a recent one concluded that human cells begin to fail in repairing themselves, especially from oxidative stress, when the circadian rhythm is interrupted. The mitochondria, or energy power house, of the cell is also affected. At issue is the ability of the mitochondria to fuse together, then divide when ready. This process, known as fission-fusion, is going on constantly within our bodies. Without this ability, health can decline significantly (Circadian Control of DRP1 Activity Regulates Mitochondrial Dynamics and Bioenergetics, 2018),

There are many empaths who like to sleep alone even if they are in a relationship with someone. Sometimes, the other person's energy can disturb their sleep. One of the things I find important for me to sleep well is to be able to lie down and feel really clean. I like to take a warm bath or hot shower first. Although, there are times I am so exhausted, I am out as soon as I am perpendicular. I think this cleansing ritual is important. It is a way of just shedding what you've picked up for the day physically and in your layered field of existence. I also love to have favorite pillows and blankets around me. It is important that everything feels fresh and clean. While I do not change my bedding more than once per week, it really begins to bother me at about that point. Essential oil atomizers or sprays in lavender or rose are a nice treat to spray each day on your pillows or comforter as you make your bed. You do make your bed, don't you? I am joking, but many people swear it changes your whole outlook if you make your bed each day. This is definitely worth a try.

Some people sleep with gemstones they feel protect or enhance their energy. They can be placed in a drawstring pouch under your pillow, tied to the bed, or even in the pocket of your pajamas if not too obtrusive. Great suggestions for stones to use would be black tourmaline which is very protective psychically. Fluorite is a great choice for dream travelers. Amethyst can help enhance dreams and it likes soft or low light.

I have a rainbow moonstone that I often wear on a twenty-four hour basis. This stone helps to energize the auric field; provides some psychic protection; and can help you dream more intensely. The moonstone ring makes me feel very connected to the moon, but also cosmic consciousness. It is amazing how it begins to glow on its own as we get close to each full lunar phase. The strange thing is that I have kept it in a dark jewelry box for weeks. If I go get it during the full moon, it's glowing without having seen the moon for a month or more. You may want to try certain stones for sleep, especially if they assist you in getting better rest.

Empaths often feel drained from incoming energies. Caffeine can sometimes be their best friend. A little caffeine early in the day could be good, but should definitely be avoided for many hours prior to rest. Be mindful of too many good nutrients being flushed out of your system with too much coffee or tea.

Low to no light in the room you sleep in is important. If you are on a schedule wherein you sleep during daylight, invest in room darkening shades and anything you may need to create a very dark, quiet environment. Do not sleep with objects that put off light. Think about at least turning a clock with a light in it toward the wall so that it is not so visible. Additionally, keep your electronic gear such as phones, tablets and computers away from your sleeping area entirely if you can. Try a new habit instead of having your phone on and beside you most of the time. It might be a great time to read a physical book or listen to a guided visualization from a small speaker or stereo located at least ten feet away from you.

I have noticed that my sleep patterns can vary with different moon phases and with certain celestial energies going on. When that happens, you just have to go with the flow. It is likely that all connected entities throughout all the living kingdoms are experiencing this on some level. This would be something you feel, but you may not always be able to identify. It could just be an energy you are picking up through clairsentience.

Dance, exercise and movement are essential for self care and regulating the body/mind/spirit complex. If we are too stationary, our muscles weaken. Even our digestion processes become sluggish. Movement of any kind, even if you are challenged physically, is important. Just approach it with what you are able to do. Consider working out with a partner for motivation and mutual support. Be happy and glad that you can move. Think about that. Some people can no longer move at all. Fill your heart with gratitude and dance around your kitchen or room. Hum a little tune that you make up of your own. All of this helps your physical body and it elevates your mood.

Cleansing what we cannot easily see is important as well. Your aura is made up of vibrations that are thought to be electromagnetic in nature. Depending on the state of your mind/body/spirit complex, it resonates a color spectrum that could be seen as the patchwork coat of many colors that Dolly Parton sang of. The reason for all these colors is that the aura is actually made of up layers of energy. We have within it, the etheric body, mental body, spiritual body, astral body and more. Together, they reflect the state of all in the wholeness of your mind/body/spirit complex.

Sometimes, the aura gets a little junked up and needs purification. This is especially true for those on the more sensitive scale that take in so much energy from others. How can you know if an aura cleansing will help you? If you are feeling stuck in negative thoughts; overly emotional; lacking direction or creativity; or even angry, this purification technique can assist you greatly.

Shamanic Smudging of Body

For this technique, a bundle of specific herbs are used. Basically, you light one end of the bundle or stick, holding the safe opposite unlit end. Allow it to burn momentarily, then blow it out releasing smoke. This is the same as lighting an incense stick — which can also be used in a pinch. It is advised and helpful to have a separate vessel that you can place the hot smoldering end of the stick or bundle into. Many people use an abalone shell with a little sand inside to absorb the heat. Smudge bowls can be made from many items you have on hand or a special one purchased just for this use.

Hold the smoking bundle or stick and twirl it around your body. Begin at the feet, perhaps sitting down so that you can pass it around the area in a circular way. Twirl and travel up the body swirling the smoke around you. Imagine it dissolving all stress and negative patterns. Allow the smoke to chase away that which is unnecessary in your auric field. As it rises into the air, see your positive dreams and desires making their way upward. Make your wishes known!

Suggested herb bundles could contain: palo santo, sage, sweet grass, or cedar. You can also burn, in a separate vessel, a few sprigs of lavender or rosemary. Resins from frankincense or myrrh are also utilized in this way.

Today, many people have gravitated toward using palo santo as their choice for cleansing themselves and their environment. From the palo santo tree which grows primarily on the coast of South America, it is part of the citrus family and has undertone notes of mint, lemon and pine. In Spanish, palo translates in English to stick. Santo is the Spanish word for Holy. So, it is revered as the Holy Stick. It is often used during ceremony for tribes and modern practitioners as well. The smoke is also effective in deterring mosquitoes and other pests.

Sweet grass is an herb I had the pleasure of using for circle ceremony with Native Americans when I was a young seeker, new on my path. My first introduction to it had me loving the smell which has notes of vanilla. It is considered to be more of a yin herb connected very much to Mother Earth. Sweet grass is braided into sticks that can also be bundled together. Intuitively, I feel this herb brings a sweet joy to those who use it. Sweet grass is great to use for a blessing ceremony.

Sage has long been used for smudging and healing. It is said to assist in ridding one's self, objects and environment of unwanted energies. There are many different varieties of sage. Some people believe certain species perform better than others. I will leave that up to your experimentation.

Cedar is also used in a smudging stick form. Ancients have used this substance for centuries for cleansing and purification. Of course, it puts off a wonderful smell that also works well to repel insects.

Finding a Reiki practitioner would be a wonderful way to heal and balance your aura, along with your physical body. Reiki is a hands on (or off) method of healing that works with clearing the energy patterns stuck in your field. Many empaths are learning this healing modality or are already Reiki Masters. It is helpful if you are friendly with a group of Reiki practitioners in your area so that you may trade serving each other at times.

Finally, for aura protection and strengthening I must tell you my labradorite story. The heart on the front cover of this book is a piece of labradorite. There was some synchronicity involved in me choosing this heart.

Initially, I wanted to draw something that would be a symbol for *The Magical Empath*. Time became condensed for me and I needed something quickly or nothing at all for the cover designer. I jumped online and perused many images of hearts. Everything looked too much like a Valentine or a cartoon. I refined my search asking for photographs only and not illustrations or vector art. I also invoked a state of expectancy that I would find the perfect thing and asked spirit to assist me as I need this now and wanted it to be right. My eyes landed on that heart and I knew this had the look I wanted.

At first, I did not realize it was a photograph of labradorite. When I looked at the photographer's information to purchase the image and use it, I saw that it was titled as such. This stone is perfect as a symbol.

Labradorite is a transparent or translucent stone, which correlates nicely. We need transparency in our world. Most of all, we need to be that way with ourselves as we heal so that we can progress.

Next, it is known as a stone of transformation. It is an excellent gem to wear or have during transitional times as it gives one resilience and fortitude. It helps the aura be more balanced as it also grounds energy. Additionally, it repels negative energy as it vibrates at a high rate of consciousness itself. As it helps in establishing a strong sense of inner worth, it may also assist in repelling our own inner negativity. It is excellent for improving intuition and psychic gifts.

This crystal has also been called a "stone of magic" and said to contain parts of the aurora borealis with its color spectrum. It has been used by ancient tribes and people for healing, including shaman. What a totally perfect stone for empaths.

Today, there are a multitude of things we can do for better self care and regulation of our sensitive nervous systems. While some of the most important ones have been addressed in this chapter, there are many more that overlap regarding energy that I have included in sections throughout.

One of the things we have to ask ourselves is why we do not perform many of these things all the time or at least on a regular basis? I have my own excuses from simply forgetting to feeling too busy. Regardless of my reasons, as I move into this new decade in this critical time of expansion, I will be using technology to set reminders for myself. If I depend upon doing it when I think of it or during certain events or seasons, it probably will not happen. You may want to set some calendar reminders too.

Another important consideration is to ask where we feel deprived in any form. Time, health, money and love are just a few areas to explore. This will show where we need self care.

Overall, regulation of our body/mind/spirit complex, by taking the best care of ourselves that we can, puts us on surer footing to travel the road of the magical empath. Our body is our holy temple. Yet, even more important are our feelings. Our emotions are everything as you will experience as we go further.

Notes – Thoughts – Ideas – Affirmations – Dreams

Working With *Energy*

"Magic is not a practice. It is a living, breathing web of energy that, with our permission, can encase our every action."
~ Dorothy Morrison

During our time as empaths, we often hear people say we just need to get grounded. What is the purpose of grounding? Certainly, we are encased in physical bodies that have their own electrical systems. These same systems can and do get out of whack. This can cause problems with heart regulation, blood pressure or more subtle signals that make us feel uneasy, stressed or anxious. Always, our physical body is striving to achieve homeostasis or regulated balance. Much of the time, it accomplishes this on its own without us being aware of it.

With our emotional body (which affects our physical), we may be aware that we feel out of sorts, but are unsure of where to begin to cure whatever it is that ails us. The starting point is always grounding our physical bodies. The act of grounding oneself gives way to enhanced clarity. It gives us the capacity to discover if something is wrong with us that needs attention. Often, it can be something in the environment causing us to feel uneasy.

Have you ever had a moment within the day, or perhaps at the end as you prepare to go to sleep, in which you just feel off? Your mood is not the same as usual. You have difficulty knowing what is bothering you. There can be a number of answers to this situation. It could stem from an intuitive warning about something. Those feelings could also be old fears or habitual negative thinking patterns creeping in. For empaths, the most common reason for this occurrence is because you have accumulated some sludge throughout the day from other people or situations. When you feel this way, mentally go back through the hours prior to this and try to pinpoint when it started or what set this in motion.

Once you identify the moment it began, it clues you in and gives you clarity on what is happening with you. You can then use your favorite clearing or grounding technique so that you can feel balanced once more.

I begin most days a tad groggy, but mostly excited for the day ahead. I have practices in place that allow me to fuel myself with positive things in the morning. Sometimes, I find myself really feeling the weariness of keeping my energy field as clear as I can. This results from being around others who cannot help themselves. Unintentionally, they can get their stuff on others. I am sure you experience the same. Here is something important to know. Do not blame them. You are only responsible for your energy and feelings you carry throughout the day.

The mature empath knows they could encounter portions and full blown dramas of what they do not like or want throughout each day. This can come in the form of the news, an encounter with someone at a store, or people you work and live with. If you are waiting for them to change so you can be okay, stop holding your breath. That is not going to happen. You hold the power – not to change them, but to fine tune yourself so that you can operate within the world and people like that. If you are around situations that are too unbearable, make the necessary change to get out of it somehow. This all comes down to making the right choices to manage our energy and deal with the energies around us.

Energy sometimes seems like a small word with broad meaning. That would be because everything is made of this invisible substance. It does not matter that human eyes do not perceive it. It does not matter that a high powered electron microscope can begin to show us its existence. It is there …. regardless. The sooner we embrace that fact, the faster and more proficient we become at receiving the energy we want around us. We also can fine tune and direct the energy we send out from ourselves into the existence around us.

You have heard that energy is vibration and this is true. Whatever substance makes up energy on a sub-atomic level is vibrating. Something that appears entirely solid such as a boulder or wooden table is actually made up of vibrating energy. This can be seen with the correct scientific equipment. It is alive and moving, even though we cannot see this with our eyes. Yet empaths can often sense energy that certain objects emit. They may receive one word or short visual impressions from things that are considered inanimate. This gift or skill is called clairtangency. Some also refer to it as psychometry.

Clairtangency can be a fun way to stretch your sixth sensory processes. An interesting exercise that I sometimes use is to pick up a geode. Clear your mind and breathe a few times, exhaling fully before you begin. Close your eyes softly while you hold the geode or perhaps a piece of quartz. Ask it mentally what its purpose is.

This object formed from sub-atomic vibrating particles and has a signature that is encoded with information. This is the same as you are — encoded with your informational DNA. When you open yourself to receive, the object often transmits an answer to you. The answer from the geode or crystal will come to you in a way you can understand. Depending upon your preferred methods of receiving sixth sensory input, this could be through mental images, sounds, feelings or words you hear in your mind.

I have enjoyed using this exercise where I allow the gemstone to speak to me. I will purchase small stones, raw or tumbled, and take a picture with my phone of the name of the stone in the store. This is because I rarely get to a good gemstone store. When I do, I want to purchase quite a few. Once I have the names of the stones recorded with the photos, I later use it to look up information about the crystal – after I have let the stone speak to me.

My process for this is so simple. Once I have my cache of rocks at home, I will wash away any vibration residue on the stone that may have occurred from others picking it up. Sometimes, I will let the stones set on a table outside at night under the moonlight to give them a period of regeneration – just like we need as empaths. When I feel ready and my own mood and field around me are decent, I will begin asking each stone its purpose while I hold it in my hand and write the answers down in a notebook.

Later, I will look up the name of the stone from my phone photos. Once identified, I check through the metaphysical meanings found on the Internet for each one to see how close they match. It is often so uncanny! This is a rewarding exercise that helps you build your intuitive skills. I have also felt that it brought me closer to the energy of the stone – almost a melding of understanding of its nature and what it has to offer.

Exercises like this can also be used with animals and plants. Certainly, they are emanating a constant energy as well. This is how some empathic people are able to be the "whisperers". Picking up on energy is a relatively quiet, delicate thing. You are tuning into some of the highest frequencies or bandwidths to see into another object, person, plant or animal. Yet, it is easier than one might believe.

Empaths are very caring souls who have incarnated here to help with energy in a positive way. At times, we can become too assisting with others. When we do this, we are not helping them, but enabling so they do not make the transitional growth needed for their own soul development. In a way, this slows the betterment of the whole. It is important that we, as empaths, learn to recognize this so that we can pull back and allow that person to unfold in their own time and way.

We must also be aware that everyone is not like us. Even as I say that, I want to warn empaths not to slip into grandiose ego thoughts of being better than. Is a student in high school better than one in sixth grade? Of course not. We all have come onto this planet at different levels and with unique objectives of why we are here. There will always be those entities that are more ahead of us and those that are behind us. Those that are ahead of us are our teachers. Some that are behind us can be our teachers as well. All deserve respect.

Many times, we may find ourselves overloaded emotionally with the feelings, duties and tasks of others because we believe they are not strong enough to handle it on their own. This is a pivotal point where empaths can invoke their codependent tendencies and begin to spiral into a situation that is unhealthy for all. We must really analyze and test what would be best for all. I will give an example.

Janet, an empath, has a twenty-three year old sister who is verbally frank in a hurtful way. She has no concern for the feelings of her family and will blurt out whatever she is thinking. She displays this behavior with parents, relatives, teachers, and more. She is difficult to be around and does not have any friends. Overall, Janet's sister is one angry young woman. Janet knows that her sister secretly hurts inside, that she wants friends and to be liked by others. She senses that her verbal attacks are a way to deflect attention away from everything she feels she is lacking inside. Despite the fact that her sister acts like she doesn't care what people think, Janet knows her sister has issues of self-worth. She loathes herself most of the time. Janet would really like to help her but it is like getting near a bomb that could explode unpredictably. Plus, her sister greatly affects Janet's mood.

What do you think Janet should do regarding her relationship with her sister? Keep in mind that Janet experiences hurt also from her sister's words.

Probably the best scenario would be for Janet to lovingly detach from her. Janet could let her sister know that she loves her as a sister, but will not be around her for any length of time until she learns to treat her with respect. For some empaths when they read that last sentence, it provokes thoughts like:

1) What if Janet's sister commits suicide?
2) What if this prevents Janet from attending family holiday events because her sister will be there?

Either of those things could happen. It is a real concern and brings up more choices and possible problems. As much as we are here to help in this world as empaths, we cannot interrupt the growth or free will of others who choose to be the way they are. It is especially difficult to save those that don't want help. To try and do so activates codependency features.

To relieve Janet of the burden she feels in closing down and detaching from this toxic relationship, here are some choices she could consider:

1) Doing Nothing – Janet does not have to do anything. Just detach and go her own way; or
2) Be very clear with her sister why she does not want to be around her. Give examples, if necessary. Janet may want to do this through a written letter or email. This could avoid her sister becoming violent or abusive during a face to face conversation; or
3) Search for professionals that could assist her sister if she chose, at some point, to make a change in her life and behavior. This could be information for local groups or individual psychological practitioners. Janet could write the information down and just place it somewhere she knows her sister will see it.
4) Depending upon the relationship, offer to go to counseling with her so that both can try to improve communication.

When we hold other people's burdens for them — their feelings, duties, or lack areas, that is all we become to them. We are like the coat rack in the foyer to dump their coat, boots and backpack upon. This, in turn, takes from them. When we take on their stuff, we keep them from knowing their fullness.

Another danger of taking this negative energy on from others is that you, in turn, can begin to create similar scenarios for yourself because you are holding this in your own frequency. Law of attraction cannot help but have this happen. That does not mean you will become like Janet's younger sister. It means you will attract more people like her into your sphere.

Taking abuse or mistreatment of any form from others is a real problem that must be addressed firmly and fast. You are the one who has to do this. They will not make the effort. Once you do so and hand those emotions and tasks back to the offending party, you will help them. As long as other people enable them, they have a slim chance of healing.

When you find yourself in or around scenes where people are angry or their extreme negativity is impacting you, leave. Detach from toxic situations such as family arguments or fights. Stop worrying about what they think if you detach. Make steps toward finding more positive people to spend time with. Go on a walk in nature. Spend time with a pet or someone else's. Go visit horses at a stable nearby. Walk alongside the ocean if near. Change it up so you can be your best. Ultimately, this is usually what your family wants for you. They just don't always know how to deliver the right environment for you to thrive.

If you do not do this, you feed the problem and it could make you very ill. So, bless them with love in your mind and hope they can come to a resolution on their own or with assistance from others. Once you are away from their toxic behavior, you will breathe easier and live more peacefully. During this time you have been trying to help them, you have been losing you. You are needed for other things in areas where help is welcome and wanted in this world.

There are the numerous personality disordered individuals that empaths seem to attract like flies to honey. This would be those with bonafide psychological issues such as narcissistic personality disorder; antisocial personality disorder and psychopathy. These are three disorders wherein research has shown there are actual physical brain differences in these individuals. Specifically, one of them is lack of empathy in those with narcissistic personality disorder or those that are classified as psychopaths. Note that an individual can have narcissistic personality disorder (NPD) and not be a psychopath. However, all psychopaths also have NPD.

These people are at the other end of the see saw when it comes to empaths. It is easy to see why they would be drawn like magnets to empaths because we have what they lack. But, it is not a good fit. There is so much literature and information available about individuals with these psychological afflictions that I hesitate to rehash it here. However, just in case you have no idea what I am talking about, let me give some quick definitions of these personality disorders.

The Anti-Social Personality (ASPD)

People afflicted with this disorder have no regard for the feelings of others. They assert their own rights easily, but not allowing rights to others. They also do not respect the law and structures that work to create a system we can live within. They can be very manipulative and when confronted with their behavior, have no remorse. They do not feel guilt for their actions. There can be significant risk taking behavior exhibited. Many have criminal charges filed against them. They feel there is nothing wrong with them and it is the way the rest of the world is set up that is wrong. Sociopaths will not seek help on their own. The causes of the condition are not clear. They vary from early childhood upbringing, genetic predisposition and changes in brain function.

Narcissistic Personality Disorder

All of us are a little narcissistic. If we were not, why would we bother to brush our hair or teeth, purchase new shoes or clothing? Most of us want to put our best foot forward for a job interview or important meetings. A small dose of narcissism helps prop up our personality as we move about in the world.

The disordered version of narcissism is built upon a weak self image and possibly brain dysfunction. While these individuals put on an air of self importance and superiority, they hide what they really feel inside about themselves. Keeping up their image is the ultimate goal all the time. They will run over anyone who tries to tarnish their image in any way and they have no empathy for anyone. They want to be tended to and cared for by others and believe they are entitled to it. They look down on others who they see as stepping stones to what they want to get. Often dominating conversations with others, they must have the last word and be looked upon as the authority on many subjects.

Psychopath

Worse than just having no empathy and exaggerated importance, these people are out to destroy you and find satisfaction in doing so. These can be the serial killers of the world. Yet, someone can be a psychopath without murdering the physical body of someone. Instead, they can destroy you emotionally and perhaps financially as well.

A commonality with all three of these personality disorders is making you believe there is something wrong with you instead of them. Perhaps they tell you that you're being too sensitive, overly dramatic. But you're not. They are now gaslighting the situation and trying to minimize the damage from their little monsters they carry within.

Basically, you are a sparkling unicorn. They are predatory in their thinking. You will know who they are by their actions. Blaming, suspicious for no reason, picking on others, talking bad about people in an attempt to elevate their own ego, etc.

Now that you know you might be dealing with one of these individuals, what should you do? Seriously do not allow this to go on. Break the chains that bind you and get out of the relationship. Make a plan and stick to it. Stay quiet while formulating your plan as they will thwart it. Be safe!

Later, I relate the spiritual experience I had about cutting cords. Basically, it is not recommended except in very severe situations. And when it is used, make sure to do it correctly so that the entire root of the light strand between you and the other person is eliminated. If you must do it, then make it a final process and do not allow that person to contact you in any form. This could be challenging with these particular individuals. They find so many ways to break you down and play upon your emotions. You will really need to own your own power and make super firm boundaries. This may mean getting the police and courts involved. It could even mean brandishing a weapon. While I know the idea of that upsets some of you, I had to do this for a short while for my own protection and that of my children. Of course, I would never want to hurt anyone, but when it comes to my kids, don't tempt the mother bear in me. Do what you must to be safe so that you can move on and live a much better life.

There are times when something happens out of the blue and you are not going to be able to easily avoid it. My parents called me once after a misunderstanding about something. I calmly and logically spoke with my father about it. Then he wanted to speak to my husband so there were three of us on the phone. My mother then picked up an extension phone at her house and was accusing my husband of things that were not true and it was a huge verbal scenario. Everyone was upset and it was all over nothing – just things that had not been communicated clearly to begin with.

After the call, I became physically ill. My blood pressure is normal most of the time. But now it was rising out of control. I tried taking deep breaths, lying down and listening to relaxing music. I wanted to go outside but it was cold and rainy in December so I stayed indoors. I had an electric blood pressure cuff so I could take readings. If it had not ended, I was going to get into see my doctor right away. I hesitated to go because I knew it was emotionally induced. I felt caught in the middle between my parents and my husband. I knew the real truth about it all, but no one was listening to each other. I felt like I could not take the irrational conflict that was going on and the residual fall out was really eating at me.

Regulation and management of incoming energies is a skill you practice and develop by utilizing mechanisms for energy balancing. Let's say you are feeling very out of sorts or uneasy and there is no logical explanation. You have analyzed every person and situation you have encountered and nothing seems to fit. Trust yourself that you are not going crazy. There is a real reason you feel this.

My husband and I had an extreme uneasiness and unknown anxiety for about sixty days before the horrible events of 911 in 2001. We spent a lot of time trying to identify what it was. Our marriage was good, finances okay, and our health was fine. We took a summer vacation to see if that would change what we were feeling. It did not. As we stood together watching our television screen that tragic morning, we instantly looked at each other and knew this is what had been bugging us.

Some empaths really feel different prior to intense storms or earthquakes. If someone you have not spoken to for awhile comes to mind during these feelings, consider reaching out to them to see how they are doing. If you live in an apartment, duplex or condominium, you could even pick up vibrations from others in your complex. The point is that there is probably a very real reason you are feeling what you are. Now, you say, what do I do with these feelings I don't want? Yes, we want to be in our grounded happy spot.

I am not going to promise you that the techniques I give you work all the time. I can tell you that many work almost always. There will be those instances in your life when something big is going to have an effect on you. Your delicate nervous system is feeling it prior to the event occurring. Even if you cannot completely rid yourself of uneasiness or other uncomfortable feelings, utilizing mechanisms for working with energy will help you cope much better.

Energy Cords - How They Work

One morning, I awoke with a complete cosmic understanding of what I could not fully see, much less understand before. It was as if during my sleep, I had accumulated or downloaded this information. My dreams of the night were a mystery to me and while I know I dreamed, I remembered nothing. All I knew is that I woke up with this incredible knowledge. Immediately, I wanted to try and communicate the knowledge my mind held. Yet, I was also overcome with great emotion. Shedding tears of joy as I sat sipping coffee, I grabbed my voice recorder to try and capture everything I knew in that moment because I was afraid it was temporary. You see, this information made me feel different ...

better than I have ever felt in my life. I knew it was meant for me to pass on. So, here is what I had a compete gnosis of and when I say that, I mean that I knew it intellectually and emotionally in a huge way that made me feel tearful with an ecstatic joy.

Even as I type these words, I am afraid my ability to convey this to you at the depth I feel it will fail. How can I recapture everything and put it into the limitation of language to pass it on? I do not know, but I will try. Please be patient with me because some of what I say here is information you may know. Yet, without saying everything, the entire idea will be missed.

Everything, literally all things in the creation of creations, is connected on some level by substance. The definition of what connects us is mutable. Basically, I saw it as some kind of light filled energetic material. For years, many in the discipline of metaphysics have called it cords. I will refer to it as cords in this writing, but also strands because that more accurately describes what I saw. Both will be used to describe connections. I saw these strands as I viewed them in a multidimensional way, seeing that they pass between physical and the non-physical.

When we become friendly with someone, a cord or strand is created between us. If we are blood related to someone, a cord already exists between the entities. If you were adopted and do not know your parents, this connection can still exist. In that situation, the strands can become thinner over time as years pass by. We have thicker strands of connection with our families of origin that we grew up with. Cords are definitely created between us and our lover, mate, or spouse. Cords are very present between our children and ourselves. These are the predominant cords of energy we deal with the most in life. But, there are many others, as all is connected.

All cords carry information. This is why we have the phenomena of thinking of someone we have not spoken with since college or the job we left three years ago and then, we run into them or they contact us. This happens to people very frequently. Even while they marvel at the coincidence, the cause is the thought preceding the action in the form of information traveling from the strands of energy between us. This person that you have not spoken to for a long time may have been thinking of contacting you for a couple of days. You pick up that thought through the energy cord. Then, you hear from them. It's really that simple and this is going on all the time. Really makes you think more about minding your thought patterns.

Let's take another example. Perhaps you go to a restaurant and find you are seated by the hostess next to the person you have not spoken to since college — the one you were thinking about for a couple of days prior. What brought you together at the same restaurant? The energy strands were telling you — forecasting to you that you would meet again.

When we are intent on manifesting something for ourselves, we often can attract situations and people to us via the energy cords. Using the same restaurant example above, let's say you have been working on manifesting a buyer for an appliance you are selling in your home. You have not advertised it yet since you are awaiting delivery of your new appliance and are still using it. You overhear the couple at the table next to you talking about their broken appliance and how they do not want to spend money on a new one. There you go, that's your opportunity to tell them about the one you have. Coincidence or synchronicity? You decide.

You put out the need — the calling — the desire. The other party has their own need or desire. These desirous thoughts travel through the white light strand energy cords. Ask yourself also, how do the energy cords of the employee who sat you next to the couple enter into the equation. It is all interrelated and when viewed from afar, coincidental to some and magical to others. This is a part of how we live magically every day.

When we have sexual relations with someone, energy is exchanged that creates a cord. This happens whether it is a one night stand, three month relationship or marriage. If you have been in a relationship with someone for awhile, the energy cord is stronger. This is why so many people experience having the feeling of their heart strings being tugged on. Literally, those strings are tugging at the place in the body where they took root initially. When you see a couple break up, then get back together frequently, they have a cord issue. On one level, they know the relationship is probably not going to work out, but they still get pulled into each other's field through this cord of emotional information that exists between them.

I believe these energy strands exist with those who have passed on. I see everything being connected, whether it is visible to us or not. This is all made of a type of fine energy we fail to see with normal eyes. Some can see it in their mind's eye or third eye as they view all the strands or cords connected to them. We are spiritual beings encased in physical bodies ... for now. These energy cords are connected not so much to our physical bodies as attached to the auric body.

We are connected not just to people, but also animals, situations, certain memories and places. Have you ever heard someone say after visiting a locale that they just really felt connected to that place?

Much of this you may already know. While I slept, I felt like I had been given further understanding about our connections to other people, situations, things, including parts of ourselves. As spiritual beings encased here in the physical, we have these invisible threads, strands or cords that are energetic, ethereal connections that have been talked about for ages.

In the metaphysical literature and discipline, cord cutting is sometimes recommended. It can seem like an easy solution to problem areas of our own lives or conflicts we are experiencing with other people. However, what I woke with is the knowledge that cord cutting should only be done in the most extreme situations. The reason for this is there is always a price paid in some way. Now, this should not create fear, but rather a karmic caution to really look at one's self to see if there is a way to heal things between the parties. Otherwise, the same situation keeps coming around or another very much like it ... sometimes worse.

Recently in the news, there was a man who publicly in the courtroom forgave a defendant for shooting his brother and killing him. Certainly, his feelings toward that defendant created an energetic cord between them. This connection would exist prior to him even being able to forgive her. I would speculate during this heart wrenching ordeal, he wrestled with feelings of anger, shock, grief and more. He probably went through a lot of dark nights of the soul to come to a place of forgiveness and love for the perpetrator. He looked deeply into her, trying to understand why she killed his brother. He went so far as to pray that she receive no jail time for her deed.

These two were very connected by those energy strands or cords. When she committed the act, she connected herself not only to the victim, but to his family and anyone that loved him. When that occurred, everyone's feelings raced toward her faster than the bullet she shot. Likewise, her feelings shot back toward them. For the most part, this all goes on unknowingly between us. Even if it took awhile to find out who shot his brother, the cords and information exist on the energetic level.

These cords, rays, threads, strands .... whatever you choose to call them — these energy beams carry emotions. They carry memories also that are wrapped within emotion. Had this forgiving brother chose to cut the cord (if he had this knowledge) it's possible he could find himself in another situation later in this life in which he was to practice extreme forgiveness. This man was a Christian and I am sure that plays a part in his ability to come to terms of forgiveness and love for this woman. He reached out to God Source for help and to forgive. He probably would not have had the knowledge of cord cutting. If he had chosen to do that, nothing would be fixed. In fact, he may have retained some sort of bitterness.

This is a touchy subject because people are always hurting each other. We don't know why we attract certain things into our lives. We don't know what the lessons are behind everything, especially when we are in the lesson or just beginning the lesson. It is only at the end of the lesson when we "get it". When we get the lesson finally, we know what is going on, what went down, what the other person needed, and what we needed. Still, there will be times we do not know and do not see the full picture until perhaps when we have crossed over and can see the situation from a much higher perspective.

I would say if you are in a prolonged period of turmoil or pain being caused by energetic connections you have to an event, person, place or thing, cord cutting may be appropriate. Yet, you need to know that when the cutting of the cord is being done, it may come around again on the wheel of life. If you don't do the cord cutting correctly, it will grow back quickly and even stronger than before. Many meta-physicians believe you must remove the root of the strand or cord. This is true. More than that, you need to heal the situation within yourself. You have to do that shadow or dark side work by asking yourself the hard questions and trying to gain a full understanding.

- Why did this happen to me?
- What do I need to know from this person or experience?
- What do I need to master so that I do not experience this again?

- Could I find true forgiveness for the other person and/or myself?
- After I forgive, can I maintain a relationship with this person or should it be ended?

You see this so often with our relationships. We get out of one where we really went through some turmoil with someone. We then find ourselves in another relationship a few weeks or months down the road. The time length doesn't matter. If we did not do the work needed to learn why we attracted that kind of person into our life, we will attract another one like them. They may not seem like that initially. Somehow, it turns into that and we are just blown away. In fact, it might be that the next time around with the new person, it is more covert and harder to see. But, it is the same dynamics at play. Until we heal these things, we cannot progress onward.

Getting back to the energetic cords -- there are ways to heal connections between you and another person. There are ways to heal the energetic connection between you and aspects of yourself such as your inner child. Healing can occur between you and a parent. This is true whether your parents are alive or dead. The important thing to know is that you can heal those cords and make them healthy. If you are willing to do this with love for yourself and the other person, you are much less likely to endure that type of situation again. It's like a graduation moment. It doesn't mean that the rest of your life will be smooth and easy. I hope it is. What it does mean is that you've mastered that one. You are ready to go on. You are ready for something better and things can be smoother as you remove the wrinkles and speed bumps you've been running up against. Cord healing will bring you something healthier for your spirit, your mind, your soul.

I want to add that I feel such extreme gratitude, tears of joy and elation this morning with the realization and finally being able to take this into my intellect, my thick skull, which is absolutely vibrating right now with aliveness. It is as if the hairs on my head feel electric. I know that I've come across something here for myself and perhaps for you. To finally understand a tough concept that is backward from the way we believe everything to be. We've been taught this, we've been told this, but we just were not fully grasping how large it is and how much we have control over it. The push buttons that work this are at our disposal and they involve our feelings. It is all fueled, all controlled by how we approach things with ourselves primarily, but also others. This information is so important. It needs everyone to know about it — everyone! Even if they cannot fully grasp it, even if they think it is crazy, the fact that they are exposed to it is important.

Being human, I am going to fall off this concept. It will take measured thought on my part and a working with my feelings to bring me back to this place. Because I like this place. This place is happy! It gives me joy and hope for the entire creation of souls. I want to share this. I want to make it available to anyone and everyone ready to hear. I know I am going to fall off the path. But this is not really the path, but more like a point on the path - reaching a high summit where I finally get it. From this high spot, I see the bigger picture, feel the broader scope and experience this visual gift. I am here in this moment and tearfully grateful for the understanding of these invisible connecting cords. I am so grateful for this moment of knowing how it all works. The knowledge that I really do have control over how I see everything from here on out brings a renewed hope. All I need to do is remind myself of that fact, moment to moment.

The intense emotions make me commit to more regular meditation so that I can be open to what Source can show me. I would not have known this two or three days ago. I would not have felt this two or three days ago. It is happening now … right now. And just as I did not know and feel this prior to this moment, what is there greater that I have not yet known or felt?

This experience brought back memories of my early training with my mentors -- those that taught to love what you fear. Love heals those things that plague us in our minds, bodies and souls. Love really does heal but we have to generate that sincere emotion. We have to be able to call up or conjure all of that love within us and that comes from understanding. Understanding and forgiveness are the keys to love. Because when we understand that someone who is hurting us is hurting also, that they have their own limitations they are dealing with, it opens up a little window to let some fresh air in. It gives us a moment of breathing space to be able to say, "I see why you do what you do." Or "I see why you did what you did." Because you have your own fear, you have your own limitations that are keeping you down.

For us to be the bigger person, to graduate and go on to a higher vibration of living, we must be able to understand that others are really not out to get us personally. It really isn't personal. It is more just the way things are for them.

In my late twenties, I met a woman who became a mentor to me for a time. She had amazing abilities with people, plants and animals. She was the consummate divine mother archetype and a true teacher with words and her constant demonstration. She was nothing short of magical and often performed miracles. On the day I met her, I observed her doing this in the small classroom we all sat within. With a gentle touch and whisper in the ear of a very emotionally distraught woman whose energy was disturbing the entire class, she flipped her 180 degrees. She did so quietly and with such elegance. I knew I wanted to be like her. I wanted to have that ability to be so empathetic, to transform through love. But, I wasn't there and only today do I see a glimpse of that in me. And those times are not as frequent as I would like them to be.

But today, this morning, I feel different. It is like someone cleaned out my pipes or opened a valve and now I see this energy exchange that can happen between us fueled by love and other emotions as well. While I knew that to be the case on some level before, I see it larger now.

Today, in this moment, I am not blocking the flow of pure energetic love essence traveling to me from Source. Today, I feel like I could touch someone with light flowing through me from that Source. Today is all I have in this moment and I relish the delicious knowledge that has been gifted. I want to hold on to it, yet can only do so for awhile. Then, it becomes something I know intellectually, but not at the same high frequency vibration I feel it right now. It's like being madly in love for the first time. Only this time, you are in love with the entire creation.

Empaths must know the difference of "being in the world, but not of the world". Those words are something that has, more or less, been paraphrased from the New Testament of the Bible. Yet, it is not an exact quote. I believe that Jesus knew we would feel tension and uneasiness over things presented to us on a regular basis. He knew that, in order to move about in this world and accomplish sowing more seeds of love and compassion, we had to retain our own individual integrity. This means holding our own power and not becoming enmeshed in things that do not serve us or in alignment with our higher purpose.

This life goes by faster than we can ever realize. We must remember who we are and keep that in our mind as we move almost prayerfully through life. We are multidimensional beings. Part of us resides here on this planet and part elsewhere. We can connect all of our essence through these cords so that we can be directly plugged into God, Goddess, All That Is. By doing this, we will experience extraordinary moments. Those moments will assist us in ushering in the new world paradigm.

Chakras

"The head is powerful, but it can only get us what we really want if we open our heart first."
~ James Doty, *Into the Magic Shop*

While it may seem that I am going into much detail about chakras, the following information is only scratching the surface. As empaths, we know that we perceive energy. It is only natural that when we become out of alignment in some way, we may notice it more acutely than others. Working with these energies and balancing of same in your field of existence is valuable. By doing so, you can achieve more magical insights, be more creative and loving. Plus your connection to others and your God Source will be more open and clear. Let us begin with an overview of each chakra. Afterward, I will give you specific remedies for balancing those seven main energy centers.

The Seven Primary Chakras

From the first chakra at the base of the spine to the seventh chakra at the crown of the head, these invisible energy spirals receive incoming vibrational information. These areas also affect what we project outward. Each chakra energy vortex vibrates at a different frequency which is represented by the color spectrum. They are connected to different physical and non-physical areas.

I will give a brief overview of each major chakra and its functionality. There are also many minor chakras you can study as well. As you read through these, take note of any chakras you currently feel may need balancing. The way you know is that the chakra area will be stagnant or over stimulated in its flow and function by challenging issues. This can be felt mentally, emotionally or physically.

First Chakra

Red is the color frequency of this chakra. It is located at the base of the spine and the element it most closely represents is the earth. This first chakra is where we feel safe and grounded in our existence. It represents our foundation in life such as our early beginnings and survival issues. Our individuality or ego is also attributed to this chakra. Basically, it is where we feel our base identity in human form. It is an important chakra as it allows energy into the rest of the body from spirit or Source.

When the energy in this area is flowing properly, you feel you have plenty of everything you need. You feel safe in your personal environment and the world. Overall, you like the person that you are and get along with most people. When we experience issues with the flow of energy into and through the first root chakra, we may feel that life is a constant game of survival. The concept of lack or never having enough is associated with this area. You may feel you are not good enough and do not measure up to others.

Second Chakra

Orange is the color of our second chakra. Located in the area between the reproductive organs and the lower abdomen, it is also commonly called the sacral chakra. Water is the element that most closely aligns with it.

Our views of sexuality are connected with this chakra. That includes our sexual desire, procreating and pleasure. Clairsentience is associated with this chakra. When the energy in the second chakra is flowing at its best, you are naturally creative. You are comfortable with your sexuality. You honor your body and create meaningful sexual experiences. When there are issues with the sacral chakra's flow, it could be you may have adverse opinions about sex that make you not want to engage in it. You could also display hypersexuality. Many people report feeling creatively blocked.

Third Chakra

Yellow, sometimes gold, is the color frequency of the third chakra which is located in the area from the naval up to the solar plexus region. The element that most aligns with this chakra is fire. As it is connected with the metabolic system, it has the capacity to transform and bring forth something new. Gives new meaning to 'fire in the belly'. The third chakra is the holding place of personal power and overall energy levels in the body. Here we also feel our emotions the most whether it is joy, fear, anger or laughter.

Magic is associated with this chakra. When the third chakra is activated and flowing with energy, you have a strong sense of your personal power which you use in healthy ways to influence and contribute to others. When the third chakra is not flowing properly, we can fall into victim status. Power struggles are evident in our lives. You have difficulty standing in your own personal power and often agree to do things you do not want to do just to keep the peace. Stomach pain and digestion issues can be common as well.

Fourth Chakra

A beautiful emerald green color resonates with the heart chakra. Air is the element that closely emulates this vibration. The fourth chakra rules relationships, healing and love. The art of self-love and the act of compassion or empathy are related to this chakra. When energy flows freely and beautifully through the fourth chakra, you are as good at receiving as you are giving. You often feel grateful for life and everyone around you. Compassion is easy for you to feel for yourself and others without it being a pity party. When there are energy flow issues with the heart chakra, you may often feel like you have to please others in order to be loved. You cannot be loved just for yourself. You could also be afraid of entering new relationships due to broken hearts in the past.

Fifth Chakra

A medium, but brilliant blue is the color of the fifth chakra vibration. Primarily located at the throat area, its element is sound. This is our connection with expressing the creativity within us. It affects communicating in well known forms such as speaking and writing. Telepathy, as another form of communicating, is ruled by this chakra along with listening to others and clairaudience.

The throat chakra is flowing and working well when you feel free to speak up for yourself, express your opinions, listen to others and communicate well. You easily express your truth. When the throat chakra is struggling with energy flow, you fear expressing thoughts and you will often go along with others so that you do not upset anyone. Sometimes, it could feel like your throat is blocked. Some people develop sore throats in a chronic way from a blockage in this chakra's energy.

Sixth Chakra

A deeper indigo blue, almost purple, is the color that resonates with the sixth chakra. Located at center of the forehead just above eye level, it is also known as the third eye. The element associated with the third eye is light.

The sixth chakra is associated with clairvoyance, imagination, visualization, seeing auras or into other dimensions of light. When the sixth chakra is flowing with energy and open, this third eye area provides you with constant guidance from your intuition. When it is not working properly, you feel cut off from your intuition. You may struggle with knowing your purpose in life. Headaches, primarily from tension, could be common for you.

Seventh Chakra

The color of violet, like white hot lavender, resonates with our crown chakra. It is located at the top of our head or crown area. The element associated with this chakra is thought. It connects us with understanding and is the area of enlightenment. This seventh chakra is where we receive information or gnosis. Regular meditation helps this chakra and allows us to connect in a clear way via consciousness.

The crown chakra is flowing and opens when you feel that wondrous connection to your God Source. You may feel tremendous gratitude and a powerful, universal love. This is your connection point where energy can flow in and reveal many things that become your beliefs. When it is closed off, you may feel abandoned by God. Or, you may not feel any connection at all and lose faith that anything outside of your human earth experience exists.

It is important to know that one chakra is not more important than another. Continued imbalance in one will manifest in particular ways or body areas associated with that chakra. For instance, problems with the fourth chakra can manifest in the heart, lungs or thymus. All of the chakras need attention. One cannot just attain enlightenment in the seventh chakra, ignoring all others. To do so, would risk peril to the entire person. All chakras work together synergistically. Although, it is normal to have a little favoritism toward one or two chakras based upon your personal preferences in life. For instance, an empath may be more heart centered the majority of the time. That would give that chakra a bit more activity than perhaps the second chakra. Our base first chakra really does assist us the most in feeling safe, worthy and grounded. Begin there …

Chakra Balancing

There are various methods for bringing our energy centers into balance. Many times, they contain patterns that are not flowing well for us and it shows up in our lives in numerous ways. The common feeling of being stuck would be one such example. Indecision is often at the root of this and as we move forward with chakra energy balancing, things immediately begin to ease. Suddenly, we have an idea and are feeling more confident about what our next move is.

Tai Chi is a beneficial practice almost anyone can do depending upon their health condition. The movements are slow, but deliberate. It makes you strong physically, but not in the sense of strong in a muscular way. Your life force energy or chi is strengthened by the movements. Ironically, it keeps your temperament soft … which is a good thing. Soft yet strong. You could attend a regular class or practice at home watching an instructor online or on a DVD.

Tai chi is not difficult, but it does take time to learn. You will be good at it empath because you are already all about feeling energy. As you strike each pose, gracefully moving your arms and legs, you will feel your force field around you. This will not only ground you into your body instead of in your head so much, it will also refill your energy well. As you eventually memorize the movements, you will feel more connection each time you engage in this energy dance. I mention this method first because I feel it works well for all chakras in general. It is especially helpful for the first through fifth energy centers.

First Chakra Grounding Energy Techniques

Earth oriented exercises work well as this planet is our foundation and supports our life. Our first chakra mirrors this. Located at the base of our spine, we can live without lower limbs, but not without this important region of our body. Nevertheless, your feet, ankles and legs are still part of this energy area too. They function as extensions also affected by first chakra energy.

Simple earth-oriented ways of coming into your own foundational space and connecting with your first chakra energy include walking barefoot on the earth; lying or sitting on grass, sand or a forest floor. Even sitting upon some rocks that are firmly attached to the earth can help ground you.

If you practice yoga, movements such as locust or half-locust work well to ground you. More vigorous movements with the legs and feet can also assist such as running, walking, or dancing.

Sound can help ground you as well. Listen to or make rhythms that feel like they resonate from the earth such as tribal drumming. Chant the word LAM or hum the vowel O as in the word coat.

The flower essences of comfrey, squash and loosestrife work well on the first chakra. Notice this is the flower essence — not the herb, fruit, plant or flower, but the delicate distilled essence from the flower. This is an important difference. Unless you have the equipment and are adept at making your own flower essences, you would need to purchase these.

Gemstones for this area include, but are not limited to, bloodstone, garnet, ruby, nuumite and black tourmaline. Stones may be placed on the pubic bone area or just above it during relaxation or meditation. They may also be worn as an ankle bracelet.

Use affirmations that put you at ease such as: I am safe - I am enough - I am capable - I am grounded.

Massage of the lower extremities can be very beneficial. Use a tennis ball for the bottom of your feet. Give yourself or pay for a pedicure.

Foods that can assist you are anything with good protein levels along with root type vegetables.

Second Chakra Balancing Energy Techniques

The second chakra, our sacral area, is watery in nature. Areas of the body like our kidneys and bladder where this energy interacts actually hold, detoxify and then rid ourselves of water. This chakra also lines up with the watery ways of our sexuality and reproductive functions. As human embryos, we grew in water within the womb where this second chakra energy intermingles.

The second chakra also revolves around the pleasure we allow ourselves and our deep feelings about our sexuality. If we are out of balance sexually, this can manifest as negative beliefs we hold about sex and even our sexual body parts. It could result in hyposexuality. In the reverse, we can see it manifest as hypersexuality and unusual notions about the sexual experience. We may use sex as only an escape mechanism or to try and manipulate others, instead of the beautiful union it provides.

Anything beneficial with water will help heal the energy in the second chakra. Simple things such as swimming, being in a hot tub, dipping your hands in cool water, Epsom or Himalayan Salt baths, showers, hot springs, even a hot water bottle placed on the area help. Have you ever heard anyone say they have some of their best ideas in the shower or bath? It is very common and I know it happens to me too. The second chakra is our seat of creativity, in a reproductive sense and in a co-creation sense. It flows more freely when we are in water.

Particular gemstones that assist in balancing the second chakra include almost anything in the coral or orange range of color since this correlates vibrationally with that chakra. Look for citrine, aventurine, calcite and carnelian. Some use snowflake obsidian, even though it is primarily dark in color, as a protective stone that also helps to balance an overactive second chakra.

It is well known that the moon is closely associated with the pull of the ocean tides and it is the ruler of the watery sign, Cancer. Moonstone would also be a great balancer of energy in the second chakra area.

Stones may be placed just below the naval area during relaxation or meditation. Carrying them in your pants pocket works well also.

Statements of affirmation for the second chakra include: I am passionate about my life - I am a creator - I am creative - I easily feel connected to others - I love that I am a sensual being - I do not deny myself pleasure - I honor my feelings - I have healthy boundaries.

The use of the herb coriander in foods assists the second chakra area. Ylang ylang is an excellent essential oil for this area as it stimulates the sexual region. Both orange blossom (neroli) and orange oil are very beneficial. Remember when working with essential oils that they are very potent and require a carrier. Try putting a couple of drops in your favorite body lotion or cream and apply to the area.

Body movement to strengthen this area physically is recommended such as Kegel exercises. This is something you can practice sitting down or standing.

Third Chakra Balancing Energy Techniques

The solar plexus chakra gives us our sense of identity in the world. It affects our personal power and will that we have available to affect things, hopefully in a positive fashion. The third chakra is perhaps the area most tested when we experience changes and transformations. We build resilience here and self confidence.

Empaths, especially, need to perform regular clearing and balancing of this chakra. The reason is because you are often challenged in giving up your personal power to others due to your sweet hearted nature. A strong third chakra area that is well balanced will aid you tremendously on your quest to be the magical empath. You will stand firmly, but express it gently, in your preferences and boundaries. You will not react to life, but direct it by being proactive instead of inactive. You will show your ability to respond (responsibility) to your life and not ignore what is important. You will regularly practice self love to strengthen this chakra.

Stones in the yellow or gold range of vibration work well for the third chakra. Since the element of fire rules this area, the following gemstones are beneficial for balancing: pyrite or "fool's gold; real gold; yellow calcite; chrysoberyl;

yellow jasper and tiger's eye. Placement of these stones on the mid-section between the sternum and naval is ideal. Stones could be worn as long necklaces or attached to a belt at the waist area above the naval. They may also be placed there during meditation.

Seasonings that add "heat" to the belly aid in activating this chakra. This would include regular black pepper which aids in digestion. If your system can stand it, hot peppers are good additions. Ginger root and cinnamon are also beneficial to the third chakra.

Aromatherapy and essential oils to balance the third chakra include sandalwood, lemon and grapefruit. If you are feeling very low in self confidence, try using eucalyptus to awaken this chakra area.

Singing, speaking and deep breathing are quick healers for the third chakra. Make sure you use deep diaphragmatic breaths.

Body work can include soft stomach massage as well as any exercises that assist you in strengthening this core region of your body.

Affirmations that can assist you in balancing the third chakra include: I speak my preferences clearly to others – My self worth is determined by me, not others – I am confident in my ability to follow my path – I set boundaries with others easily and with grace.

Fourth Chakra Balancing Energy Techniques

Now, we come to the heart chakra. While I mention how important it is that you view each chakra equally with the others, I think you will find that this particular chakra needs quite a bit of focus in today's world. This is true for everyone, not just empaths. Yet, it is a very large reason there are so many empaths here on the earth today.

Our heart chakra is the center of our experience of compassion, joy, gratitude and universal type love. It is the wellspring of inspired kindness and understanding. When empaths are feeling balanced in the fourth chakra, they will practice self love which, in turn, allows them to love others with more intensity. Ruled by the element of air, love flows invisibly all around us. Indeed, we are the culmination of love from our Creator Source.

Located in the middle of the body, this chakra has three below and three above it. It serves as a bridge between physical aspect chakras and those more closely associated to spirit. It speaks in the language of feelings. We know that there is an imbalanced fourth chakra when we experience problems with the heart, lungs and blood pressure regulation. On a milder more mental level, when we are expressing ourselves in a codependent way, this also is an imbalance here — as well as the third chakra. Of course, any feelings of hatred, malice, etc., would indicate a problem with the heart chakra.

One stone I highly recommend is malachite which is a brilliant green and will help balance all the chakras. However, it really resonates well with the heart area. While green is the color of the heart chakra vibration, many gemstones in other color ranges — especially pink work well also. A necklace may be worn and if your stone extends down to the heart area, that is good. Since arms and hands are also affected by this chakra, it is easy to wear bracelets and rings that assist you in balancing the heart chakra. Stones to consider include: green aventurine, rose quartz, green tones of peridot, and authentic green jade.

I recently began using rhodonite and instantly felt like it was assisting my heart chakra. Using the intuitive reading method I mentioned in an earlier chapter, the stone gave me impressions of peace and tranquility. While I am wearing it, I feel more compassion and understanding of others, including myself. It seems to impart a feeling of acceptance for where everything is at and a peace associated with that. Some people believe that rhodochrosite is more effective than rhodonite in removing hard blocks from the fourth chakra area. It is also more expensive. These two stones are very closely related. I would recommend trying the less expensive rhodonite first. If you then feel you need something stronger, you could decide to invest in the rhodochrosite.

Aromatherapy and oils can quickly help you balance your fourth chakra. Geranium essential oil is a good one to choose just for overall clarity and balance. If you are experiencing a particular heart wrenching time, the calming effects of lavender are good for this area. Feeling blase? I have always found the scent of rose to be beneficial for opening up and activating the heart chakra.

Affirmations that are particularly good are anything that involves love, compassion, joy and gratitude: I am loved - I am capable of great love for others - I love myself - I feel gratitude for all around me - Joy flows through my veins and is pumped continually by my heart - I have understanding on a universal level for all

Fifth Chakra Balancing Energy Techniques

Located in the throat, upper shoulders and neck, it regulates our ability to share our voice and thoughts with others. It is also the first of the three spiritual chakras. A well balanced fifth chakra allows us to speak our truth easily and be very authentic with others.

Self doubts, false programming, limiting beliefs all affect this chakra in a negative way. One of the best ways to balance this area is to continue to learn, gain knowledge and meditate regularly. These practices allow us to come into who we really are and able to express that eloquently. We can then feel more at ease setting boundaries and allowing others to know we value ourselves and what our preferences are. A balanced throat chakra will also allow you to be a better listener when others are communicating with you in any form.

Basically, the fifth chakra supports the lower chakras. While it is not the center of creativity in the body/mind/spirit complex, it is the expressive outlet for same. Stones I love for this area are larimar, blue topaz, blue sapphire, aquamarine, blue opal, sodalite, turquoise, azurite, lapis lazuli and blue lace agate.

If you have a hard time allowing others to speak, chamomile taken either as a tea or the essential oil added to a lotion you place in the throat and neck area work well. This will calm your overactive need to speak over others, which you may not even realize you are doing. You may have so many thoughts that you feel you need to get out quickly that it is not apparent that you are not allowing others to play back with you in this communication energy dance.

Essential oils or products containing peppermint or rosemary awaken the fifth chakra. Chamomile and blue tansy calm this center if you are overly talkative.

Singing, speech, humming and chanting all help open the throat chakra.

As you might suspect, foods that are blue in color such as blueberries, blue corn and blue-green algae are highly beneficial for the fifth chakra energy.

Affirmations can include: I communicate easily with others - I speak with authenticity - I listen to others and try to understand - I communicate well through my chosen avenues - I know that communication helps expand community

Sixth Chakra Balancing Energy Techniques

Also known as the third eye, our sixth chakra is the energy center that allows us to connect with our inner thoughts and those floating around outside of normal conscious awareness. Intuitions and insights are possible with a sixth chakra that is open and balanced. Clairvoyance is also associated with this area. Even if you are not clairvoyant, strengthening this area will assist you in creatively visualizing the manifestations you wish to have come to fruition.

Stones that assist in balancing the third eye include labradorite; amethyst; lapis lazuli; azurite; moonstone in blue to purple range. Other stones for this area include purple fluorite and the metaphysically friendly stone, sugilite.

Essential oils that really help open and balance the third eye include patchouli, myrrh, frankincense and sage.

The element of the sixth chakra is light. Being outdoors and getting into the sunlight each day really assists the sixth chakra as it helps activate the pineal gland. Stay away from water with fluoride if possible. Switch to a non-fluoride toothpaste as well. Fluoride calcifies the pineal gland.

Foods include anything that looks like the pineal gland or pine cone in shape. Think pineapple! Also, walnuts are great. I also include almonds as helpful for this chakra. Foods with purple coloring such as eggplant, red cabbage, plums, grapes, raisins and dates.

Flower essences for the third eye include amaranthus, chamomile, green rose and dill.

Essential oils for the third eye are palo santo, bay laurel, chamomile, jasmin, melissa and rose.

One of the best ways that we improve the receptivity of the third eye is keeping our mind/body/spirit complex in balance. All things spoken of here propel us toward that goal.

We learn also to recognize when we are not balanced and put methods in place to correct it, a sort of spiritual homeostasis.

The third eye area which is governed by the sixth chakra can be prompted or teased into more activity. First, it is good to balance all the chakra energy areas so that you may feel balanced within the imagery or flashes of knowing intuition that will come to you. Meditation is a prime way to activate the third eye. Often, you can even feel that area begin a dull hum, especially in the beginning. While not really painful, it can feel like a distant pain at times as you meditate, but it corrects itself if you just stick with it.

Eliminate fluoride which is in most municipal water supplies, many toothpastes and it is also in some anti-depressants. Aspertame affects your corpus collosum, an important part of your brain that helps both hemispheres communicate.

Be aware that we live now in this digital world where we are constantly around electromagnetic frequencies that do not always jive with the human body. The more you can remove those invisible distractions, the better your health and well being. All of that certainly lends to more intuitive you. If you can sleep in a room free of those influences, that is best. If you can turn off wifi at night, that is even better. I realize this begins to get into people and their habits. Perhaps, reevaluate your habits to have a better, clearer connection, if desired. Sometimes even slight changes can yield significant results.

If you feel you need to detox the glands of the brain, some people use turmeric with potassium iodide. You can also try lavender or mugwort tea. Cacao is a beautiful food for your third eye. I favor distilled water. Some like mineral water. Most calcium supplements leave deposits in the bloodstream. Try to intake calcium each day from natural food sources. Cilantro (but a lot of it) can be juiced along with other vegetables for detoxification.

Affirmations could include: My consciousness is in balance -- I trust my intuition -- I have great discernment to know the difference between my fears and intuition -- Everything I need to know comes to me easily -- I am focused and calm.

Seventh Chakra Balancing Energy Techniques

When you were born, your skull was soft and each of the bones that make it up were not fused together. This ingenious design allowed you to pass through the birth canal. As you grew, those bones began to combine and fuse together. However, until you are around the age of three years, a portion of the top of your skull remains open. It is believed by many that the consciousness of infants and small children is part here and part in 'heaven'.

Our seventh chakra gives us direct communication with our God Source, spirit, higher self ... however you wish to think of it. Thought is the element for the crown chakra and it is the fastest form of energy known, even more so than light. In this chakra, we receive direct information from Source. I call these downloads. They are life changing and emotionally intense in a good way.

Because, we are not always connected, are we? We find ourselves embroiled in a ton of drama or wrapped up in worries. One of the best ways to balance this area of ourselves is the practice of mindfulness — staying in the now. When we add a regular practice of meditation, this area flows even better.

The crown chakra's vibration carries a color that vacillates between a light lavender or a more white hot violet range. It is crystalline in nature with touches of this violet color.

For balancing with gemstones, look to clear quartz and amethyst crystals; also selenite and diamonds.

The seventh chakra is associated with the central nervous system and cerebral cortex. The pituitary gland is ruled by this area as well. Foods that can help these body areas will include things of a lighter nature and raw is preferable rather than cooked. If possible, use the highest quality ingredients that are organic and non-gmo.

Exercises for this area are more mental, but can include every part of the body and chakra system.

To open this area, try deep breaths while viewing something you consider very beautiful, perhaps an idyllic mountain, forest or beach scene on the screen of your device as a background. You can also just try deep breathing with eyes closed and visualizing for a couple of minutes something that makes you feel extremely peaceful and happy. As mentioned, a regular meditation practice helps keep you connected to Source and greatly facilitates reaching states of gnosis.

These communications are a gift. When I have experienced them, it felt like grace poured into and over me. The information I received is something I could not have known on my own or studied with another. It is like an experience on another level. Suddenly, you know something. When this happens, it is hard to always translate into language what this blissfully entailed. I have found myself attempting to open farther in an attempt to take in everything I can. This would include all the feelings, any visions, information that came with it, knowing it was all going to end soon. While the afterglow lasts awhile, soon it is back to the normal world. May you be blessed with many such happenings!

As I said at the beginning of this chapter, what I have gone over here with the chakra energy system touches the surface of what can be learned. There are many good books dedicated to the subject. The best chakra information, in my opinion, has been gathered and authored by Anodea Judith

(1987). This book has over five hundred pages packed with detailed and is extremely informative on the chakra system. I first read it back in the late 1980's and it has stayed on my bookshelf since. I highly recommend her later works as well.

Notes – Thoughts – Ideas – Affirmations – Dreams

Filtering & Protection

"May the force be with you." ~ Star Wars, 1977

There is so much information available about empaths needing to protect themselves in a spiritual way from malevolent entities or just other people's moods and energy they give off. Sometimes, the information presented can produce more fear and anxiety in the practitioner than they felt originally. We have come to think of negative energies as things that can reach out and touch you in an invisible way. We may believe it can curse us, hurt us in some way. Rest assured, I have learned that this can only happen if you are in a place that would attract it. This means that your current vibration has turned dark. And, let's face it. That can happen. The empath who is experiencing this needs healing to get back on track and attract beautiful positive things instead.

Early in my twenties, I was mentored by several others on a spiritual path. My Baptist upbringing tugged at me repeatedly as I had been programmed to believe that anything supernatural in nature was bad or "of the devil". My spiritual friends assured me that when I felt fearful of things, love fixes all. It was presented in a simple form because it is not complex. It is as easy as understanding the Law of Correspondence (The Kybalion: A Study of The Hermetic Philosophy of Ancient Egypt and Greece). In this law, we commonly attract entities, environments and situations that match what we are vibrating. This is because like attracts like and whatever is our dominant thought feeling comes forth to mirror this to us.

When I was told to simply "love away" anything negative that felt like it was trying to make itself known, this was true advice. Yet, if you are vibrating in a place where you attracted it, how do you do that? How do you just use love to make something vanish? This would fall in line with another principle: the Law of Polarity from the same referenced book, *The Kybilion*. This law essentially states that all is one and manifests according to where it is vibrating. Imagine a pole. At one end of the pole is divine consciousness love. At the other end is deep seated hatred. The distance between these two polar opposites has many different degrees of either love, hate or perhaps indifference in the middle. In order to dissolve the appearance of hate in your world, you would need to change your frequency moving toward the other end of the pole — moving toward unconditional love.

Basically, this is what I was taught in a short hand fashion. We must recognize where we are vibrating and be responsive to changing that if it is not what is desired for our inner self and our outward manifestations. If we change our frequency and resonate from a very high state, we will attract much greater and positive things. We are able to look at something negative, either with our human or spiritual eyes, and feel its pain. We are able to send it unconditional love and ask that it go toward the light and love of the one infinite Creator. When we do this, it cannot have anything common in frequency to attach to. It becomes an incongruent situation. For the empath, you must get into that high state and really feel that inside for this to work well. Do not let fear creep in. You are capable as you open your heart. It may take a few attempts, but once you know how, it gets easier. You also have the ability, at anytime, to ask for help from others in this world and in other realms.

The Kybilion is a book of sacred practices for living magically. These laws are at times cryptic as they were taken from ancient Egyptian teachings given to us by Hermes, a teacher who may have lived during the time of Abraham or even Moses. His books, *The Corpus Hermeticum* and *The Divine Pymander,* were translated into Greek and then later into other languages. The study of alchemy comes from

Hermes' teachings. Often referred to as hermeticism, many well known persons have made it a study including Carl Jung and Sir Isaac Newton. I bring it up in this chapter and others because the laws contained within it have the capacity to expand our understanding of why things happen to us. For those times when we are attracting what we do not want, we would look at our own self. We would ask questions like:

1) What am I feeling at a core level?
2) What mood dominates me now?
3) What or whom has upset me?
4) Do I feel resentment or bitterness toward anything or anyone?
5) Do I feel extreme anger? If so, at who or what?
6) Do I believe or suspect someone around me hates me or holds jealousies?
7) What do I fear?
8) How can I find balance?

All of these are self-examination starting points toward healing the situation with love. Go as deep as you can with yourself in looking at all aspects. Journal about it if possible either through writing, drawing or a combination of the two.

You may be getting tired of my personal stories, but I can only advise through my own experiences. Once, I was in a dark place with my thoughts and I knew it. I told my husband about it without revealing all the details of my thoughts I was not proud of. He understood and was sympathetic, but had no real solutions for me at the time.

Someone had become very angry and hateful with me and this was not the first time. On this latest occasion, it had escalated to such a fever pitch that it had me grinding my teeth for many days afterward. Since this person is a bit mentally compromised, I had no way to work things out with them verbally and they would never apologize to me. I seethed with angry, destructive thoughts about the situation.

During these days, there were a couple of times I experienced some strange phenomena. The first time was at night where I felt a dark presence. I did not see anything, but felt it and slept with crystals around my neck. I placed myself in a white bubble of light as I fell asleep. The second occasion, a day later, happened when my husband and I were looking for something. We were standing in the kitchen and looked at every inch of the counter tops. Each of us had searched extensively. Finally, we had given up. Within minutes, the item we were searching for appeared on the counter top next to the sink. Ironically, this was a clear area where nothing else stood before. We would have seen it. So, we laughed and jokingly said we must have a little poltergeist activity.

The next day, I was trying to relieve myself of stress and bad feelings still. I was actually doing a pretty good job of it, although I had mentally worked myself into a frenzy over the previous days. I took a bath in scented Epsom salts and placed a stool beside the tub. My bath was relaxing. My thoughts were centered and good. In fact, I never thought about the situation that had been bothering me during the entire bath. I stepped out and dried off quickly. I then sat on the stool beside the tub and continued drying my feet and lower legs.

Suddenly a mirror that had been on the wall of the master bath ... some seven or eight feet away flew in a sudden projectile motion toward me and shattered on the floor beside me.

I called to my husband who came and helped me clean up the mess. That mirror had been there for years. The way it flew, as if someone had picked it up and hurled it, was amazing. I looked at him and said, "There is no rational explanation for this that I know of, but we will try and think of one just to relieve our minds." We did try to logically explain how it could have occurred, but could not come up with something that felt true in any way.

Did I make the mirror hurl toward me? I don't think so, but I really do not know for sure. Psychokinesis like this is something we would imagine from a movie, but it happened to me in real life. Did the other person's anger make this happen? I was not sure how any of it came to be.

For me, it was a wake up call. I had to find true compassion and forgiveness for this person that hurt me. I had to love them because evidently they were hurting and all they could do was get that hurt over everyone around them. I began to work on this healing immediately, from a pure space inside my heart that forgave and loved them unconditionally. After that, nothing strange happened again. In fact, I made a point of being kind to them and letting them visibly know I cared about them. If we want to examine where the negative force was coming from, we can spend time doing that. No matter where it originated, I knew I was the key to making it go away. If I was resonating from a compassionate, loving vibration, it could not exist around me.

The fact is that we are usually our own worst enemy and have a hard time knowing that on a real level. We would not attract someone or something negative into our sphere if we did not have something there that we needed to look at ourselves. It's impossible to do this based upon the Law of Correspondence. Remember, we are working with "the force" and it can go either way polarity wise.

We do not so much need protection from things we perceive as negative as we need healing of our own emotional states and beliefs. Remember that when you feel spiritually fearful. You can go through motions, just as I did, that make you feel safer and there is nothing wrong with that. In fact, I encourage it. You can call on angels such as Archangel Michael to come to your side. Yet, eventually you want to get down to the real causal factor which is what you are attracting.

Love repels hatred and anger. It has to stay at the opposite end of the pole. Light shown on the dark illuminates it and it is no longer a shadow. Be love, be light in your nature and judgments. This is the magical empath's way.

Butting up against other undesirable energies from other humans is a common situation for empaths. There are methods and ways of dealing with this to minimize effects on you. This commonly happens in situations where you are meeting new people or put into some type of situation with groups of others. We do not want to live holed up in our home or restricting ourselves only to the company of select people. To live fully, we must get out in the world. Here is an interesting way to think of this.

When you make coffee, you generally use something to filter it. You want the coffee, but you do not want all the wet grounds floating inside the liquid. It is the same with tea leaves. They must be filtered in some manner to keep from having a cup of tiny leaves floating in the brew. If we, as empaths, want to continue experiencing life and what it has to offer us on every level, we should consider filters instead of strong barriers that nothing can break though.

The Poncho Experiment

Imagine a poncho that you wear covering your arms and torso. Instead of it being constructed by a thick blanket like material, see it made from a light, sheer fabric. If you are good at imagining things, pretend this poncho covers you when in your next situation with other people. Imagine this is your filter that nothing can pass through unless you allow it.

You may even want to wear a poncho in your home environment to practice this technique. Ponchos are easy to construct if you would like to make your own from sheer fabric. By wearing it often, it will be much easier to imagine having it on at your next meeting or gathering with others.

Basically, you are providing yourself a boundary that is not so harsh as to make you unapproachable. It gives you a sense of control in that you can decide which energies you allow to come into your torso area. Empaths, as a rule, have boundary issues because we tend to always want to be perceived as nice. Perhaps, we should appear a little more mysterious rather than so open. Having good boundaries does not mean erecting a concrete wall to keep people out. It is about having an honor and respect for your own feelings. It also involves being cognizant about your own energy field and that of others.

With your acute nervous system, the poncho experiment makes you feel that the delicate energy that feeds you is protected. On a mental and emotional level, it assists you in maintaining your sense of self when people or situations are not the best for you. Wearing this filter as a reminder, you know more than ever where you end and others begin. This assists you in standing in your own power until you are stronger and need no filters. By using this mental or real poncho as a filter, you may then determine for yourself what you are willing to allow in.

Eventually, your goal as the magical empath is to be able to transmute energies coming toward you that are undesirable. Instead of absorbing them and holding them in your emotional system, you mentally kiss and bless them, sending them out into the vast vibrational world with love. You do this by utilizing the practices in this book so that you are ever increasing your frequency.

Much of the time when we are put into new situations or enter an area with other people, we are unconsciously scanning the information field for how it feels and what impressions come to us. This is all occurring at lightening fast speed. We are not aware we are doing it until we get a hit from someone or something. By that time, they could be in our auric field and making their way closer. It is very likely they do not realize they are in your auric field. They may just feel a pull toward you. What if you were to change things up and take the speed down on new situations or places? If you could begin to practice this, it would give you great strength as you would not feel bombarded by the energies of others.

In order to accomplish this, you need to give your ability to focus a work out on a regular basis. Focus is critical for accomplishing many tasks in life. The more you can focus your attention, the better results you will have in not feeling so overwhelmed in crowds or parties by all the energy around you. In fact, focus is absolutely required for many things you may choose to undertake in your life changes you make toward the magical empath.

When we are in a space that is crowded with people and we are not focused, what happens is we lose our ability to shield. We are open and receptive to every thought that other people are generating in that space. So, the more that we learn to focus our own thoughts, intended actions, and what we are doing, the easier it is to keep from absorbing so much from others.

Imagining you have your poncho covering you or actually wearing one turns into a tool that assists in focusing. In your mind's eye, see yourself as a self-contained unit that has energy flowing freely within and around it. Realize that occasionally your light energy will mingle with others in that space. Pull it back and self-contain it for the gathering you are attending. This is also a practice point to begin working on focus of your energy.

Here is an advanced technique to practice checking out the energies of others to determine if you want to engage with them or not. It does take practice and while the concept is very simple, doing it deliberately can be tricky at first. You cannot fail at it though. You can only get better each time. It can also be an interesting challenge.

Ball of Light Technique

When you enter any situation, workplace, room or meet someone at the grocery or mall, instead of being "so nice" as you usually are, place your feet one step back from where you would normally stand. Always when we come face to face with another person that were are meeting or greeting, we tend to go a certain distance into their space ... or they into ours. Deliberately stay one or two steps back from what you would normally do. As they look at you and/or speak, imagine holding their energy just outside of yourself. See it as a ball of light or a cloud, whatever you want to imagine it as. What color is it? Does it provoke any thoughts in you? Most importantly, what are the feelings you get? Does this person's energy remind you of anyone else's energy you've ever known? That is a very important question. Remember, those that have lessons for us come around with different faces until we master the lesson.

Another advantage of learning to use this method is that it will make you feel a little more secure and in control of situations. Instead of you being a sponge absorbing every incoming energy, you are holding it a bay, examining it and letting it tell you more about it before you get closer. So, basically all you are doing is holding that energy that is coming toward you outside of your auric field so that you are not absorbing it so easily. If you get an icky feeling from the energy that has presented itself, make your excuses to the other person and send that light ball or cloud away. Send it back with love and compassion to the other person. Smile, say excuse me, and exit stage right to another person or situation. This may sound odd, but you have to decide if you are going to be more mindful and watchful of your own energies. You also must determine if it is more important for the other person to have their needs met or for you to have yours tended to. As empaths, we are often nice to a fault and it ends up affecting us.

Your journey to becoming the magical empath involves a shift in perception. It requires clearing away all the old patterns you have been operating under. A warrior mindset is needed in the sense that you see the way forward as something that may have a few interruptions, but ultimately results in victory. When the empath finds they are slipping back into an old way of thinking or being, they utilize course correction to get back on the road toward finding and owning their own magic.

Luck Energy

"Scientists have calculated that the chances of something so patently absurd actually existing are millions to one. But magicians have calculated that million-to-one chances crop up nine times out of ten." ~ Terry Pratchett, *Mort*

How can we attract situations into our lives that are described by many as luck? After all, we have all these energies swirling around us. Why not make them go in our favor more of the time! There are people who have made a study of luck and some of the common findings they have observed are outlined below.

Lucky people exclude rational thinking more of the time, going with their "gut" feelings. As they trust their intuition and pay attention to cues around them, they often walk into lucky situations. By spending more time in the vast unconscious areas of the brain, the lucky person is open to more intuitive flashes or even downloads that produce a gnosis wherein they are receiving information the average person does not.

Those we consider lucky do not hesitate to grab opportunities when they happen. They recognize when something is being presented that is a potential for attracting some good luck. Many people who are luckier than most often carry an anticipatory feeling of something good happening for them.

Skepticism can hold back lucky occurrences in our lives. Resonating differently, we could be preventing strokes of luck. If our message inside ourselves is not to expect something good because that way we will not be disappointed when it does not happen, we are effectively shutting down potential luck. If we secretly do not feel 'good enough' for it to happen, this is just one more way to keep good luck at bay.

Some may fear being branded as living in a fantasy or being unrealistic. How tragic would that be? Live out your fantasy — even if it is only in your mind. Because that is where your story takes root — in your mind. Be mindful of your thoughts and feelings. They count!

My own conclusion is that people who appear to be incredibly lucky are resonating differently than the masses. There is an underlying belief they hold. They are fairly content and happy right where they are. They are not devastated by a losing situation. An incredibly lucky person may see it as a game and they know they will play again and have a good chance of winning something. Deep down, they feel gratitude and may even see themselves as a luck attractor.

Those addicted to gambling are often not lucky. They are too attached to trying to make something happen whereas the lucky individual is waiting to be signaled by their intuition. Those with gambling problems become emotionally involved at a lower end of the vibratory scale. They are way too vested in it emotionally. When they first began gambling, they experienced that beginner's luck many of us have heard of. They had no expectations attached then. The naturally lucky individual can go with or without the prize, yet they hold an anticipatory feeling that good things will come their way.

Attitudes affect our luck or the lack of it. Our self talk and basic feelings we are resonating with can determine so much. Our core beliefs and what we say inside ourselves is projecting that frequency outward. That vibration attracts what matches up with it. Keeping our self talk good is a worthy endeavor. One of the easiest ways to do that is by utilizing positive affirmations or mantras.

Other things that help are mindful practices where we try to stay in the now. This is especially helpful for those who project into the future a lot with worries. If we can find something we love to do where minimal analytical thought is required, this helps reframe our attitudes. By spending thirty minutes to an hour doing something artistic or participating in some sort of craft, we can begin to quiet down all those other thoughts and get in a great zone. Going somewhere outdoors where we can feel the magic of life is a wonderful way to change up our thought patterns and refresh our attitudes.

Carry something on your person that is your token of luck. Many people ask St. Christopher for the right parking space. Amazing, how they often get it. I began doing this even though I am not Catholic and must say I have experienced at least an eighty percent success rate. How many people bury a figurine of St. Joseph to help sell their home? There are endless ways people put some intent out into an object where they are attempting to have good luck, a successful day or final outcome. Many top athletes report similar activities. Whether it is a particular bracelet they wear or something they carry with them, many in sports not only invoke visualization to see themselves making their athletic goals, but may carry objects with them that make them feel lucky.

Sharing the news of your good fortune

Have you ever hesitated to tell a friend or relative good news that has recently happened for you? Whether it was the new vehicle you won, saved for and bought or that promotion that happened at your workplace, did you hesitate to share with them? Chances are you had a mental pause about it because you know they may harbor resentment or jealousy about this new fortunate situation you manifested. You may really love this person and want to continue your relationship with them. However, you know what you feel from them is real and it kind of rains on your parade that they refuse to share in your joy. What is the wisest way to approach a situation like this? Let us look at some choices.

First, you could just go ahead and tell them. We often intuit their true feelings about our new item or good fortune, even if they covertly cover it up. Second, instead of speaking with them personally about it, you might just post it on social media or send an email to several friends or family members with the same information.

You could choose not to tell them. When they see you in your new vehicle or found out you won a trip to Bali from the photos you posted on social media, they may ask you why you did not tell them. At that point, you could become unauthentic and say you were too busy getting ready for the trip; or your mom was sick; or a million other excuses.

What if you told them the truth? What if you told them in the highest way possible? What if you said, "Sometimes when I share my good fortune or news with you, I feel like perhaps you are not really very delighted about it." Chances are, they will dispute this and you have the opportunity then to respond that this is just a feeling you picked up from their comments or tone. Agree with them that you may be wrong about it. Because you might be. However, it is something they will think about, even though they may have robustly denied it. If they gaslight you and say you are crazy for thinking that way, you know this is a more extreme form of denial.

Ultimately, we cannot be responsible for how others react as we manifest things we want, have strokes of luck, or advance in any form through our lives. This is your life. You do not have to play small to keep from upsetting other people's apple carts. If they lose their grip over good coming to you, then it may be time to reevaluate the relationship. You can control the amount of exposure you have with this person via boundaries. Set your preferences so you may enjoy the glory and bounty you will manifest.

One thing I have learned about other people and the relationships we have between us is that one or both of us change over time. Sometimes, those changes are incongruent and it is difficult to continue to enjoy the company of one another. Sometimes, this is temporary. Take adolescents for example. During this rebellious time of trying to find themselves and assert independence, they will often pull away from their parents and grandparents. This happens for several reasons. While this is happening, you may not feel as close to this child. From a communications standpoint, you may not be. You still love them greatly and they have love for you, but their path they are traveling is changing. They do not even know where it is leading them. It can be the same with adult friends and relatives. In these types of situations, it can be beneficial to keep the relationship ongoing, supportive and friendly, but not as frequent as before. This can be difficult because you miss the old times of the past and how much you enjoyed each other. Yet, we have to look at what is currently happening and adjust the relationship frequency and depth to fit that.

Ultimately, luck is a mood or vibration we carry with us that says good things are on their way. The more we can maintain those types of thoughts for ourselves, the more we will experience good luck.

Notes – Thoughts – Ideas – Affirmations – Dreams

The Flow of Money

"Believe in your heart that you're meant to live a life full of passion, purpose, magic and miracles."
~ Roy T. Bennett, *The Light in the Heart*

Before we create, we actively think about something to manifest into our reality. Sometimes, a thought comes to us and we catch it in our mind. We then use physical and mental energy to create action upon the thought. This is how we create on a physical level. We are so used to doing it, we do not even realize it is constantly going on. And, we learn that we attract what we focus upon the most and hold patterns of belief about.

Money is a representation of energy. It is not true energy. It is merely an exchange system for your creations. If I like the service you provide, I will consider giving you money so that I may utilize it. You may then use the money I gave you in exchange for your service to purchase products you want or need. This money exchange does have a certain energy to it, but it is not pure energy itself like thoughts or feelings.

Paper money and coins are made up of substance or matter and thereby contain some form of energy. According to the numbers attributed to each bill or coin, some have more exchange value than others. These values are assigned by those in charge of monetary systems. Likewise, money we never touch and has no form in matter still requires energy to exist. When you access your bank account from a machine, electricity is fueling the banking systems that keep track of those debits and credits.

In times past, the exchange may have been made by using sea shells, gold, silver, grains or livestock. There is a value placed upon those exchange items by either a governmental body or the merchant. If you wanted something you could not or did not create on your own, you would need items of exchange to get it elsewhere.

Lack of money is never really the problem. Nor is lack of creativity. While many have numerous creative ideas, they may not exert the physical and mental energy required to manifest their idea into reality. We are creating with our minds and belief systems all the time. What comes into fruition for us matches what we project the most on a deep level. If we spend the majority of our time immersed in self-talk that promotes lack, we will not have enough of whatever it is we need or desire.

There is a reason that money is often termed currency. This word comes from the Medieval Latin word currentia. It is closely related to the word *current*, when used as a noun, relating to the steady flow of water, air, electricity or something similar. On our planet, currency, in the form of money, is flowing with a strong force constantly twenty-four hours a day, seven days a week.

It is only logical that we ask ourselves how well we are flowing with the current of money. Are we saying that money is bad, that it is the root of evil? If this is a core belief, our ideas about money and its availability to us will be very limited as we try to swim upstream against the current. Does the flow of money start and stop for us? Do we experience times of it flowing freely, only to find at certain intervals it stagnates against a high walled damn? Energy needs to move — always on all levels. Money will follow, like water, the path of least resistance. Money flows toward value, whether real or perceived. This brings us back to our creations. Are we providing enough value that money will naturally flow toward us?

Basically, this is how the world of money works. However, there are instances where we have money flow to us magically. This could be in the form of a winning lottery ticket, an unexpected large inheritance, or something else out of the blue that people would see only as a fluke or extreme luck. When that happens, truly you should be grateful as it is like a gift. Somewhere inside, you had to have held a belief that you value yourself enough to be the grateful recipient of it — whether you realize it or not.

Do you see, however, how your creativity plays a key role in creating value? This same value is what others will eventually recognize, want, desire and buy. If you are not receiving the money you believe you deserve, then we would want to look at where the flow may be stagnated.

We cannot speak of creativity without mentioning vocations or businesses we create to make money. Like all energy, we need to make sure we are an open channel for money to come into our lives. In our current societal systems, it is the way we survive. Empaths often have a tendency to feel bad about having wealth. This needs to change because money is a wonderful form of exchange that you can use to transform your life and the lives of those around you. Whether you donate to causes you feel are worthy and have an affinity toward, or give money to people you know need it, cash is just an exchange system you may utilize to give. There is no reason for empaths to not experience prosperity.

When it comes to occupations or endeavors to make money, find your calling. If you have a job now that you use to pay your bills and stay afloat, do not quit that endeavor. Rather, allow your interests and guidance you receive toward your life purpose to flourish alongside it for awhile. I have built a few businesses during my life. Some succeeded, some did not. It takes time and money to do just about anything. The worst thing you could do is put your empathic self under extreme pressure by quitting a job you need now and end up losing the soul based business you could have had later due to money woes.

If you are in a different position where you have the financial means to stay afloat and dedicate your time to your soul's mission, this is wonderful and ideal. Carpe diem! Make a plan, begin and keep going!

Your ultimate goal is to design your life around doing your soul's work — the reasons you came here to help. The best way to do this is to lock into your intuition and pray or ask for guidance. Additionally, be very general in what you want initially. The plan spirit has for you may be something you have not even imagined and would love even more.

Just take notice of your main interests, talents and abilities and begin asking how they can be utilized to help others in a way that those same people would be willing to pay you for that service or product.

Develop practices to get more in touch with what your higher purpose is. Even if you already know that, we always hit forks in the road or complete road blocks and need assistance to know what is the next step. Think of how many times a great inventor fails before they have that experiment that works out. Being disciplined and staying connected with Source will greatly improve your odds over most geniuses in our past.

Incorporate some type of body movement into your daily routine if you are physically able. This could be simple. Walking meditations not only get you outside, the practice will get your blood flowing, improve your cardiovascular function and you will probably experience some ideas while on your walk. Just by quieting yourself and taking advantage of this practice, you will be propelled toward greater things.

Movements such as tai chi are extremely beneficial. You learn discipline, focus and working with subtle energies. Martial art training such as Qigong is beneficial too. Like tai chi, you are working with energy plus many of your body systems. I was surprised there are forms of Qigong that even the invalid can practice to strengthen themselves.

Yoga - need I say more? The shortest path to connecting with Source is through meditation or quieting the mind. Be silent so that you can hear. Breathe so that you can oxygenate the brain. This provides the least resistance and will assist you in having intuitive flashes and ideas for improving your money flow. These thoughts could occur during exercise or meditation. Often, they happen within a day or two afterward.

To master money, figure out your value in the world and what you bring to others. This can be accomplished in a work setting with others or in an endeavor you create on your own. It could be both for awhile. The more energy and value you are putting out there, the more money will flow toward you.

Once you have created something — even your upgraded self — connect deeply with it. What are your gifts you bring to a work situation or company? How do the services or products you create offer solutions for others? See the value of what you do or create. Ask yourself constantly, how can this item I created be better? How can I be of more value to others? Each time, you are leveling up and increasing your chances for attracting more money.

Develop a deep sense of self-worth. Train your brain to feel worthy, because you are! This is true not just of money, but anything you want to manifest for yourself. Realize that your self worth is not equal to your net worth. You can have a zero bank balance temporarily and still value who you are inside.

Once you begin to receive more money, have a real plan on how to utilize it. It has been suggested by many to pay yourself first. This means take a certain percentage of each portion of money you receive and put it away just for you. Attack any debt you have because it ends up costing you more money. Make money work for you by learning about ways you could invest it and the power of how it compounds over time.

Keep your expenses in check. Do not deny yourself, but move forward with major purchases only when you know you hold a very secure amount to fall back on if needed. Because things happen to our personal flow of money. Sometimes, the sun dries up the river bed until heavy rains come around again. Even the tide of the ocean has low and high points. So, it is with the flow of money.

If you learn to pay yourself first and grow an amount of money that makes you feel safe during leaner times, your ability to keep creating will be not be stifled. However, if you are worried about how you are going to pay the bills, you will push yourself into that lack territory and your creative juices will not be flowing.

Finally, realize this is a game. The money game is nothing more than you having the God given opportunity to create. You get to create a better you, a better service, a better product, etc. Money is given to you in exchange for your creation. Nothing more than a game! And, it is not like Monopoly where there is only one winner. Everyone keeps the currency of money flowing and can participate in it. Yes, some will have more, some less. But, if all were equal, what would we feel compelled to do or create?

Receiving Energy

"Until you make the unconscious conscious, it will direct your life and you will call it fate."
~ Dr. Carl G. Jung

Open your palm and look at it. Is it ready to receive? Empaths are notorious for blocking their own good. Plagued with feelings of worthiness and often afraid they will take something from another if they receive it instead. We must learn to be open to receive the abundant lives we deserve. How can we do this and feel a true comfortable feeling about it? It is only by confronting the issues at the core stories of our life. In that way, we transcend what holds us back in all ways, including abundance. This includes, but is not limited to, lack thinking; worthiness; and eliminating our fears of asking or requesting what we want. Using our intense feelings, we are in a position to visualize what we desire into existence, putting our faith, beliefs and expectation behind it.

Currently, some call it the art of allowing and there is a book by that name as well. It is really important to keep in mind that in order to allow the good things into your life, you must be open to receiving. This is a requirement because when you are vibrating in a receiving mode, the good things can be allowed in. Otherwise, your vibrational signature is setting up blockades of different types that keep it from coming into your existence in miraculous, and often magical, ways. Let us examine each of these lower vibrational frequencies that keep you from receiving that good.

Lack thinking is generally a habit first formed from fear. These fears lie at the root of whether or not we are worthy. Deep inside, we have patterns held that for this reason or that, we do not deserve. These outdated, but held beliefs, could have begun with our family of origin and often do. In frustration, parents often repeated things to us as children that were said to them. These negative messages are not true. They are the product of poor parenting techniques. If you were subjected to abuse (and many empaths have been) you will have more patterns to clear. Over time, rid yourself of feelings built upon false premises which unconsciously became your beliefs.

Often unknowingly, our parental and authority figures said or did things that made us feel not good enough. We spend the rest of our lives putting up sticky notes saying we are good enough. It does take retraining of our brains as we replace those old beliefs with new ones that are true.

We also buy into the theory of lack when we feel there is not enough. Again, just hearing our parental figures state there is not enough money for that item you want or to take a vacation began to form the lack ideas in your brain. Hearing of people in the world who do not have enough food or other necessities put ideas and beliefs into your unconscious. "You better eat your brussel sprouts, there are children starving who would love to have them."

Lack thinking is a lower vibrational frequency. Along with the fear of not having, we find the fear of having. This is the same pole, just opposite ends. They both lock out your good and must be transformed. Within the fear of having, you worry that you may upset others who do not have the same. They may be jealous, talk behind your back, and a myriad of other responses you would find negative. You might even fear you will be abandoned in some way in relationships if you receive what you really desire in your own life. If you have a wonderful home with a swimming pool or that chalet in the mountains, what about other people who are homeless? We all receive what we are open to and have worked toward on some level. Many people living on the streets do not even want to have a place of their own because it would require that they make some changes. Of course, this is not true of all people that do not have a home to go to. However, it is a very frequent statement from quite a few.

Why deny yourself anything in life because others are not where you are mentally, physically or even spiritually? When you improve your situation through receiving, you are then in a position to help those who are lost, physically challenged or in need. There are many people unable to walk. I have a grandson unable to speak. Does this mean we will spend our lives not taking walks or not speaking because we do not want to be unlike the least of us? Of course not! Instead, we should utilize all the tools and talents we have been blessed with to make this a better world by being open to receiving our good that we can share as we see fit. If you will not conquer lack thinking and receive the things you really desire, how will you ever be an example or teacher for someone else to emulate, follow or learn from? How could you assist others if you will not assist yourself?

We have no control over the responses of others. Often, their response is temporary and just knee jerk reactions. As you stand in your God given personal power and be who you are, others will, at the least, respect you for your position. However, if you are groveling and in lack most of the time, they will not.

What you decide to manifest as a magical empath is your desire and up to you. Whether it be simple and Zen like or huge and over the top, it is your dream — your life. Be open to receiving. In your willingness to have what you desire, you are then in a better position to share and help others.

Here is something important to keep in mind: you need to progress toward higher vibrational feelings surrounding receiving in steps. In fact, this is true for everything you are endeavoring. It is difficult to jump from "I don't deserve" to "I deserve whatever I desire". The easier, longer term effective route would be to just go a little higher at first than the feelings of not deserving. You may move mentally and emotionally to "my feelings of not deserving are unjustified and rooted in old thought patterns. I will be shown what I need to clear away to receive my true desires."

Become aware of your self-talk and habitual feelings that hang on due to old patterns that need to vanish. We all participate in this. I have a jar with a lid that sits on my desk. When I feel discouraged or like I am not in any way good enough to do something, I write that thought down on the nearest scrap of paper and put it in the jar. Once a month, I go through the jar and burn those pieces of paper. Sometimes I read them first. Often, when I see those thoughts I had, I realize they were momentary lapses in judgment — that's all. They are only silly little negative thoughts that don't mean anything. And the burning of them releases them to be transformed.

Right now, as I am typing this chapter, I am going to pull one of those notes and tell you what it says. Here we go: "I honestly wonder how I can finish this book with all the interruptions and hours of caring for my grandson I am engaged in. God, Please help me do this." Do you know what has happened since I put that note in the jar? My daughter has picked up many more hours taking care of my grandson because the business she was employed at closed suddenly. For a reason unknown, I experienced less interruptions from my husband and family so that I could complete the book.

Sometimes, you have to give your problems or negative feelings up to a higher power and just surrender that to them. It still will probably require you participating in your new reality creation too — such as with setting boundaries, etc. I could have sat in front of my computer and cried that day. I could have just closed the door on all of it and not finished the book. But, it was and is very important to me. Even when things are not working magically for us, we can transform the situation by letting go of what we cannot control in that moment until we can get a handle on our thoughts and emotions. We move forward with a confidence that tells us that somehow, something is going to break open for us to receive what we want whether it is time, money, love or friendship.

When we learn to care about monitoring our self talk and feelings on a consistent basis, we are in a position to make adjustments along the way. It always comes back to us. No matter what is going on externally, it is our game we play with ourselves.

Another thing we fall victim to is consensus thinking. This is where our thoughts and beliefs are based upon the collective ones of other people. If everyone in your family believes a particular thing about your genetics, it must be true, right? Reexamine that belief. Thoughts held for awhile turn into beliefs. If your family believes that you will likely develop Type 2 diabetes because it runs in your family, will you? What if the foods prepared and lifestyle lived within the family unit is the culprit actually contributing to this? That changes everything about the belief.

We can be held back and tamped down by the words being spewed from the media. Did you ever notice that almost every media outlet is using the exact same words? Words are spells cast upon the public to make them believe in a certain direction or way. The mass media knows the power they have with regurgitating the same phrases and words repetitively. Our brains are computers. Garbage in … garbage out. Now, a part of you may be popping up with the thought, "But it's true. What they are saying is true." Is it? Perhaps six people died at the hands of someone else. That could be true. But are the motives, manifesto provided, social media postings, and everything else about the story true? You really do not know, do you? It could be … or not.

You decide what is going to be true for you. This is a powerful position to be in. You decide to remain open to other versions of history and her-story. You decide to be a lightening rod and feel the strike, but wait to deliver judgment on what direction it came from. It is a wise and magical act to suspend judgment and belief. When put into daily practice, this will assist you in reexamining all the beliefs you have ever held about anything. Further, it begins to allow you to divide up thoughts. There are the thoughts you actually think and the thoughts that you are receiving from outside sources. Knowing the difference is powerful as well.

When you feel anxious or confused about something and do not know the course to take or what to believe, give it some time. Surrender it to your higher self, angels, God Source ... whatever feels comfortable to you. Then, go and do something fun or relaxing. Or, stay on a project you are engaged in. In other words, drop the worry. As you do so, you open yourself to receiving in a new way .... Receiving thoughts and solutions from a higher source that will come to you later.

Your inner being or higher self already has the answers to all your situations. You just need to stop holding onto so many unfruitful thoughts and worn out beliefs to let those answers come through. This is the main secret to opening yourself to receive.

There is enough air for everyone to breathe. The planet is full of water, bountiful food and resources. Political decisions are keeping many in slavery or devastating conditions. Money is now made up and digital most of the time. It's a current — flowing or backed up. Make it flow to you by having your palms open mentally, ready to receive. Do this also with love in your relationships with others. See yourself, arms open, ready to embrace those around you.

Visualize
Believe
Expect
Receive
Give Back

Managing Energies

"Magic is believing in yourself, if you can do that, you can make anything happen." ~ Johann Wolfgang von Goethe

What some have perhaps made you feel is your weakness is your power. Sometimes it has been criticized greatly. You may have been subjected to statements such as:

- You wear your heart on your sleeve
- Chip on your shoulder
- Overly sensitive
- Too emotional
- Need to let things roll off your back

The fact is emotions are the fuel you put into the manifestation engine. A magical empath has learned to direct their emotions into productive channels. An empath who is just discovering themselves or who is in earlier learning stages is trying to cope with their emotions and all they are picking up from others unknowingly.

Most of you reading this book may fall in between these two points. You are looking for balance daily in your walk through this dense earth plane. Because you are empathic and caring, you are easily a target for some of the more treacherous individuals who seek to steal your energy. You also feel so much at times, it is just overwhelming. You do not know if these feelings are yours. Are they true? Are they coming from somewhere else?

This is where practice and discernment come in. When I say the word practice, I am literally conveying that you need to do certain things to build the inner dynamics required for coping. Instead of hiding away, we must put the things we try to avoid into different contexts. Allow this example:

I awoke at 4am, earlier than usual, and decided to begin my work. I felt it would be beneficial for me to meditate first. As I sat in my meditation posture, random thoughts of things I needed to make priorities kept popping into my mind. Most of it was personal things to take care of that I had perhaps not made note of somewhere else. I would let the thought occur, acknowledging I would make a note of it after meditating. The only problem was, I was not able to meditate. Thoughts consumed me and I finally stopped resisting, made notes of those items and began my work.

For the life of me, I could not get into a blank space as more and more things filled my mind. This is a common occurrence when you first learn to meditate. However, I began this practice decades ago. Honestly though, I had not been doing it very regularly. Unlike riding a bicycle, when you fall out of practice, you have to rebuild those abilities again.

At a very base physical level, I know that meditating is super healthy for me and it keeps me connected to the divine in a larger way. My problem is that I am just well enough attuned that I sometimes take that connection for granted. I have pretty good discernment now and excellent intuitive skills. I am conscious of energy around me and when I need to do some filtering of it. Yet, I am missing out on some magical opportunities for the miracles and synchronicities to not only continue, but increase. Because I am not regularly slipping into that deep state of meditation and opening to the one true Creator, I am losing my edge or advantage.

My resistance or lack of disciplined habit in this regard is holding me back from being a magical empath more of the time. It is most likely what causes my fluctuations in feeling connected or in the flow or experiencing days of just feeling "off".

We must acknowledge also that we have internal and external challenges around us that are part of what is vibrating into our essence or being. There are hormonal fluctuations. Hormones are a very powerful thing that can affect our feelings and behavior. There are others around us experiencing hormonal fluctuations. Yikes!

We go through short and long phases along with our galaxy. There are full and new moons, lunar eclipses, and challenging astrological aspects at times. When we are experiencing these, we can only surrender to the tide that is present and mimic its qualities in order to find peace within ourselves.

Some are surrounded by others who require extra consideration and help such as those with physical and mental challenges. There are many things that can tug on us as we begin to try to achieve the balance we seek to make each day as magical as possible.

It is important that we not allow ourselves to drop into victim mode. No one plays victim better than an empath! But, a magical empath would not indulge in this for very long at all. If you catch yourself going there, realize you are still responsible for everything coming at you on one level or another and stop. Examine where you are leaking your power and how you can correct it. Look at the chapter on Building Trust. Also review the Self Care and Regulation chapter. This is the time for it -- when we begin to feel sorry for what we perceive is our awful plight and how no one really appreciates us.

The point of managing our energies is to turn what others view as your weakness into a powerful strength that fuels the magical life you desire. The easiest route to this is three-fold: meditate, say positive affirmations and utilize creative visualization.

Being a magical empath holds a balance between polarity energies. In other words, you cannot be all yin or feminine in your energy and accomplish your goals within this life. Nor can you be entirely yang or masculine, using techniques to mold things the way you desire. There is always a surprise element present from your higher self who knows what you need when you need it, if you will only listen.

Utilizing the two practices, meditation (yin) and creatively visualizing with strong emotion (yang), can bring you into energy alignment. With meditation, you are in the receiving mode. When you use your imagination through affirmations and visualization, you are in the directing mode. Meditation can be approached in several ways as there are various methods. Reach out for help from others who teach this if needed. The benefits outweigh the trouble you may expect that it will be. Take advantage of guided visualizations if you have trouble at first using your own mental creative visualizing skills. There is one requisite for both of these activities - time dedicated to yourself.

The main point of meditation is quieting that voice within us that is distracting our magical focus most of the time. The more we meditate, the higher we raise our vibration. It also assists us in quieting the resistance we are putting forth so much of the time. This helps us open and receive. There are numerous physical benefits to quieting the mind during meditation like decreased stress or anxiety levels, enhanced immunity, more relaxed brain wave activity, decreased blood pressure and putting yourself in a better mood.

For those really having a tough time getting into a deep meditation due to noise, busy thoughts, etc., try a walking meditation. This method falls more into the mindfulness category, whereas the other meditations described below would be considered a concentrative approach. During your walk alone or silently with another, allow your mind to let go of thoughts about the past or future. For instance, if you begin thinking of what you will prepare for dinner, this is a future thought. Likewise, thoughts of what happened that morning or at work yesterday are of the past. Stay in the present moment.

Look at things very closely. Examine the structure of a leaf or flower in detail. Entice yourself to drink in mentally everything around you. Feel how wondrous the environment is.

Other forms of body movement can be conducive to a relaxed, meditative state. These can include dance, tai chi, qigong, You can even practice mindfulness meditation while washing the dishes or gardening.

If you are in a physical condition that makes it difficult for you to walk, sit in an outdoor area and again, really examine all around you. Drink in the flora and fauna. Listen to the noises of nature and focus in on them, ignoring sounds from passing traffic, etc.

For a more concentrated traditional approach to meditation, know that you do not have to sit in lotus position. In fact, I would consider your first priority to not be uncomfortable as this can interfere with removing internal thoughts. A comfortable chair will suffice. I always like to have the soles of my feet touch the floor as I ground myself mentally in the first chakra. Often, I sit with my palms upturned toward the sky in a receiving position. My eyes are closed.

Begin by taking deep breaths, through the nose, that expand your belly. Exhale through your mouth. This is not fast breathing — it is not super slow. It is more on the slow side and measured. Experiment with your breath to find what is comfortable and relaxing to you. It should all be relaxing and not feel taxing on your system.

Focusing on breathing only the first few times you meditate may be beneficial. In other words, do not put any other expectations upon the experience now. Just get comfortable with the process for you. Typically, I inhale through my nose until I feel my belly expanded with air. I then hold that air for 5-6 seconds. Upon exhalation, I allow my jaw to drop open and begin letting the air out, almost pushing it a little at the end. Meditation performed in this way is close to the Zen tradition which is minimalist in structure. Another physical benefit is the deep lymphatic breathing. It assists your body in moving toxins through your lymphatic system for eventual removal.

Those thoughts, those thoughts, those unrelenting thoughts! Yes, they can be an issue when you are doing any type of meditation, even the walking exercise above. Instead of attempting to reign them in, let them move past you. When you see, hear or feel the thought arise, just say, "uh huh" — let it pass on by without worry or judgment. You can deal with it later. You might even visualize passing it by as if you were traveling in a vehicle and just noticed a billboard.

During meditation, many people find it helpful to chant while they are breathing. This can be a faster way to reach a deeper state. A traditional way to do this is to repeat the word "om". Allowing the sound to resonate from your diaphragm, you may also choose to use a mantra or affirmation. If you feel self conscious about that, you can focus on a noise like a fan you hear running, something that is constant in nature. There are also many selections of music to choose from that assist in beautiful background noise for meditation.

Some people are able to meditate with their eyes open. Usually, they are using something visual as a point to focus on. This could be a large screen television or display of snow falling, a waterfall, or ocean waves rolling in and out.

As you become more comfortable slipping into a meditative state, you may experiment if you wish with other forms. I will cover those in more depth in book two of this series. Yes, I have been told there will be a second volume of information to assist us in being magical empaths. In fact, book one is proving to be preparatory for the information coming next.

Creative Visualization (1978) is a metaphysical book I read back in the day. I loved Ms. Gawain's approach as she explained to us so much about how energy works or what we knew of it at that time. Today, we know a little more. Yet energy still remains mysterious. One thing I (and others) have discovered is that our feelings fuel manifestation. What we focus on with some sort of intensity, we receive — negative or positive. It may not always be an exact thing or person. No matter how much we put emotion into dating our favorite television, movie or rock star, it does not mean we can override their personal choices and make that happen. However, it could mean we attract someone who embodies much of the same attributes that we admired in that star to begin with.

In 2004, I found myself grabbing morning coffee and a croissant in the area of St. Vincent's Hospital in Greenwich Village while visiting New York City with my oldest daughter. She had been living and working in Manhattan for a few years. We were there to pick up items she had in a storage unit as she made a career move across the country to California.

In the early hours while she slept, I walked the streets and passed a corner that was covered in painted ceramic tiles of remembrance for victims of 911. I felt an intense heavy grief in the area. I picked up my pace and with sunglasses on, tears welled up in my eyes and I was very overcome emotionally. My daughter asked if I wanted to visit ground zero during the trip. This solidified my decision not to. It was just too overwhelming. I had to avoid that corner in the village each day thereafter. In fact, I made myself walk on the opposite side of the street. It held an energy and it was permeating through my skin into me ... or at least that's what it felt like. And this is how it is for empaths. I think I still would have felt that sad energy even if I had not read a single remembrance tile. I only read a couple. This was three years after the tragedy. Energy hangs on, especially where we memorialize it in some way.

I loved the energy of New York — bustling around the clock and such a diverse population of people. I could live there if I chose. There would be a lot of changes I would need to make internally. I am lucky to live in a secluded area, but I could do it and still find my solace. It would be interesting each day.

A vast number of empaths seem to have high functioning intuition. In fact, many are telepathic and either feel, hear, see or have a knowing about what others are feeling or thinking around them. This aids in knowing if someone is not being truthful or attempting to manipulate us or others.

Often, an empath can meet someone for the first time and although others may feel that the new person is perfectly fine, the empath senses something is not quite right. They may or may not be able to verbalize exactly what it is. This feeling comes to them and later proves itself to be true to all involved.

This psychic skill of empaths has sometimes been pushed down out of the way inside of them. Why? Because it requires that we feel and often we don't want to take on the feelings of others. There is a way to step into and toward another and peek into their inner world without becoming part of it.

Exercises for stepping toward energy without absorbing

Project Loving Strength – During your daily life, visits with others and general moving about in the world, you are going to come upon those with distorted views that are divisive in nature. This often cuts against the empath's ideas. As you think about how screwed up the other individual is, you are missing the opportunity to display a broader, more loving view. Granted, sometimes you are dealing with a more toxic individual or situation and there can be no immediate influence. For example, during a holiday visit with family, one person spouts off their political views and alienates about half the people present.

A loving, empathic approach would be: first, acknowledge in your mind that each person is an accumulation of what they have come to believe as truth. While holding certain truths can be subjective and based upon the experiences of that person, truth always rises and shows itself. Instead of immediately taking sides, here is what can be done. Find a point of agreement with that person that is true – not something to placate them, but a true statement that reflects a larger view. You could say something like, "It is true that each of us, in one way or another, have the capacity to make this world a better place. It is our choice to do this or not by the amount of love and tolerance we are willing to feel for others."

This type of statement may even be misinterpreted by the other person(s). It could change the subject or propel the conversation into another direction. The point is not to dig your heels in and defend your viewpoint.

Leave it at that. Time to change the subject or excuse yourself into another room or conversation. Generally, this person that brought the polarizing subject up wants to hammer it and debate it. They may even enjoy a good argument.

No Real Response -- Why respond at all? Why not be a gray rock and say nothing. That is a second possible choice. It may feel safer to remain uninvolved in the conversation and not engage to begin with.

If you find yourself feeling frustrated with that person and angry at yourself for not speaking up, developing artful dialog would be something you want to build toward. This way, you can be in many social settings where you do not leave the situation feeling like you were not true to yourself and your core beliefs.

Diffuse -- A third response that I have used at times to diffuse another when they are trashing someone, whether it be a political figure or another family member. Buddha says about those we can find little good in: "even his exhalation feeds the flowers". I love this metaphor because it is inclusive. It brings things instantly around to the idea that we are all in this.

Transmute -- A fourth option is to change things up and transmute the negative energy. Most people don't know why they may be feeling really bad. Empaths sense negative energy in many rooms, buildings and situations. You can assist in transmuting the energy in a situation by utilizing positive pointed thoughts, humor, placing objects of beauty and positive vibrations in the area. Adding music, playing in the background, can change the mood instantly. Light a candle or two also. See how the vibes change.

Allow your sensitive nature to be a skill that is honed instead of something toned down to meet the ideas of others. See how this expression of your feelings can be shared in an artful and creative way that is in alignment with your purpose. You might walk over to the person at the event who is trying to upset things and say, "I really appreciate your passion about this. While everyone here may not agree with you, I am sure you would be just as passionate about defending their right to hold their thoughts and beliefs."

You must decide which approach works best for you to diffuse the negative energy you can find yourself in the midst of suddenly. Remember, you have the power to choose what you want to take on and what you do not. All of the methods above work well also when combined with the imaginary poncho technique.

Before, During & After The Event

When we are in difficult situations, it can be hard to think swiftly and know what to do. In your daily life, consider wearing or carrying on your person gemstones that assist you. I have found certain gemstones really assist me in having an entirely different mentality when carrying them on me or wearing them in a pocket. Here are a few suggestions, but go with what you feel drawn to. There are many and I will not list them all as it would be another book unto itself.

Lapis Lazuli – Edgar Cayce recommended this stone saying it assisted with higher spiritual attunement and aura maintenance. It is a meditation aid as well. Use it to strengthen your energy field and clear negativity.

Pyrite a/k/a Fool's Gold is great at blocking lower energy forms.

Calcite assists you in clearing the energy around you. It is also a stone of amplification in the sense that it allows you to speak your mind and set clear boundaries.

Lapidilite helps relieve anxiety from feelings of overwhelm and PTSD. Look for Lapidilite with nice tones of pink and lavender. If you are prone to picking up feelings and impressions or have absorption issues, this is a great stone for filtering those effects.

Rainbow Fluorite can assist empaths on all levels of their being. This magical mineral is found in a myriad of colors: pink, magenta, white, purple, yellow, red, green, black, blue. The rainbow version has multiple colors in one stone meaning that it is equipped to clear and balance multiple chakras.

Sugilite is a crystal which originates from South Africa. Ranging in color from an opaque pink all the way to dark purple, sugilite is perfect for empaths to use often. First, it helps with allowing us to feel more grounded. It is often used for protection as a shielding stone. Sugilite also assists in wiping away negative patterns and thoughts.

Black Tourmaline is excellent for absorbing negative energy and a great protection stone.

Rhodosite has been one that instantly gives me feelings of peace and harmony with everything and all people. It feels like it really activates something in me. It has been said that it is an excellent stone for empaths.

Labradorite as on the front cover. A must have stone for empaths!

The Empath's Inner Power

What is inner power? More importantly, let's define what it is not. Inner power is not the same as having a lot of energy, although your physical energy in your body will definitely increase as you move through life in an empowered way. Inner power is not having a lot of charisma. Yet, many will be attracted to your vibration not even knowing why. Some will be repelled by it. This may happen because it reminds them of their polar opposite of what they are currently experiencing. They may secretly wish to be more like you or want to avoid what you are. Often, this avoidance is because they know on some level it would require them to make significant changes. As humans, we often have a wall of avoidance pop up around change.

Inner power is certainly not displaying some type of control or authority over others whether overt or covert. It is not coming from a position of having to manipulate to operate well within your life.

So what exactly is it? Inner power is a state of being where you do not sabotage yourself. You move forward with things and craft your life in a way that is enhancing to your mind, body and spirit. Because you are self-focused on this, your influence may affect others that come into contact with you. However, that is not your mission. If that were your goal, it would be born more of the ego and looking to manipulate others.

The way to grow this inner power is through continued inner seeking, assessment and outward actions taken to ensure it is not trampled or lost. Finally, however, we must feel confident standing in our power and not allowing others to manipulate us. This is difficult for empaths, but very doable.

Discharging Unwanted Energies

As empaths, we are at times filled with so many confusing emotions that do not feel good. We may try to pinpoint what is bothering us, but cannot. Even mature empaths can have this occur. However, it happens with more frequency when you have not become aware of energies and the management of them. The best thing you can do is find quick ways to discharge the unwanted energies you have picked up. There may be times you wonder if it is your stuff rather than someone else's feelings you have picked up. If it is your stuff, it will come back to visit again. For now, let us find ways of relieving the discomfort. Here are some quick fixes:

Music is vibration and it has the capacity to reorganize the energies around you very quickly.

Place your hands and/or feet in the dirt or sand. Touching the earth is very beneficial. This is a great time to plant some seeds or flowers, weather permitting.

Venture outdoors and try to find a wonderful tree to lean your body against. Trees are such majestic, loving entities. They will allow you to discharge that energy by placing your hands on them.

Sit beside running water or the ocean, if possible. Enjoy other natural sounds like crickets chirping at night.

Any creative endeavor such as painting, designing, building helps discharge blocked energy and change focus.

Epsom salt body or foot baths — add the music too — something uplifting for your vibration.

Visualize yourself covered in thick mud and then step into the shower. In your mind, see the mud washing away down the drain until you are clean and renewed.

Often, we really do not know where all these emotions are coming from. Sometimes, we believe it is the people we have to be around (or think we have to be) that we are picking up from. Periodically, check in with yourself about the people you are around. Go over each of them in your mind. As you think of each person individually, ask yourself how they make you feel? With those who affect you negatively, is there a way you can distance yourself a bit from them? Is there a way you can eliminate contact entirely? If not, what solutions could you put into place?

Discernment

How do empaths, with their exceptional abilities to read people, get fooled? There are many ways for us to be aware of. They always involve us not being totally in touch with ourselves and off track in some manner. The more balanced we can be, the harder it is to fall into that trap. If it does happen, our own egos, can be a factor.

Falling for a trickster often occurs in conjunction with us operating out of codependency. We need someone else to make us feel of value. Our people pleasing kicks into high gear with us abandoning our own needs first.

Whenever we feel this happen, it should be a warning sign that we are out of balance and need to come back home to ourselves and honor our needs first. This will give us a much more stable piece of ground to stand upon so that we can begin to determine if the relationship we are engaged in helps or hurts both parties. For even when we are helping someone we know is not going to change, it is enabling and hurting their development.

We can also be fooled by people who are just really adept at convincing us they are someone they are not. With you being an empath, there will probably be some little signals going off for you that either this person is too good to be true or something feels incongruent. Take it slow — at a snail's pace. Be mysterious instead of too quick to accommodate with the relationship. Consult others whose opinion and discernment you respect. Feel the energy dynamic going on between the two of you. It is important that we are clear with ourselves and the intentions of all parties and not in some form of denial about what is going on in relation to energetic and emotional levels.

Notes – Thoughts – Ideas – Affirmations – Dreams

Walking Backward

"It is only through mystery and madness that the soul is revealed" ~ Thomas Moore

When we visit our own earth beginnings and personal story we experienced, we begin to find clarity. Examining our growth from infancy to childhood, and then into adolescence and adulthood allows us to piece together what shaped us. This peek at the past shows what gave us the outlook and inner feelings we hold within. This is often painful for many. Yet, if we feel ready and able to perform this inner examination, the rewards are numerous. When we approach this in a deep unfolding way, we finally begin to uncover our true purpose.

Many people want to know why they are here and what is their purpose. For empaths, this is often a deep calling. They know they are here to do something, but what is it? How can they know or uncover it? It is only by walking backward through our lives and viewing things from a different perspective. By pretending to be a high flying eagle and soaring above our life situations, we can stay a little more detached. As we gaze and view the dynamics that passed by us before, we realize it was because we were in our story. By rising high above it with eagle eyes instead of human, new ways of looking at our life open to us and give us profound vision.

Once we identify the patterns in our early caregivers and life experiences, we see what it was shaping us into. We can then begin to contemplate the purpose of a person who experienced that type of past. Soon, our purpose(s) begin to unfold before us. Our purpose comes unannounced in the form of sudden ideas, desires and opportunities that are shaping us further. In other words, once our consciousness has cracked the code on our past and the why of it, we are then open to begin naturally attracting our future.

It is necessary to walk backward into the dark in order to find the light we are seeking. Yet, we must also know what it is we are looking for. This differs with each individual. Primarily, we are looking for how you picked up certain ingrained patterns. The next step is to completely bust those myths wide open that are not serving you as true solid beliefs. Finally, look at what things you continually struggle with time and again. Really examine this because often these items vary with different people or situations, but basically it's the same core issue. These are patterns not serving you picked up from the past.

No one can tell you your purpose. It is a discovery you must make. Sometimes, the ego can lead you astray. Even if that happens, it is perfectly alright. Events will shape around you that try to lead you back toward your purpose. This often shows up in our relationships with others and in sudden, unpredictable events.

However, there are some common questions that allow us to explore and discover from our early roots to now, uncovering clues of our greater purpose. These prompts serve as a broad beginning of uncovering how your past relates to your purpose. They may be questions you want to ponder over a few days and journal as well.

1) Look deeply at family of origin situations. If you were a soul getting ready to come into this world and you had certain things you wanted to accomplish or lessons to learn, what kind of family would you be born into?
2) What gifts or natural talents did you seem to possess from a young age?
3) What challenges did you encounter? This list could be exhaustive, but begin with challenges encountered at a young age.

4) What are the core feelings you held about yourself as a child? Are any of those feelings still present?
5) What event(s) had the greatest impact upon you up to the age of adulthood; and after adulthood?
6) What did you want to be as a child? This may be several occupations or items. Take each one and list the benefits a person would receive if they were that.
7) What do you want to do, but have not accomplished for whatever reasons?
8) As a child, what characters or archetypes were you drawn to? Specifically, what was the attraction about?
9) If you were now 100 years old, what would you say to yourself?

By journaling and exploring many of these questions, common themes will begin to arise for you. While you are actively engaged in this searching of your past, you may also experience many other events such as lightening quick revelations at some point. Just try to flow along with the process in an unhurried way. As long as you are doing the searching, what you need will come to you at the perfect moment.

Meditation is key to getting outside of your thinking mind so that insights and downloads can come to you. By meditating, you will be able to shift your state of awareness to something that is outside of time and space. Who you think you are and what your purpose is can sometimes be extremely limited. This is because you are using your mind as the vehicle to try and figure it out. If you allow your awareness to expand, who you are becomes not only infinite without the restrictions you experience now, but limitless in the ways you can manifest and express yourself.

When you perform the examination of your past, you are uncovering karmic ties that reveal things you need to master and overcome. You are loaded with gifts, even if you do not believe you are. Those talents can be developed further. As you do so, your spiritual and physical progress speeds along exponentially. You came into this life with a precise thought form that was very focused. Once you get here, it is so easy to be distracted by the dense human experience that you have a hard time finding your original reason for being here.

It is like you set out on a trip across a great land in your vehicle. While you are traveling, your human body needs energy just as your vehicle needs fuel. You become distracted by all restaurants you pass and finally make a decision to stop and fuel up at one of them. While there, the food is so intoxicating that it has an effect on your mind and you forget where you were even traveling to in the first place. In fact, the meal was so delicious, now you believe your sole purpose may be to try every restaurant on this highway. You became so attached to the delicious food, you have forgotten your original desire. Distraction from purpose is not uncommon in this human experience. Yet, the energy strands we are bound to in the realm beyond always have a way of pulling us back toward our purpose.

For empaths, the higher purpose they feel called to complete is vital. Without embarking upon it, they are apt to feel unfulfilled in many ways. These common threads I suggest above to explore are not all inclusive, but a start to unwind the real reasons you are here and assist you in discovery of that so that you may move toward fulfillment of same.

Selflessness = Less Self

"A piece of writing is like a piece of magic. You create something out of nothing." ~ Susanna Clarke

Empaths are so giving in nature, they assume that when they need help it will be there. They can find themselves disillusioned, angry, bitter, resentful and even ashamed of the love they have given over time when they realize that is not automatically the case. In the alternative, they may slip into a dark time of depression, not really sure who they are any longer. This happened to me.

I went through a long period of losing many parts of myself. This was a good thing and bad. I knew it was happening, but felt powerless to change it. I lost myself in others too much of the time. I was not in my personal power. Awareness of this finally came from two of my grown children. It was shocking for my second daughter to look me in the eye and say, "Mom, I don't know what has happened to you. You are like a shell of yourself." Daughter one asked me on the phone, "Where is the strong woman with ambition and ideas galore? What happened to her?" I really could not give either of them a clear answer. I did not know myself. All the things that had changed in my life had sucked me dry.

I had to really begin to see my part in allowing this to happen. I had slipped into codependency -- again. Since my diagnosis of codependent behavior decades ago, I had spent many hours studying the subject and working to eradicate it. I believed it to be something I had conquered. But, it happened again when I was not paying close attention.

My extreme codependent behavior probably resurfaced when I began to feel without clear direction and that my life was out of control. Simultaneously, my husband was diagnosed with stage 3 cancer. Our income dropped drastically. I spent months saving our dream home from foreclosure which was a monumental project. I resolved tax debt and penalties — another stress ridden task. I attended college again to try and find a new direction, only to discover that I wanted to pursue my dream I had envisioned all along — to be a writer.

With so many health and financial issues in my day to day existence, I had no idea where to begin. Stress keeps us from thinking clearly and it certainly blocks much of our intuitive abilities. Following the lead of Julia Cameron's book, *The Artist's Way*, I used my time in the morning with coffee to journal about everything that was going on. These pages were filled with things I felt strife about. Some mornings, it was a full blown pity party. Yet, I noticed something. Some mornings, once the negative thoughts were out of the way, something cleared in my mind. During those moments, I found myself writing more profound things that I was elated about. Those writings led to more words. Eventually, I knew I was headed somewhere with words that were good enough to be shared.

My husband was finally and thankfully declared cancer free. About four years later, he began to have heart issues and went through a quadruple bypass. Of course, this required me to put anything I was pursuing on hold while I helped him recover and get back to normal life. Then, our youngest daughter announced she was pregnant — on purpose and not married. She expected us to be delighted with this news. The reaction was mixed. She then became a mother while living with us and gave birth to a beautiful baby boy. Within the first three months, we could tell her enthusiasm for motherhood had wained. I found myself stepping in to make sure this child was taken care of quite a bit of the time. I still help care for him, but I have instituted boundaries with my daughter. This is not only helpful for me, but her as well. She is then forced to step into her role as a mom. But, she does need help and he does as well.

Currently, he is non-verbal and diagnosed on the severe end of the autism spectrum. He does understand many things so I hold hope for continued progress from therapies he receives and us working with him at home.

Watching all this play out in my household, the empathic part of me kicked in that wanted to be the fixer. My whole life began to revolve around extreme care taking of others, instead of myself. It has taken time to wean everyone, getting back to a life that seems normal again. It is all about boundaries and I am still setting them and reinforcing my preferences consistently. I must strike a balance in my life between what I should be doing as a grandmother, instead of taking on responsibilities that are not mine.

I am thankful daughters one and two were very pointed and frank with me. It was my moment of waking up out of some strange people pleasing slumber I had fallen into. Even if we are thoroughly embroiled in codependent behavior, we can turn things around and come out of it.

Another Empath

Allow me to tell you about Rhonda. She and her husband John have been married forty years. Rhonda recently discovered that she is an empath. During their early years together, she raised the children while John worked full time. As the children reached school age, Rhonda began working part-time in the school cafeteria, adding to the family income so they could afford a better home and material things. She made sure her work hours were situated so that she could still be with her children after school and during the summer when they were off. This also allowed her to get them to all the different extracurricular activities they were involved in.

As evening approached, she would fix dinner without help from the children or her husband and often be up late folding laundry for the next day. Her husband would go to his job, come home, sit in a chair and do what he wanted to do. He never asked her to go on a walk with him after dinner and instead have the children wash the dishes. He stopped bringing her home little gifts like he used to. Soon, they would stop having sex altogether.

Now with both of them in retirement and the children gone, Rhonda finds she is still waiting hand and foot on her husband and assisting him with every little stomach ache or pain he suffers from. Yet, if her back is killing her, he pouts and acts like he cannot even make himself a sandwich while she has some downtime. He attempts to make her feel guilty and she allows him to, finally slowly moving from her spot on the bed and dragging herself to the kitchen to fix him food.

Empathic Rhonda is still anticipating her husband's needs, checking in with her now adult children as to what they may need her to do as well. Rhonda is busy, very busy. She is still cleaning the house almost like she used to. Thankfully, there are more machines and easier systems for flooring than the old days. She is still doing laundry and planning the next holiday event when they will see family. For the most part, Rhonda is focused on everyone except herself and when anyone won't lift even a pinkie finger to make her feel better, she is completely perplexed and wondering how in the hell they can be this way?

There is a great feeling of loneliness that Rhonda carries with her. She does not understand why in the world her husband would not be more attentive to her at times. He never offers to rub her shoulders and she doesn't ask because the last time she did, he did so very begrudgingly making her feel horrible for asking in the first place. It took all the healing capacity out of the rub.

"Is this what life is going to be until I die?" Rhonda asks herself. "Will I just feel all alone, even though he is here with me?"

One day, the call of freedom rang in Rhonda's ears and tickled her brain in a new way. Liberation soared through her veins as her husband was driving miles away from her now, headed north on a hunting trip with work buddies from the past. How different everything felt. The house, even though it needed numerous repairs now, was vacant of his energy which seemed to be thick like a fog that blanketed the entire structure at times.

Yes, she felt free and if he had a fatal accident, she would consider it a blessing. How could she be so evil? It was not that she wished for John's demise. It was more so that she just wanted to be out of this relationship that was holding her down and she had no graceful exit. He will be back though, she thought. When that happens, would Rhonda be brave enough to just tell him that she is happy without him and wants a divorce?

So used to not feeling freedom, Rhonda found herself projecting into the future with worries and concerns. Again, if John did not come back for some reason, she would work whatever jobs she had to, sell whatever she needed in order to be free of his overbearing energy he put her through all the time. She didn't like where they had gone in this marriage and it was a hell of a travesty because no one had ever captured her heart like he had in the beginning. There was not a man anywhere she would have even considered marrying, except him.

Now, everything was in ruins where their feelings for each other were concerned. But for today, she could pretend. In fact, for the next few days – she could imagine life without him permanently.

With her home space clear of her husband's energy, Rhonda began to break down exactly what had occurred during their marriage and the woman she had become. She felt she was following society's norms by staying home and making that house the center of her family's world. She was always there to assist their children with homework, social and sporting events, teacher conferences and more … much more. She did not regret doing this for her children. She did wish her husband had taken more of an interest in their school and activities. Rhonda could see that, in John's mind, he had followed what he believed was normal for a husband and father to do: go to work and provide financially for his family.

But, things were never quite what they should have been. Rhonda had previously prided herself on being a wife that did not have to go to the beauty salon on a regular basis or have her nails done. No, she had gone without those things and even certain items of clothing or shoes she needed at times. Anything for the cause. She could see that she had more or less ignored her own needs living some type of martyr lifestyle to appease everyone.

Now, she was open to changing some things at home. She needed to stop waiting on her husband all the time. If he had the energy to hunt, he could do for himself a bit. He was a grown man who could get up and fix his own lunch … and breakfast too. In fact, she wanted to be taken to dinner at least once per week and have him begin helping in the kitchen as well. She anticipated a show down on these issues when he returned home. Rhonda took the time to think of the way she wanted her life to change. These changes needed to happen. Unknown to John, this was just the beginning of changes Rhonda would fight for. Her people pleasing days had ended. It was time she began to enjoy life for herself.

How do empaths fall, often unknowingly, into people pleasing? At the basis of this is fear. They fear being unloved, not needed, or not having significance. This is because the empath has never been taught that, for them, love of self in a manner that is healthy is paramount. If they truly valued themselves, they would never engage in extreme people pleasing behavior. They would have expressed what they like and what is not acceptable to them. The situations they find themselves in would not exist. As much as many of us would like to stay in denial about it, this extreme people pleasing stems from not loving and valuing our selves.

Instead, we find it easier to be agreeable when we really do not agree. Our motivation is to be loved, not disliked or even hated for expressing our own requirements and opinions. The empath examines their surroundings and reaches out to make sure the needs of others are met. This way they know they have some sort of significance. Empaths are nice people with loving hearts and they need to give, but must be very careful not to do it to a fault or until they are enabling the people around them. When their need to give to others is used to validate their worth as a human being, they are giving of themselves in the wrong way. Let me repeat that for hard headed people like myself: if you are giving to receive self-validation, you are on the wrong course.

Initially, when the empath gives to another, they get a mental boost, perhaps even a little dopamine rush. There is a certain satisfaction in helping others and this becomes a fast revolving ferris wheel they cannot exit easily. In order to feel their internal worth, they must continue taking care of the needs of others instead of their own. So, they end up burned out at a certain point and either depressed, resentful or both.

Another reason that empaths jump on the ferris wheel of people pleasing with all of its ups and downs is that they are afraid of losing out somehow. This could be something that compels them to keep giving, even when they know they should curb it or stop. It could be they have fears of being abandoned in some way. Some may feel they will be blamed or held responsible if they do not continue the people pleasing or extreme caretaking. An example might be that if they are not the parent that constantly takes care of the children, something could go wrong. If they do not tend to all their physical, mental and emotional needs and the kids suffer, they will be responsible.

In my younger years, certain people around me with personality disorders used my fears against me to get me to perform this people pleasing behavior. However, I will not put all blame on them. I did it willingly ... for their love, admiration, or to try and eliminate my fear of being abandoned. When we can finally understand why we are doing something and it clicks for us, we can begin to change it ... and do so without blaming the other parties involved. After all, we've been showing up and volunteering for the job.

Where is the division line? How can an empath know when they are just truly giving to be kind or succumbing to people pleasing behavior? Here is the essential difference: Are you doing it out of love or fear. It always comes down to that. If you are doing it to gain their love, that is still fear. If you are doing it because you already love yourself and are committed to limiting how much you help, then that sounds a lot more balanced. If you are giving to another to feel worthy or important in any way, that is fear based. All of these considerations are important distinctions that should be made.

If you fall into people pleasing and extreme caretaking because there are individuals who really need your help, set boundaries. In situations where there is a child with learning challenges, enlist others in the family, medical field, community services, even sitters for an hour or two to assist. This is much wiser than trying to take it on yourself solely. If one of your loved ones are ill or incapacitated in some way, they do need your help, support and love. Again, measure it out with boundaries. Realize if you do not take care of yourself, you will eventually be of little help to them. Get assistance from other sources to balance things out.

Another item I had to work on is shared responsibility. Whether you have a family, spouse or roommates, everyone should pitch in. When we take on the responsibilities or shared portions of what other people should help with, it is usually because we want to avoid their negative comments and energy.

They get flustered easily and act overwhelmed from being asked to chip in.

Because we often do not want to listen to their whining or woes, we find it easier to just do it ourselves. The problem is that we end up overwhelmed with all we are doing for everyone else. We should not have to sacrifice our time and energy so that others do not feel any discomfort. It's all about energy. You will possibly help others build character by relying on them to pull their weight in the situation.

When we realize we are allowing their 'poor me' attitude to manipulate the energy, we can make a change. Once we really see and understand that, we can decide it is time to play another role. We may have to retrain the people we live or work with. At the very least, we must ask them to do their share. Then, life becomes more managable. We stay in our personal power and are not enabling them any longer. Yes, there will probably be some complaining during the retraining. There could be things that are not accomplished. Let them take the responsibility for it.

How can we as empaths be helpful to others and still remain assertive about our own needs and preferences? How can we stop the extreme people pleasing that we can slip into? The first step would be to look at our life now and determine where we may be engaging in people pleasing behavior in order to receive some sort of emotional pay off.

By reflecting on this, we are able to determine our motives for doing things. We can also begin to stop ourselves before volunteering to please and fix things for others so much of the time. We should determine if our interaction is really in everyone's best interest. Remember, they need to be self sufficient too.

We must also reclaim our dominion to deal with authority figures or anyone we feel might hold some type of power over us. That must not be. We must be in our own personal power.

We need to make sure we are not just being agreeable to get along with others out of fear. That is giving in for the wrong reason.

When it comes to people pleasing, most allow situations to build. Indeed, they are often long patterns of behavior. It can seem daunting to change and retrain those around you that you expect something different. Empaths do not like rocking the boat or making anyone upset. We will talk a lot more about that in the chapter, Fear of Conflict.

To honor ourselves, we must not allow things to go on and build. If we address it immediately, it keeps things from feeling too large or out of control. We have to learn the language and approach for these situations. Empaths truly can communicate their likes, dislikes, requirements and such in a beautiful, eloquent way. And, it is very important to do so. Otherwise, we will find ourselves walking around with an angry or resentful vibe that a smile cannot cover up. Worse, we lose our personal power which is going to be needed to live as a magical empath.

How important are your needs? Do you go around putting the needs of others above your own most of the time? What are you trying to gain from this dynamic? What is your payoff? What are you afraid of if you stopped doing this? When can you know if this is truly something you need to do versus something that is falling into a codependency mode of living? Do you find yourself saying or thinking?

"No one understands me"
"I do everything for them, what do I get in return?"
"I don't even understand myself"
"Why can't they just _____" fill in the blank.
"No one really loves me."
"They don't appreciate all I do for them."

Beneath all of these thoughts is something not so pretty. It is self pity, anger and resentment. This puts on a false martyrdom that is unhealthy and punishes not just you, but others around you. If you really seek to help those around you, this is something to work on so you can stop engaging in that manner. Even if you do not portray your thoughts aloud to others, they feel them in your actions, lack of action, demeanor, etc. Here you were thinking that you were doing something for another and in the end, this animosity has been growing like weeds. Why do we do this?

Empaths are notorious for falling out of balance with themselves and suddenly finding that their inner well is running dry, if not empty. An empath operating with low inner power cannot walk in the steps of the magical empath. All the energy and resources you are giving away take a toll on you. That is how you find yourself falling into feelings of not being appreciated and loved. It is just your nature to be helpful to others. It is not solely that you are a nice person. As an empath, you are picking up on levels of discomfort around you from that person. When you feel their situation and problem, you want to fix it so that you can stop feeling uncomfortable.

Again, the danger of it all is that you are setting everyone up for a fall – not just you. As resentment and anger build, you may react in a couple of different ways. You could become passive-aggressive; take on a cold icy demeanor, or become overly aggressive and explode. Once you learn to trust yourself to set up your game rules effectively with others, you will no longer be falling out of balance and enduring the inner turmoil that comes along with that. Those boundaries make it possible for you to have a strong inner trust and richer experiences with others. This is true for all people, whether they are an empath or not.

Resentment held within ourselves becomes a thick stone wall that keeps our good away from us. As long as we are focused upon what we feel deprived of or angry about, we attract more of that. The only way through this is setting preferences or boundaries, coupled with forgiveness of the other person, situation and yourself for participating in it.

But what about those specific traits empaths seem to struggle with? Specifically, taking on another's emotions and energies can seem very bothersome at times. Think about the control factors this may bring up in the mind. Are you expecting the outer to be a certain way in order for you to feel better within the "inner"?

For a less mature empath, we may see them staying in feelings of self-pity and personal torment. This is also a passage into egocentric thinking. How can we know that? Look for payoffs. What emotional or physical payoff is the empath receiving to be in that state of mind? Is it poor me? This serves the negative ego and keeps the empath away from their greater purpose and being a light to others. It may reflect a personal drama they are playing out from past experiences ... or even past lives. This needs to be acknowledged, recognized and worked on in order to progress.

Instead of chastising one's self for any self-defeating behavior, surrender to what is around you and ask to be shown the catalyst or lesson within that circumstance. Also, ask to be shown the next step to transcend the situation. Always, the answer lies within. It is not about waiting for others to change. It is waiting for the empath's inner change in thoughts, viewpoints and feelings.

Self Love & Self Care

Sometimes, a set of words that are great concepts to embrace become such buzz words they feel meaningless and over used. At times, I wonder if this has happened with self-love and self-care. If you are involved in the healing community, you will hear those terms often. It almost feels necessary to come up with new words so that these words do not just run through our brain and we think, "Oh yeah — okay, blah blah blah."

Self-love and the act of caring for self are the absolute set point for being your best and shaping the existence you live within. It is so important that we must keep it at the forefront of our minds. But, let's explore both a bit. What does it all really mean?

To some, self-love could sound like narcissist indulgence. Yet, it is far from that. It is holding favorable opinions of yourself; feeling good and believing in yourself and what you have to offer in terms of abilities, skills or talents. Self love means you can look at yourself in the mirror and not feel disdain. Instead, you may feel like you are looking at a very good friend – your best friend.

Having an adequate amount of self love means we do not let the opinions of others define us. We stand firmly, owning who we are and if other people fit into that in order to have a relationship, that's great. We do not need the relationship or their approval to feel good about who we are.

Remember the golden rule to treat others the way we would like to be treated? Most empaths follow that. The problem is they need to treat themselves the way they want to be treated. Instead, many empaths are overdoing for others and ignoring their own needs.

If you develop more self love, you will not have a problem expressing your opinions or preferences. You will make better choices in all ways because you truly value yourself. When challenges come or someone is hurtful to you, it won't be quite as bad because of the security you feel from loving yourself and knowing who you are.

The concept of self care will easily begin to take form when you conquer self love. Better self care will not just feel necessary or something you need to do. Instead, it will occur as a natural result of showing yourself appreciation and acknowledging that you deserve.

When we know we are worthy, lovable and have value, we treat ourselves differently. We eat better, try to curb our addictions, and generally show concern about our own welfare on all levels. This self care stemming from self love creates a natural balance in our lives and it allows us to free up space to love others more deeply.

Forgiveness & Understanding

As we build on ways to truly love our self, it allows us to truly love others in a deeper way, including those that perhaps we could not before.

If we can learn to love what we fear or hate, it heals those things that plague our minds, bodies and souls. Love really does heal, but we have to generate that emotion. We have to really be able to call up, conjure all of that love within us and that comes from understanding. Forgiveness and understanding is the key to love. When we understand that someone who is hurting us is hurting also — that they have their own limitations that they are dealing with, this opens up a window to let some fresh air in. To give us some breathing space and say "I see why you do what you do." Or, "I see why you did what you did."

We all have fears and limitations keeping us down in some way. For us to be the bigger person and graduate, go on to a higher vibration of living, we must be able to understand that others are not making it personal. It is usually not personal at all. It's more just the way things are for them.

Empaths, starseeds, lightworkers, and more are humans born without the full veil over their consciousness connections. They sense, see, hear and feel energy. Sometimes, their thoughts and feelings manifest as a viewable force. Remember, we are working within the Law of Polarity. We must curb our unwarranted people pleasing which is born of fear. Otherwise, we will find ourselves wallowing in low, dense energy. We will be under fueled and unable to retain a full charge. Instead, we must strive to stay high on love and light at the other end of the spectrum. We do this by having the courage to know our intentions of why we do what we do.

Notes – Thoughts – Ideas – Affirmations – Dreams

Building Trust

"Self trust is the essence of heroism." ~ Ralph Waldo Emerson

As empaths, we often seek to insulate ourselves from other people and the outside world. This is necessary for us to do on a regular basis to regenerate. Yet, we must be cautious not to build a complete wall around ourselves. Somehow, we must learn to reach a balance between interacting with the world and short retreats in which we recharge our energies and attitudes. This involves a respect for ourselves coupled with well thought out rules of engagement with others. When we can achieve this delicate tight rope walk of loving our own self and allowing others certain freedoms with us, it gives us an inner trust. When we know that we will protect ourselves where necessary, it also makes us more trusting of others

If we have been betrayed, treated poorly or abused, it is easy for us to erect a wall around us and say "no more". At times, this is an opportunity to go inside ourselves. Instead of building that wall, we may take time (lots of it if necessary) to analyze and be introspective about how the event occurred in the first place. What could be done in the future to avoid this happening again? In other words, how can we trust ourselves to not get into that position again? The answer almost always lies in setting boundaries.

Boundary setting is very difficult for empaths because they want to be helpful, useful and accommodating. Empaths are sometimes uncomfortable making rules. What are the most common reasons they feel uncomfortable making rules? Many times, they do not want to be perceived as mean, hostile, unbending or uncaring. With appropriate words and actions, empaths can remain friendly, approachable, and still seem caring to the other person while still maintaining boundaries.

Another reason empaths have issues with making preferences known is they want to be approved of and liked. We need to rethink this because no one is likable to everyone. There are always going to be people that do not care for us and they may not even know why. Perhaps we remind them of something they dislike or it is just a particular vibe they get from us. Again, if our self love is strong, other opinions will not matter to us.

If you are an empowered empath, which could equate to a certain amount of success in navigating your life, this may remind the other person of what they do not have, but want. Everyone responds differently to others. If I meet someone that has a quality I would like to have, I am in awe of them and may even try to follow them like a new pup to find out how, why and experience it more. For others, they know that whatever they are lacking would require them to make uncomfortable changes. As long as someone is around that reminds them of what they want but will not go for, they may reject the presence of that person. This way, they can continue to stick their head in the sand and tell themselves it is not achievable.

For those with particular personality disorders, the empath's preferences do not matter to them. They will test those boundaries because that's what they do. They are more apt to tuck tail and go pick on someone else when they realize the empath will not be compromised or budge. It's very difficult to resist some of these people. They are often so complementary and charming in the beginning. But that will end and truth makes an appearance. That takes quite a toll on empaths.

There is an incredible attraction between empaths and those with certain personality disorders. This includes, but is not limited to, those with narcissistic personality disorder, sociopaths and psychopaths. As empaths, we see the good in others no matter how minuscule it appears. Be on the lookout and watch for signs of these individuals. They can be so deceiving as they mirror back the greater portions of ourselves that they want to steal from us. All of them have the ability to appear more like us initially. Truly, they are mirroring our empathic qualities back. Yet, they have little to no empathy for anyone. It is an act. Ultimately, those we have in our lives with personality disorders like this are showing us where we lack boundaries and trust in our own instincts.

When we let others know that we will not be treated a particular way or we will not tolerate certain things — and we do so at a high level - even a very firm level - we negate what they are trying to dish out. They will have to either go somewhere else or change their behavior. Unfortunately, they do not change their behavior very often and there are so many other people out there that they can play against.

What if every empath or person that had codependency tendencies in the world knew this information? What if 85% of them knew and those with narcissistic personality disorder were unable to find anyone to feed off of? What would happen? This is an interesting question. How different would our world look? How would it change?

You have either found or could find yourself immersed with someone suffering from a personality disorder. These relationships seem so idyllic in the beginning. You were made for each other. It's a match made in heaven. But, it isn't. It is more of a match made in hell. You soon find out. They initially appeal to your helping side. You want to help them. You know if they just "got a leg up" they would be alright. If you could just show them the way or fix something for them. It always involves doing this or that for them emotionally, monetarily or physically on a consistent basis. What you will find is they do not give back.

What I found in one of the longest relationships I had was that he threw me bones occasionally to keep me quiet or content. It was his way of keeping me under control. Often, the real part of me would come out and say, "Hey, this isn't right, fair, etc." That is the time when he would own up and say, "I'm sorry" and throw me some kind of a bone. It could be fixing my car that was broke, buying me flowers or other gifts. He would take me out when he didn't really have the money. At times, he would have me go on rides out to the forest, knowing that it would make me feel better. Getting me out in nature he thought would subdue me ... and it did.

He had me absolutely convinced that I had a problem, not him. But yet, I was the one going to a job everyday. He wasn't getting up until five in the evening when I was about to return home with my children from work and schools. I was the one taking care of two children, one of which was his. This was a totally screwed up situation. These people with personality disorders do not give back. There is a gross unfairness. When they do give, be careful. That's the bone they are throwing you to keep you under control. When you have your next argument, it will be, "But I gave you that ring; I took you to your favorite restaurant; I fixed this or that." Big whoopee do! You are the one constantly giving, giving, giving day and night to this person. You are probably the one holding most everything together. In a relationship like this, your self image and confidence erode slowly day by day.

Now, if you are dealing with someone who operates more covertly, it can all seem confusing. Do not blame yourself ever! You're a good person at heart and in your spirit. It is so easy to fall in love with someone and to love what you see that they could be, not what they really are. That is slowly revealed to you. Those parts that first attracted you begin to disappear and you know if you just love them well enough, they will appear again. Wrong!

They know the right things to say and ways to act. Later, as you see the real them, you realize they are not going to change. It is the turning point when you know this is the way they really are and what you saw initially was a rouse. You have a choice then. If you stay with them, you will be miserable. You may even fall physically ill because of it. You could even lose your sanity over the relationship. And in some cases, people lose their lives through violence. They lose their fortunes ... or their potential to have or build wealth.

You have another choice - you leave them or make them leave you by booting them out the door. Chances are they are mooching off you — you're not mooching off them. If they do have a security chain tied around your neck because they are the breadwinner, you need to get a plan. You need to find a way out. Remember the movie with Julia Roberts, Sleeping With The Enemy? (1991) She slowly banked money, saved and made a plan. She left the oceanfront dream home with the monster she was married to inside. Her husband was crazy, showing a definite personality disorder. She got out and found freedom, joy and happiness away from him. While this is just a movie, it is going on everyday in real life around the globe. If you are a woman in a developed nation on this planet, you have options. It is possible. You can do it.

An Example of Imbalance

Maria is always assisting her boyfriend when he has problems, which is often. Whether it is just talking things out with him, giving actual physical help, or even lending him money, he knows he can count on her. The problem is that Maria's boyfriend doesn't really reciprocate. He seems to do just enough to keep her from getting really upset. He is not volunteering out of the good of his heart when she needs him. What is worse is that Maria is often afraid to ask him for help. Maria wants to avoid his complaining responses and she really fears him saying no. Her boyfriend has no problem setting boundaries.

Maria is smart enough to know this relationship is probably not going to work out and turn into something permanent. Yet, she feels boxed in and cannot break free right now. For one thing, her boyfriend still owes her quite a bit of money for his car repair and he is only giving her a little back each week. If she broke it off, she would probably never see the loan repaid. And, there is her fear that she will not find someone else. She's no spring chicken anymore and guys today can get women so easily. In fact, she feels her boyfriend would be hooked up with another woman in no time. She would then have to deal with feelings of jealousy.

Maria's situation above is very typical. Simply change the names and the particulars and it is the same story. There were never enough boundaries in place for Maria to require her boyfriend to toe the line or move on to the next woman. Instead, he is making the rules in a passive aggressive manner. Maria fulfills his needs all too willingly because she feels that may draw him closer to her in some way. Perhaps, they will become more bonded as a couple with everything she does for him. This is one rationale that plays through her mind as she does more and more for him.

While she holds hope that he will change, Maria also believes she is out of choices. She is unhappy with the situation but unsure what to do about it. Feeling stuck, she does nothing and just goes along making the same mistakes with her boyfriend. She is in danger of finally blowing a fuse as she experiences more feelings of being taken advantage of.

What Maria does not know is that she does have choice in this. They may not be easy decisions to make, but in order for her to turn around her trajectory and come out landing somewhere much sweeter, she will need to consider ending the relationship and not worrying whether she recoups her money that she loaned out. Trying to wait for him to pay it back so gradually may cost Maria much more in her personal integrity as time goes on. It's sort of like smoking or another addiction, the longer you put it off, the harder it is to end it.

In the alternative, she could make new ground rules that she enforces. If her boyfriend does not abide by her requirements, she does risk still having to end the relationship. Often, we see this happen because people don't change. The fact that you are now making new rules will not make them be different. It only sets lines in the sand that state what you are not willing to tolerate in a relationship. When people cross over those lines, there have to be some type of consequences.

On a flight, I sat next to an adorable 18 month old girl and her mother. They were on a return trip home after visiting the child's grandparents. She spoke of how her daughter was the first grandchild and I knew that was very special for the family. I was friendly, complementing her on how intelligent her daughter seemed. She was already babbling words and was particularly curious about me and making frequent eye contact. I would smile at her and she would smile not just with her mouth but her beautiful eyes too. At one point, I said to the little girl, "I bet you will love being home again, playing with your toys. You probably miss them." The little girl just looked at me and the mother seemed to grow very distant. I looked ahead down the middle of the plane from my aisle seat and did not push or engage in further conversation as I felt a nerve had been hit for the mother. She looked out the plane window and seemed to have a worry come over her. I wondered if she was treated well in her relationship with the child's father as she had stated earlier she was married.

Unfortunately, female empaths are very prone to finding themselves in relationships that they thought were about love only to find they were more about ownership and a strange type of enslavement. This enslavement can be on a psychological or physical level. At times, both elements are involved.

I have personally wondered, but have no measurement, if male empaths have an easier time setting boundaries. It is possible they are more skilled within job and social settings. However, they may still struggle in romantic relationships or with family. Male empaths have the advantage of being men. Although gender biases are changing, men typically are taught as boys to seek respect. Some demand it. Female empaths may have grown up with the idea that to be cherished and cared for is a higher priority. If so, they would be more oriented toward wanting to be loved. All want to be appreciated. When setting boundaries, it may be more important to be respected than liked or loved as far as stating your preferences goes.

Relationships that start out feeling so different – you thought he or she was the one. Most relationships begin with a level of excitement that is intoxicating. Truly, it is difficult to tell what is real at this point. There is a huge advantage to those who are good friends before becoming lovers. When we are in the stage of falling in love, we can begin to fool ourselves into thinking that real love has no boundaries. It is so easy to fall into love and even easier to believe that you don't have to set specific rules.

Without you possibly knowing it, you are setting boundaries from the first contact onward. Whether someone calls you when they said they would is in the realm of boundaries. Let's say a person you are interested in has told you they will call on Saturday around 11 am. The time comes and goes without a call. What response can you make that would be appropriate to set the boundary that you consider appointments and promises important?

What about male empaths who are engaged in a relationship with a female who has a personality disorder? Male empaths often stay and try to make it work for several reasons. First, if there are children between the two, leaving means not seeing those kiddos as often and perhaps not being able to have much influence over their upbringing. He may be required by a court to offer substantial financial support to her and the children plus maintain a new place to live himself. I am speaking in a statistical, generalized way. Certainly, there are instances where the female empath may also have concerns about having to pay their partner alimony or support for children.

If you are in a marriage with an individual who has been medically diagnosed with a disorder, that fact may help you in a legal proceeding to gain custody of the children due to possible detrimental effects of the other parent. At the least, you should be able to obtain joint custody.

Whether you are male or female, when engaged with someone who displays hateful, violent or harmful words and behavior, begin getting a plan together. Document incidents that arise. The best way, of course, would be video. At the very least, keep notes of these happenings. However, video is going to show all the dynamics and give you some peace and protection if later embroiled in legal proceedings.

The largest reason that empaths stay in relationships that are unhealthy is energy cord connection combined with familiarity. All humans can have the tendency to want to stay with what they already know. You do remember the good times with this person and still have fun moments with them. You also have that energy cord connection with them that we spoke of in the chapter Working With Energy.

Often, those with personality disorders are very adept at winning you over after treating you poorly. Common things they do is often referred to as love bombing. This would include seduction, sex, gifts, promises to change, etc. Frankly, it is wonderful when the love bombing occurs. Finally, this person is acting like you hoped they would. It is these types of temporary moments or days that give you hope they are changing. Yet, things revert back and you feel the let down inside. You may feel angry with yourself for believing that it would be different. You may feel ashamed for believing them.

If you would like to explore counseling or therapy with your partner before making a permanent split, do so. If they refuse to go or quit suddenly when the therapist points something out to them, you probably are not going to be able to make any headway.

You will know when someone is stealing your inner power. The first inkling you get of it, you need to put up boundaries. That will show you who they are. If they do not respect that preference you've stated to them or if they give you extreme resistance, this is showing you something significant. If an argument ensues, this too is telling. If they suddenly walk out, abandon you or engage in a cold withdrawing, this is a bad sign. Some with personality disorders may leave and not tell you where they are. They could be going home to mom, staying with friends or sleeping with someone else. They are putting you through turmoil. They KNOW they are doing this. Its a punishment because you drew your line in the sand. I lived this for ten years with someone. This is the way many of these people operate. It has nothing to do with how attractive you are. It has nothing to do with how smart you are, how kind, giving, etc. It has nothing to do with any of that or with you. It is about control. They are refusing to make the change or adaptation to your preference or boundary and they are going to punish you for it.

When you are finally done with them, they will do this to someone else. This is how they conduct their life. It is truly sad. So, it brings back the question regarding knowledge. If everyone knew about those with personality disorders, how could things be different in our world? If most knew what measures to take to protect themselves, what would these people do — start feeding off each other? Those with personality disorders would have to make some changes to blend in. Many of them are adept at that. The thing is, they can only do it for so long. It's not the real them. They are putting on a face. That face is what they want you to see.

The word boundaries has so much overplay. Yet it really only indicates what we are willing to accept and that which we are not. It is easier to think of it as preferences. When we get a new electronic device such as a computer or phone, we have the ability to set our preferences so that the screen is the way we want it and the apps we want are there. We know that we can delete many of the preloaded applications taking up room on the device if they don't match up with our needs. If we try to think of these boundaries as nothing more than our preferences — the way we want to experience our world, it might make dealing with them and the implementation of same easier.

This chapter is called Building Trust, but the building of it is within you, not others. The point about boundaries is this:

If you cannot trust yourself to take care of you, how does that make you feel about your own inner capabilities?

If you cannot be emotionally whole without having to rely on another to make you that way, what does that say about your current inner state?

If you allow someone to push your boundaries or completely ignore them and there are no repercussions for that person, what does that say about how you value yourself?

For true empowerment and to live a magical life as a healthy adult empath, boundaries must be mastered.

And you will falter at times because you are genuinely good inside and want to help others. Just realize it, make the correction and go on.

People pleasing can be so prevalent with the empath personality because on a deep level, the empath fails to fully love, appreciate and trust themselves. They are looking for worth and validation outside of themselves. This always produces disappointment. Other people will know how far you will go. They will test how far you will bend to be acceptable and liked by them. This becomes a repetitive behavior where you actually get an addictive fix by doing something for someone when it is not perhaps what you really want to do, just to try and make yourself feel better about whom you are. You are putting your eggs in someone else's basket and then looking at them holding their basket and saying, "Ah, see how much I'm worth."

Don't be ashamed if you are engaging in this silent reward behavior where you are allowing your worth to be mirrored to you by another person or group. Find ways to stop continually giving to them to the point of it being a fault. Just objectively recognize the behavior and use the exercises in this book to transform it.

In the beginning, you may be clumsy and even sharp with others as you draw these lines in the sand. Relax with that. You will find more eloquent ways to express yourself and set your rules of engagement. As you do so, your trust in yourself will grow along with your confidence.

You may be saying, wait a minute…. I thought this was about trusting other people. Having a solid foundation of trust with ourselves flows into and actually stimulates situations where we can trust others. Of course, we are always using our own talents of intuition and discernment, plus any other psi abilities that we are gifted with.

Adopt new, perhaps unspoken, requirements of accepting others into your inner circle when it comes to trusting them. Allow others to earn your trust. Don't be so quick to share your inner thoughts, resources, and time with people until you know they are worth it to you. Work on establishing what those items are. What are the ideal standards you would want with each category below? Do this exercise and I have provided some examples to get you thinking. Perhaps take a notebook or journal and go over each of these prospective preferences. Change them and make them your own. Expand on each one by asking who in your life follows these boundaries and who does not.

Good Friends

- Ideally, in order for me to trust a friend, they need to:

- Be willing to listen to me as much as they need me to hear them

- Be able to keep a secret. If I cannot trust them to do so, it will affect the level of friendship we can have together, almost really changing it to an acquaintance level. This is because I will not share secrets with an acquaintance.

- Have similar values about significant issues like honesty and integrity.

- Never intentionally hurt, belittle or abuse me.

- Never lie to me. Be honest even if it hurts.

- Treat me in a respectful manner

Lover or Spouse

It is very likely that everything you required for a good friend, you also require for a romantic partner. You could include all or most of those items and also add other things. Ideally, in order to be my romantic partner or spouse, they need to:

- Be faithful sexually

- Be able to kindly communicate if something is not working for them in our relationship or if they feel dissatisfaction with me or themselves.

- Honor that sometimes I need to be alone and understand that is just the way I am wired.

- Be financially responsible.

- Be emotionally available

- Have boundaries also that are acceptable to me and in alignment with what I believe.

These decisions on what your standards are is an exercise in showing how much you value yourself. The act of writing them down gives them more strength. Your next step is to live by your standards by drawing those lines in the sand with yourself and others. And this is where you can feel very uncomfortable and slip up.

Often, this arises because we don't want to make waves by letting someone know, "Hey, this is a requirement with me." For example, you are just meeting someone online or for an actual date. As you converse, there are clear ways you can let that other person know what your standards are without being completely overt. You may say, "One thing that is important to me in a friend or romantic relationship is honesty." Time will show you whether the person you are contemplating getting closer to is able to be honest with you or not. Just one more reason why it is advisable to date for awhile before getting too wrapped up in someone.

Often, you are afraid of appearing bitchy or too particular. Females are often raised to be accommodating to others. Somehow, we think it is our job to make everyone feel good, except ourselves of course. No one taught us in school about boundaries.

There are many ways we fool ourselves. False stories serve a purpose. They help us avoid making boundaries with people. When we lie to ourselves this way, it gives us some temporary feeling of validation of why we are doing what we are doing – even though we don't want to do it. Essentially, we find ourselves distorting the facts in our minds so that we do not have to feel uncomfortable in speaking up for ourselves. But how can we come to trust ourselves if we cannot even count on us to take care of our needs? These are excuses made for others where perhaps we should not be so understanding or compliant. After all, you are feeling what they are holding inside. You tend to be compassionate and understanding toward their problems while ignoring your own needs.

While we may rationalize the requests or behavior of others away, there is always that part of us, as empaths, that knows this is not right. We sense we are not being true to ourselves. This creates an inner conflict that we often experience as confusion and anxiety. Thus, the other person gets off the hook with their needs being met by us and we are left holding onto some degree of inner turmoil.

We fear speaking up for our needs. By making excuses and lying to ourselves, we won't have to get into that uncomfortable zone of saying, "No, I'm sorry I can't do that." Or "No, not today, perhaps some other time." Or just, "no."

Many people gravitate toward you and this is often happening in an unknowing way for them. They feel you are an understanding soul, someone they can vent to, unload on and we all need a friend like that at times. Yet, we don't want to become the garbage can for everyone's trash they want to get rid of. What will that leave us being inside?

At times, there are those that want to feed off your good energies. These people have often been referred to as energy vampires. Essentially, people that feel the need to suck the life force out of you are low in it themselves. These parasitic types do not know how to develop it through their own spiritual evolution. They seek it from you like a temporary high. It raises their dopamine levels and allows them to feel better for a short time. They often do not know it, but their basic nature is to be an energy drain. You cannot fix these people …. ever. You do not have the power to change them. You must send them away from you in the best way possible and keep them off your path. Further, you must learn to recognize the energy vampires when they appear on your path. Frequently, they are quite charming in the beginning. It only takes a little time to see what they are really made of. As they say in Texas, these people are "all hat and no cattle".

This stresses again the importance of getting to know people over a period of time instead of instant friendships and lovers. Take time in establishing relationships. Test it in different circumstances. With a potential good friend, you could reveal something to them privately asking them to keep it secret. What you reveal is not really important to you, but for the test, it is. If you find over time they did not reveal it to others, that's a good sign. This will make you feel more confident about moving forward with a meaningful friendship.

Listen to your body when you are around people, or just afterward. Do you feel drained? Now, I know it is common for empaths to feel this way in crowds, certain situations, etc., But do you feel like that person took an emotional toll on you of some sort? Remember, the charming vampire type could seem very different in the beginning. You could feel very elated during or after being in their presence. Again, time always tells. Truth always rises to the top. You must slow down in your relationships – on and offline.

The price is high when we do not have boundaries. At the lowest spectrum, it can affect our self esteem. Worse, it can send us spiraling into horrible relationships and situations with people that could have been avoided if we had stuck to our own set of standards and rules. Always, to not speak our truth and stand up for ourselves affects our personal integrity. It means we cannot trust ourselves to put the stop signs up in the neighborhood. Therefore, don't be surprised when people are speeding through intersections, getting into collisions and even running over one another.

You have the power to choose who will become your good friend and who is your spouse or lover. This all comes down to valuing yourself as the incredible person you are now and the one you are constantly becoming.

Family

When it comes to many other people that we encounter, we are pulling the wild card. Family is a prime example. Our family of origin, or the lack of family, can bring up so many issues for us. We may be close to one or two persons within our families and have trouble getting along with many others. Or, we may enjoy the company of almost all of our family, but then there is that one person who cannot be trusted. This is very common. Most empaths have been through many situations within family units that are extremely distressing at times. It is also not uncommon for you to be the scapegoat in the family due to your propensity to be the nice one, please others and as they say about you – wear your feelings on your sleeve.

We cannot change our family. But, we can regulate how much they are active or not in our life. Due to the fact that certain family members can evoke such intense feelings from us, it could be a situation where distance is needed. If there is a true toxic situation, your boundaries might even include no contact with certain members on a temporary or permanent basis.

I am a proponent of The Law of One philosophy as some of you may know from reading my memoir. One of the major tenants is that we must treat others the way we wish to be treated. This is also what Jesus taught. It is amazing that if we all did this, the world would work so smoothly. The problem is not everyone does this all the time, including myself. Further, there are people who do not do it at all. And, guess what empath? They are looking for you. You are easy for them to manipulate if you refuse to get on board with boundary making. I know it is difficult. I struggle with it too at times. But, it must be done for you to live that empowered life that is available to you.

It is not your fault that you lack ability with boundaries. You have actually been raised to believe that pleasing others and taking people as they present themselves is something you get a good scout badge for. It means you are a kind human. It shows that you care about others. Please, please, please understand this: If you do not care first about yourself, you cannot be your best for others.

If you do not love and value --- yes cherish --- yourself, you will be a doormat for others to wipe their feet on any way they like. Are you helping them to grow and be their best by becoming the doormat? No. You are enabling them to continue poor habits or behaviors. You must make you the centerpiece of your life – not anyone else. Trust that you can do this as I know there is a true aversion to it that you feel. This will mature you, balance you and give you an absolutely smooth, magical, beautiful life.

Forgiveness and Boundaries

When someone transgresses you, crosses your line in the sand, you may forgive them. In fact, I encourage you to do this as quickly as you can. However, the line was crossed and they will most likely do it again. They have shown what they are made of. Don't extend the trust. Trust yourself to know that you need to make a decision depending on the situation.

For example, you may need to downgrade the good friendship to less interaction or even take it to an acquaintance level. You may need to explore with a spouse what motivated the transgression to begin with. Is it something that can be repaired or fixed? Would counseling help?

Many things that occur within a marriage should not send us rushing to the divorce attorney's office. Rather, they should be analyzed and sorted out, preferably with the help of a professional non-partial third party. Yet, there are some things that the divorce response would be totally appropriate. Each situation is different.

Do you honor the boundaries of others? What is your real response you feel when others have to tell you no? Most empaths do not ask for the help, favor or assistance they would like to have because they are afraid of the response they may get. This is a clear signal that you may be dealing with someone who is attracted to empaths because they are primarily takers in a relationship. They know they can get by with giving very little back.

If you find it difficult to forgive someone who has crossed a boundary any person should know, even if you did not state it, such as violence, it can really be difficult to feel forgiveness. Try to look at the situation in a new light. Perhaps they are serving you in a way you never considered. After all, they have made themselves a catalyst that is requiring you to make some decisions. This could involve standing up for yourself in a way you never had to before. It could push you to institute some type of legal action to make them accountable for their actions against you.

It took long time to forgive some individuals in my life that hurt me. To speculate how or when you should forgive would be presumptive of me. It is part of a journey toward wholeness that is self-determined.

Body Awareness

Try to recall a recent time when you felt your boundaries were being tested. When you would rather tell someone no or decline something with another person, how does that make you feel inside? In other words, do you feel any discomfort and, if so, can you pinpoint where in your body you actually experience this? If you do not feel anything in your body, what emotions are you experiencing when you want to say no, but are having a difficult time doing so? Write down what you feel in as much detail as you can.

Now, recalling that same situation. If you said yes, when you wanted to say no, how did that make you feel? What thoughts occurred to you? Do the same as above with remembering whether you felt anything physical within your body or any emotions that occurred after you agreed to something you did not want to. Write it down.

Accepting Confrontation or Disagreement

Are you always apologizing, even for nothing? What are the effects of this on you and how do others see you when you do this? You are walking and someone bumps into you – do you have to say that you are sorry when they bumped into you? Determine how often you are saying sorry. After awhile, it does not hold the same weight and meaning. Apologize only when you really need to for some transgression. Otherwise, it is like you are affirming that you are sorry for taking up space, having an opinion, or existing at all. This is living in disempowerment.

Whenever we set our preferences, there will be those who do not like it. There will also be those that test it once or repeatedly. Empaths want to avoid conflict. They are looking to have peace in life with no added negativity. Yet, to move forward, you must become comfortable with some resistance.

Journal this thought: When I think of the people in my life, _____ is the one I have the hardest time saying no to. Ask yourself why.

What are things I am willing to compromise on? For instance, which restaurant you go to or what you and your partner prefer for dinner should not be a situation where you have to put up a boundary. This is a compromise situation and it is healthy to do so. The more you learn to negotiate, the better all your relationships will be and you will experience an inner knowing that you are able to trust yourself to find ways to have your needs met.

Journal this: Now that I am becoming more adept at setting boundaries, what will I now not compromise on?

These are the things that you allowed in the past and regretted after you agreed to them. This is where you really need a clear boundary.

What things could occur or what could another person do that I would feel is the point of no return for me in the relationship? Write it down—that's your boundary. For some persons, it may be cheating, lying, abusive actions, and more. You have to find your deal breakers. Make sure you write them down because you need to know them now.

Many empaths find the most difficult thing they take on is accepting the fact that to stand in their power, they will run into confrontation. Many times, negotiation skills can be utilized to have all parties find a win-win. However, there will also be times when this is not possible. You will make some people upset with the rules you have in place for yourself or the preferences you have enacted. Acceptance that this is their situation to resolve, and not yours, is of the highest good for all.

Notes – Thoughts – Ideas – Affirmations – Dreams

Acts of Transformation

"Learn the alchemy true human beings know. The moment you accept what troubles you've been given the door will open."
~ Jalaluddin Rumi

Many empaths had trauma inflicted upon them. Most humans have experienced being a victim of something or someone. These happenings often leave deep grooves in our psyche. Removal can seem daunting at times. Yet, in order to transform from victim to victor, we must take active responsibility in our circumstances.

One of the first concepts I learned in my metaphysical studies is personal responsibility. I am 100% responsible for my experience I am having. My interpretation is that I have the ability to respond to any situation, stimuli or phenomena as I choose. It does not mean I am responsible for every situation on this planet around me. Responsibility, as I was taught, means my ability to respond and how I choose to do that.

Part of being a victim is feeling out of control and that things are not working for you. Yet, if you look closely, you will see that there are many things working in your favor. Depending upon the type of trauma inflicted, this can be difficult to take notice of.

In my memoir, *Dreaming Synchronicity - Journey of an Empath*, I revealed vignettes of trauma and abuse I endured. I spoke of the ways that my own gifts helped me overcome some of the shame, blame, grief and loss one can experience after such incidences. Never afraid to explore the darker elements of myself, I still make it a constant mission to engage in the act of knowing myself.

Since trauma and the level of it can vary for everyone, I always suggest that people begin with what feels easy. New ideas can be added as you ramp up your healing recovery. Even though my trauma healing began decades ago, I still remember how it feels to be where a person just starting out might be. It is the same with any type of trauma you have experienced in life. Start out with easy and then move forward. This is one of the ways we can begin to feel victorious, instead of controlled by the dynamics of something that happened prior.

Trauma healing takes a lot of time. There are little gifts along the way in which you make tremendous head way in a short time. For the most part, however, you need to be patient with yourself. Often, it can begin as a change in how and what you are focusing on. Exploring that, what could you begin with that you know you can believe? Let's start with your physical body, because you are alive.

Right now, there are thousands of processes going on to keep your physical body in homeostasis. You are not aware of them. You don't even think about them. Can you see how there is something greater than yourself taking care of you all the time? Even if you are ill, injured, paralyzed, think of the parts that are still working correctly. If you have cancer in one or two parts of your body, think about all the healthy cells that make up every area of your body except those one or two. What a miraculous thing the human body is. On auto-pilot, it is constantly guided to heal and find homeostasis.

Look at your environment. Have you ever thought deeply about an element like water? Water gives life and is essential to it. Water can become so extreme and powerful that it can take life. Yet always, if you tried to pick this liquid up in your hand, some would slip through your fingers. Water is so soft, yet the constant movement of it can cut through rock. Water can become hard when exposed to the right temperature. Likewise, it can evaporate right before your eyes when exposed to enough heat. You cannot be water, but it is a good portion of what forms you. It is beyond a chemical. It is a compound element that forms the basis of life. How miraculous is that? Who or what makes water happen? Think deeply on this to feel the depth of miracles in your environment and in yourself.

What if you just decided to go through an entire day feeling lucky? Try navigating with the thought "I always have good luck. Everything I need comes to me easily because I am so lucky." Repeat that little mantra to yourself over and over. If you do this, first you will notice that your feelings begin to change. Putting emotion behind it makes this happen. If you're driving to work, yell out "I am so lucky!" If you hit a traffic jam due to a wreck ahead, say to yourself "I am so lucky that I am here and not in that wreck." You can turn many situations into your good fortune. It does not have to be something where you are more focused on being late. Maybe you are lucky to be late. Perhaps you avoided something by being where you are. You are lucky – think it – say it with emotion – feel it and you'll find yourself in a lucky mood all day.

These simple ways are the start of the new, better you and an enriched life. It is the reframing of attitudes. These different ways of looking at things are just the beginning of silencing the victim memories and reaching out toward something greater that is already inside you, just buried and in need of retrieval. You were born for your own greatness and it is there. Begin anew each day and practice positive things like this over and over. Through rote and repetition, you will become so different than you were before. You will begin to heal that part of you that has been retaining its hurt for too long.

During this time of reinventing yourself, fill your mind with healthier thoughts and feelings fueled by intense emotion. Give up that which is not serving you. Walk away from watching negative things on television that are not propelling you forward to the new you. Fill your time with thoughts of the future – hopefully very near future. Look up places you would love to travel to. If possible, collect photos of these places and start a vision board for your new adventures.

Imagine people in your new life who are supportive, loving and healthy in their responses to you. Daydream about this each day and you will attract those people to you at the perfect, right time. Affirm "I attract people to me that are loving, healthy and supportive of each other."

See yourself handling your finances with a new finesse you did not have before. You deftly take care of balancing accounts and keeping track of things responsibly and with care. You save money for yourself and invest in things wisely. You give appropriate sums of money away with forethought and without needing anything in return.

What do you fantasize about that you have not accomplished? Make a bucket list of items you want to do within the next few years. See yourself doing them.

Try changing some of the music you listen to. Ever notice how many songs croon of lovers done wrong and victimhood? It is so pervasive and much has been said about people wanting to wallow in their misery. Yet, realize you are programing your mind each time you engage in this. There is something to be said of sorrow, grief and loss, but we don't want to stay there in it. What if you listened to something that evoked different feelings in you? This could be music that held feelings of triumph, power and true tender love.

Daydream and see yourself fully functional with opportunities constantly for you to grow. See yourself ready more than ever to handle whatever situation you find yourself in. See yourself surrounded by relationships and people who are understanding and loving. Light an inner fire inside to recite affirmations you can believe in. Trust that even if you hear doubts arise in the beginning, these are just memory reflections stored in your subconscious and they will finally subside and go into a long sleep or disappear entirely.

Almost all empaths are haunted by something they feel they are here to do. At times, they believe they know it and many act upon it. For others, it may seem like a hazy fog that hangs over them. They cannot get a clear picture of what they are here to accomplish. When you feel like this, it is good to create a mantra for yourself. Affirm things are just where they need to be. Here are some examples you could use:

- Each day I am better at being me and fulfilling my purpose
- I stay connected to Source that loves and guides me
- Everything is always working out for me
- I am always at the right place at the right time

By using affirmations like this at various times of the day, you will soon see results in your life. Ideas will enter your mind. Invitations could come. Someone will say something on the radio, television or in person that sparks something inside of you. Keep reciting the affirmations and watch things begin to change. The more you can put your feelings into that mantra, the better results you will see.

Exploring Your Shadow

Behind this nagging feeling of something you are here to accomplish is the urge to do good. You feel constant urges to be a helper to others. Yet, in order to live that life, you have to get past your own personal story. You must transcend and transform the old thoughts that hang on playing that story over and over in your mind. This often happens to us without us even knowing it.

That story is a part of you, but it is not the totality of you. You are so much more! You have uncovered a good portion of it, but sometimes you must go deeper into the pond, into the darkness and examine it again to see how it may be affecting you. How can you help others if you do not perform the rescue upon yourself? Especially if at a core level you feel not good enough or flawed in some way. You do this by exploring where you hold onto the negative and notice when you are thinking that way in your mind. Trauma, neglect, abandonment issues often lie at the bottom of this. As you shine light on these shadow issues you have been carrying deep within, healing begins to occur.

When you feel angry, do you express it? If so, is it an appropriate expression? Do you meet anger with anger? Do you create or remind others of the boundaries you have in place? Do you just vent to someone about your anger that can do nothing more than listen?

We must actively look for or create solutions to alleviate the anger we feel in our lives. Often, we find that it is us. There is something we are either doing or not doing to allow the anger to exist. This deep dive into the shadow side of ourselves is necessary to heal and become the magical empath. You can explore many emotions you find limiting, debilitating or just plain negative and do this deep analysis. Some of those may include: emotional pain; grieving; shame; confusion; emotional hurt; self-destructive tendencies; greed; jealousy; depression and despair.

How do you get through this maze of negative emotions and be the empowered empath you are meant to be? It is through personal analysis combined with new habits and retraining of the mind.

We have the capacity to burn away that which plagues us. We always have the choice to take the higher road in circumstances. We are on a personal growth journey toward our best selves and the only way this can happen is by encountering some adversity and meeting it head on where and when we can.

To begin, try viewing people and events as catalysts for learning, change and growth. It is really about each of us choosing to disrupt or bust apart the patterns in our lives that no longer serve us — the habitual ways we have acted in the past and are letting continue on auto-pilot. Everything we explore in our life has purpose. We are advancing our tools for dealing with our past, even when it was as recent as yesterday. As we heal our mind/body/spirit complex, we transform our lives. When we truly understand that the more we change internally and do the work, we see things change externally. People, circumstances and events take on a new look for us. Things that are in our current field that do not match up with us vibrationally begin to fade or disappear. This does not happen because we make it so by some external spell, ritual or force. It happens because whatever "it" is that transformed does not match up now vibrationally with the old.

For your new life ahead, remember that you are responsible for how you feel, not others. You always have the power of choosing how you will respond. This is a simple, yet tough concept. People do things that make us feel hurt emotionally or actually inflict physical pain upon us. There is a point … a strange, but freeing point where we transcend this.

Notes – Thoughts – Ideas – Affirmations – Dreams

Blessing or Curse

"Real magic can never be made by offering someone else's liver. You must tear out your own, and not expect to get it back." ~ Peter S. Beagle, *The Last Unicorn*

Being an empath is wrought with dichotomous feelings of blessing or curse. When our intuition and skills are working for us, our gifts are a blessing. When we are ignoring our intuition and painting things in a different light than what it is, our emotional gifts are viewed as a curse. Always, we are being shown how we need to love ourselves more so we can be that shining light. We are being shown our wounds that still need healing. And we are offered information from experienced souls who want us to heal so we can be at our best.

We love in such a wide, inclusive way. Empaths see the good in others and sometimes give it priority over their less positive traits. We even love what some would find unlovable. Constantly seeing the good in others, we are guilty of missing warning signs of those we need to think twice about. We see this mirrored in tales like Beauty and the Beast. She sees something else in him that everyone else does not. I happen to feel that this particular tale is damaging to girls and young women because it sets up a false idea that we have the power to change someone into something more pleasing or better through our beauty and/or love. Have we not tried that a few times without success? Was that not the last relationship where we eventually stomped off into the sunset and joined the nearest recovery group?

For those that have the love relationship under control, they may struggle with emotional information incoming from others in their day to day life, whether it is a co-worker, boss, relatives or people passing you on the sidewalk. I remember when I used to work in the city each day and walk down sidewalks. Many times, I could detect what others were feeling as I passed them. At times, I could hear the thoughts of some. I never mentioned it to anyone because I was sure it would be collected as evidence that I was. When emotional information is flowing toward us from other people, it can be very heavy to feel the thoughts and feelings coming our way. This is especially true when we know they are expressing something distasteful or even directed toward us. Yet, there are so many other instances in which those deeply intuitive urgings can save us. Sometimes, they prevent an accident or even save the life of another. I would never wish for this ability to go away ... even if I don't openly talk about it to others. And I totally trust it. Why? Because it has always been right.

    The blessings of being an empath are many. We often know the truth instinctively whether we are watching the news and feel it is slanted or misrepresented. We know when others are not being truthful or hiding something. At first, this may come as a suspicion that we have no proof for. Later, it reveals itself in numerous ways.

    Janelle felt her husband, Blake, was having an affair but could not prove it. Blake worked a late night third shift at an automobile assembly plant. He had been putting in a lot of overtime lately. One night, she dreamed she saw him dancing with another woman. In her dream, she saw them not just rubbing bodies together but kissing and groping each other while on the dance floor. Janelle recognized the bar in her dream. In fact, it was like she was there. She felt the shock of seeing them together and could hear the clanking of glassware along with sounds from the band's music. Suddenly she awoke and on a whim, quickly changed into some other clothes and drove like a mad woman to the familiar bar. She felt stupid as she sought to find a parking space on the crowded street. I am going to walk in here and find nothing, she thought, and that will be a good thing.

As she entered the door, it was noisy with the band's music and conversation of the crowd. A bit on the short side, she could not see the dance floor from the bar's entrance area. She made her way toward the band, knowing the dance floor was right in front of it. A shock wave of anger hit her right in the face as she watched the scene unfold in front of her ... just like in the dream. They were so entrenched with one another that her husband did not even notice she was there. She pulled out her phone and took about thirty seconds of video of the two of them. Turning, her face red hot with emotion, she made her way out of the bar and to her vehicle where she broke down crying. Hard as the situation was, Janelle felt the dream saved her from just wondering and being in the dark. While tapped into the "field" in her dreamlike state, she knew the truth and took the action of actually driving there so she had physical proof to confront him with. Though the revelation was crushing, her empathic abilities to know she was being deceived are a blessing.

Another blessing for empaths growing toward greater empowerment is self awareness. The magical empath is always working on personal growth through various means. They check in with themselves frequently and clear out negative patterns that are affecting their life. They are seekers of truth within themselves.

Many humans, if not all, are creative in some way. Yet, empaths have the unique ability to fuse or meld feelings into their work whether it be music, painting, writing, dance or pottery. Whatever way the empath expresses creatively, their feelings drive this endeavor and therefore it has a larger effect on those that engage with it. It is rare to find stale art produced by the magical empath.

Healing also comes natural to most empaths. In fact, many have done so unconsciously since they were small. I remember having a wart on my right hand when I was young and my parents telling me I would need to go to the doctor and have it burned off. This sounded horrible to me as I visualized fire or something very hot burning the wart away. I spoke no more about the wart and each day I looked at it and rubbed it some wishing it away. And, away it went on its own.

Many empaths feel drawn to the professions of healing whether those be traditional western style; alternative and holistic; or a combination of both. Often empaths know when something is wrong before others do.

I remember picking up one of my friends for an outing years ago and as she rode in my car I could smell feces. I asked her if she had been feeling okay. She mentioned that she had felt rather constipated lately and didn't have her usual appetite. I said nothing for a few moments because I was not sure how to give her my impressions, but then told her later that I thought she needed to see a doctor because I felt she had an impacted bowel. She was not insulted by my comment and later began vomiting at home that night. She did go to the emergency room and indeed had an impacted bowel.

I believe it was from a heightened sense of smell that I picked this up from her. There could have been other elements as well, but I definitely could smell the back up she was experiencing inside. Now, on to nicer smelling subjects.

I would rather travel with or as an empath. We are scanning our new environment constantly. With our strong senses, we can be alerted to potential dangers much of the time.

You can never find a better person for a friend than an empath. They strive to understand and know you in a deep way that is kind and compassionate. When the empath is feeling good and in their power, they spread light naturally to others. They shine!

Have you ever been in the presence of someone and knew they were thinking something quite horrible or negative and it was about you? Have you been tempted to confront them with your impressions? What is going on in this type of situation?

This is a reflection process of the other person mirroring back to you something that you secretly or openly fear about yourself. It can be deep rooted and upon initial reflection you may discount this saying, "No, this is not true about me". The fact is it may not be true about you. Yet, the fear of it ever being true is what compounds you and shows itself to you through the other person's thoughts or even words.

To take this level of responsibility as an empath can initially seem to add a burden upon you that weighs heavily on your psyche. Yet, once you work through these shadow side issues, you will find liberation from this aspect and a new page can be turned.

During our lives, we will have many little things like this come up. Often, they repeat in different ways. This is simply the universe pointing out a contrast to us. It's a color we don't want in our artists' palette. It's something to transmute into a very positive aspect. By knowing this side of ourselves and our fears, we grow in ways we could not imagine before. We begin to see that things we initially thought felt like a curse have a blessed side to them. Us knowing is us growing.

And then there are the true aspects of being extremely intuitive or psychic. Of being able to receive warnings about people, places or situations to steer clear of for now. This is certainly a blessing to experience all of these wonderful urgings and it is part of our magic entourage for living.

One of the most basic, yet common, things we experience as empaths is living in our heads so much. Often, we are engaged in mentally surveying everything to know how we feel. This habit has most often been developed from early childhood, perhaps even infancy. During that time, we could have been with family members or others who did not often act in our highest good as young members here on the planet. For that reason, we sought personal safety. If that meant knowing what others were thinking and feeling so we could adjust our behavior, we would do so. Our primary objective could have been to not be neglected or receive abuse. Our young minds, set in a psychic receiving hypnagogic state much of the time, were constantly surveying the environment for how we could best navigate and not be hurt. It also did this to see how we could get attention we sought from others. We could still be doing it now as adults.

Part of breaking this cycle is a simple, yet very effective, technique. The first part is realizing what you are doing. Begin by discharging your worry energy. You can do this quickly by walking outside and touching the ground or dirt with your hands. If that is not an option, go to a sink and run cold or warm water on your hands. Close your eyes during either of these tasks and breathe in through your nose and exhale deeply through your mouth. If it does not seem too strange, allow your exhalation breath to be rather loud, a guttural release of energy.

As you touch the earth or water, imagine you are looking at your root chakra area. Look at your feet. Stay grounded with being in your body. Squeeze your buttocks momentarily several times. Feel yourself inside your lower chakras and body. Ask yourself: "What do I want right now? What can I do right now to make myself feel safe and loved?"

All of this may seem like a lot to do at first, but I promise you it can be done very quickly. Except for loud exhaling, no one will even know what you are doing. It gives you a moment to discharge all the worry energy and reconnect with yourself in your physical body. You are here in this world and for a reason. Listening to your body's cues and grounding yourself back into your lower extremities and torso will assist you greatly in coming out of this anxious mode.

Now, there are times when you need to be engaged in scanning your environment, not in a worried way, however. In a new situation, especially if it feels precarious, you need to be scanning the vibes and figuring out what you resonate with and what you don't. You need to be listening to those intuitive impressions you hear, feel, see and know.

If you want to live magically everyday, this practice can become invaluable for inner guidance. You may come up with other techniques that assist you as well. Share them with others. The point is, you must have a go to response when you catch yourself going into overload with thoughts, worries, feelings of others that you encounter frequently such as at school, work, home and such. Much as empaths would love to stow away like hermits. We need to engage with others also. Part of living magically is being able to be present with others and bring that magic with us.

If you have or are experiencing a lot of anxiety right now, this may seem terribly difficult. Yet, the grounding techniques do work if you apply them. You will get some relief initially and more as time goes on and you continue with these quick little exercises. Try patting a small amount of dirt or water directly on your third eye area. Reiki can be used as a method to clear this area and feel better quickly.

When something significant or traumatic has occurred, such as severe loss, a death, abuse or violence, go ahead and hole up like a hermit for a bit. Yet again, try to ground first and ask yourself what your current needs are to feel safe and loved. What could you do right now, under your current circumstances to achieve that? If you are able to get off by yourself and feel that is what's needed, do so. Meditate, sleep, cry, journal and do whatever is needed during your recharge time. When you have been feeling something deeply that is traumatic in nature, you need plenty of time to release and recharge your energy.

The process of surrender is a wonderful tool during trauma. To lay the situation, feelings or problem at the feet of God/Goddess/All That Is and say, I surrender this to higher powers to remedy. Because we cannot fix everything. We are not here to be fixers, we are here to be helpers. And there is an important distinction between the two.

Creating A Sacred Space

You may find it necessary and very beneficial to have a sacred space where you live to recharge and connect with yourself and Source. It does not need to be large or elaborate. Let me give you some examples of what this space could do for you.

This is an area that is just your spot on the planet – your safe spot. The size can be tiny, small or large. It can be something in a corner, on a large table or desk, or take up quite a bit of a room. Make it the size that fits your desire and space available.

Transform your chosen area into a shrine of all you love, find comfort in and brings you joy. You may want to begin with a piece of cloth as a table cover in a color or design that pleases you. Place items in this area that make you feel happy or joyful. Items to consider are a photo of someone you really enjoy and love. It could even be a picture of you – perhaps as a child, teen or later in life.

Place a vase with your favorite flower. This could be a fresh flower you replace every so often or a silk one you can easily obtain at so many different stores. Add something that smells good, whether it be your favorite cologne, perfume, incense, scented candle or other aromatherapy products. Place something that connects you with your spiritual or religious faith, if any. This could be images of the Buddha, Jesus Christ, Mother Mary, an angel, Goddess archetypes -- whatever is appropriate for you. If you do not subscribe to anything like this, consider a beautiful landscape photo from a place you have visited or would like to visit. You might place a picture of your favorite super hero – one that you feel closely identified with and would be if you could. Any archetype you feel drawn to.

How about adding a physical book --- one that you know you can open anywhere within it and read something valuable. I would have a notebook and pen available too. Add something soft you can hold if you want, or just stroke with your hand if you are feeling anxious. This could be a small stuffed animal, a folded baby blanket you have kept since childhood, a beanie baby that calls to your heart. And speaking of hearts, place an image of that on your table as well. How about a favorite rock, crystal, gemstone, sea shell or even a piece of jewelry that brings you joy?

These are just some ideas and I know you are going to come up with better ones, especially those that are closer to what pleases you. This sacred area must be about you and what brings you feelings of contentment.

You might want to place a soft rug in front of this area for your comfort when sitting. If you prefer sitting in a chair, maybe you have room to place it beside your special area.

Now, what is the point of this little shrine? It represents all that you love, trust and find joy in. It is also a physical place that you can touch and go to when you need to transcend what you are feeling and be in the now. This is your sacred space. It is an area that holds special meaning just for you and you only.

When you feel fearful or are experiencing any distressed feelings, go to your shrine. If possible, sit cross legged on the floor in front of your joy area. Touch and hold your items. Journal any thoughts you have at this time or speak them into a recorder on your phone.

Breathe! Through your nose, take deep, but comfortable, breaths that expand your belly. Then allow the air to blow out your mouth. In through the nose – out through the mouth. As you exhale, see all negativity in your mind's eye leaving your body. Do this several times.

If possible, play soft relaxing music that assists you in calming your inner self. Repeat in your mind. "All is well. Everything will work out for me. I may not have all the answers now, but they are coming. All is well with me."

Did you play hide and seek or chase as a child? Remember, there was always one place that was base? This is your base – your safe spot where nothing can touch you. This is your go to spot during times you need for renewal.

Balance

"There is magic, but you have to be the magician. You have to make the magic happen." ~ Sidney Sheldon

Balance is the bridge to your inner well being. It is what keeps things from going haywire in your life and gives you the foundation you require to fulfill your purpose. In beginning gymnastics, the balance beam seems impossible to maneuver as you try to stand in the middle or straddle it. With the right coaches and fellow team mates, you can begin to walk the beam with grace and ease. You may also develop some tricky moves that make it seem astounding.

Balance is achieved by building your inner power and peace of mind. It requires practice at the very least. A coach or mentor can definitely speed your progression and agility. However, most of the time, it is a challenge because you are often bombarded with the feelings and needs of others. They gravitate to you because they know you can often be counted on. To find balance, ask first: Who is most important to you?

If there is not a well balanced you, how can you really be effective long term in helping anyone? If you have found yourself falling into the role of putting others' needs above your own, just know there will come a time when you realize on a grand scale that you cannot continue forfeiting your needs for others. If you make yourself the priority first, others will still benefit. But you will learn to have more discernment on who to give your energy to.

A more compelling point to be made is that the more you are at your optimum, the whole world benefits. This is how spiritual evolution works. As we change ourselves, we change our world.

Let us look at a technique for building inner resilience and keeping your mind and body in balance

Fishing For Energy Technique

Stand with your feet about six inches apart and posture fairly straight. It does not have to be perfect .... That's not the point. Just stand straight with a little space between your feet. Or, if you are physically challenged, sit or lie as straight as you can comfortably. You should be relaxed and not strained. Take a few deep breaths.

Place your palms facing your chest, but not touching. Close your eyes and feel the energy from your body. Hold this position with eyes closed for about twenty seconds or whatever feels right to you. This can also be done with one hand instead of two. But, if you have two, use them until you feel more adept at this.

Next, quickly turn your palms outward and push. Simultaneously, imagine yourself pushing your own energy out into the world. As you do so, tell it to bring back what is out there so you can scan it. Take your hands from the push position and turn your fingers up in a receiving position. I want you to imagine that this fishing expedition is bringing you a ball of energy that you can roll around in your hands and decide what to do with it.

Visualize you are holding those emotions out from you. This little energy fishing method works very well but may take time for you to feel smooth with it. You may latch onto this immediately.

If you practice this, you will learn to move about in the world not taking the problems of others inside you so much. Of course, you may not want to do the actual physical movements around others. Again, if you practice this, you will find that you can do it all through your mind. And, it works just as well.

The physical movements are only to lay down memory lanes for you to accomplish this mentally. Practice!

The next time you walk into a room or situation where things feel stressful or uneasy to you, visualize catching that energy in your hand and dispensing of it how you see fit. Here are some ideas:

- Mentally toss the energy out of a window or door
- Mentally toss it back where it came from
- Mentally transform the energy with white hot light and watch it begin to melt and then turn into butterflies

You see, there are so many things you can decide to do with that unwanted stuff. You really do have choices magical empath. Conjure your inner wizard who is trying to maintain a balance, an equilibrium that is needed to perform their work. Because the perpetually unbalanced empath is lethal to themselves and those around them. We are here to heal. But we must maintain balance within our mind/spirit/body complex in order to be effective and live fully magical lives.

Notes – Thoughts – Ideas – Affirmations – Dreams

Patterns

"True magic is the art and science of changing states of mind at will." ~ Douglas Monroe

My youngest daughter has a fairly lightweight portable greenhouse that she has attempted to start seeds in for two years now. It stands about six feet tall and is probably about three feet in width and depth. This morning, I walked outside to see the entire greenhouse once again lying down on the deck after she just replanted seeds yesterday. Unfortunately, the wind has other ideas and many of the seeds she plants do not come into fruition.

Going against the wind, she places the greenhouse in areas where it will not receive too much heat or sun, yet she is unable to secure it in some manner. In her defense, it would require her to poke holes through at least two corners of the greenhouse covering to tether it to another object. Then, wasps would get into it and build a nest inside because they are already buzzing around looking for a way in.

There is a simple solution, but each time I suggest it, she resists. Finally, she relinquishes and takes me up on the idea of placing it in the screened porch. She can then secure it in place with a piece of outdoor furniture making it more secure against the wind. She has a pattern with this for two years now and it prompted me to think of ways we all go against the wind in our lives.

This world we live in is absolutely made up of patterns everywhere. In fact, it is so pervasive that we totally take it for granted. Our entire physical experience is founded on patterns of sacred geometry.

- -We have circadian rhythms and sleep patterns.
- -There are centrific ring patterns that make up the trunks of trees
- Space has patterns we call solar systems, galaxies, and astrological signs.
- Snowflakes each have patterns and weather systems hold patterns.
- Songs are made of patterns of vibration.
- Light holds frequency of vibration patterns and we call it colors
- Wind has patterns with the most spectacular culminating in a vortex.
- Leaves have unique patterns and so do our fingers.
- There are patterns to the seasons and revolutions around our sun.
- Information and communications systems work off a basic pattern of zeros and ones or on and off.

We use patterns and templates to make things, often in a repetitive fashion. We study patterns that relate to physics, finance and even criminal profiling. We display behavior patterns that we call habits. We have all heard that when you keep doing the same thing over and over, expecting a different result, that is a definition of insanity. We have patterns in how we treat money. How we make it, save it and spend it.

My favorite toy I remember as a toddler was a device that contained many multi-colored gears. I was drawn to the colors, yet more enamored with the way the gears worked synchronistically together to produce a result at the end. While I don't remember my questions on how the result was produced, I do remember my father explaining to me about how the gears worked together, each doing their own task – touching each other to work in harmony.

Patterns establish a flow of energy and life that moves forward toward a result. These patterns stay the same most of the time, only some things can alter them. Usually, this is a force of some sort.

There is no one reading this that is immune to patterns. On a pole of negative and positive, patterns can rest anywhere on that spectrum. The only meaning of good or bad to patterns is what we ascribe to it. Yet, we often see that something is not working and is not in the best interest of a person. It is then that we can see that resistance is happening and a pattern needs to be either heeded and worked with or changed.

Humans have the unique ability to analyze these patterns and change the ones that are not serving them. We can actively choose to establish new thoughts. By ingraining them in our minds as new patterns, we outwardly change our behaviors and experience. This is the path of the initiate. To know one's self and begin to follow one's own flow, instead of going against it, brings us in balance. Otherwise, we can easily stay in states of resistance.

When we expect someone else to be different than the patterns they have displayed prior, such as dishonesty or being abusive, we must assess our motives. If they have made no real succinct attempt to change their behavior, we are hoping the greenhouse will stand on its own and survive all the winds that blow our way. It won't. That goes against nature. It takes tools and maybe moving your greenhouse to a completely different location to keep it standing and productive. People can and do change. There are many who will tell you they have changed or will change, but do not enact new patterns to develop such a metamorphosis. You, being empathetic to their words and perhaps even fooled by the way they change temporarily to convince you, are sucked in. Once again, you hope the relationship now has the strength to withstand gusty wind.

Our propensity of attracting someone who does not serve our highest good in a relationship is also a pattern that must be looked at and changed for a different, better experience. You see, relationships are patterns too. They are like a mirror that shows us something we need to learn in our life. If you have a relationship with someone who is supportive and loving toward you, this would indicate that you are supportive and loving of yourself.

We get used to our habits we have created. It is only when we look at them and ask if they serve us well or not that we can determine their usefulness. I make myself a fruit smoothie almost every morning. On days I do not, I don't feel quite as energetic. This is a habit that serves me. When we want to try a new diet to gain better health, we often dive so full force into changes that are not sustainable for us. We fall back into our previous patterns because enough effort (force) has not been put into erasing those behaviors. Success flows more naturally, without so much resistance, when we gradually replace the old with new, better patterns.

You may have believed this relationship was perfect for you in the beginning and for a period of time. How has it turned into something so awful? Guess what – it was perfect for you. Your vibration and patterns that you hold unconsciously attracted the perfect relationship that you needed to learn something significant about yourself. All those patterns and behaviors you did not like that you saw in your mate were mirroring something you needed to learn and surpass, either together or separately.

Just like photons of light vibrate to form what we perceive as a certain color, you vibrate unconsciously to display a color of your own. Certain others are attracted to your color for reasons usually not even known to themselves. Where you are resonating, the pattern or frequencies you are generating attract into you what you need to experience. This is happening to hopefully initiate conscious change. To take the unconscious things you are doing and transform them into knowledge first, and then acting upon that with new patterns, habits, feelings, thoughts and ideas. These, in turn, become the new you. You look for patterns not serving you and bust them, making sure you replace them with what does facilitate your progress.

This is powerful information to know and live. When you set up new patterns of living and being, those people that were there to show you something toxic often disappear. This can happen because you do not allow it in your world any longer. You interrupted the pattern. It can also occur because they are not serving their unconscious purpose with you any longer. They do not get the same level of stimulation or are not able to feed off a situation any longer because it has changed and doesn't exist. It changed because you transformed it.

Where you feel and see resistance in your life is the area to analyze and determine if change is needed. Life will be smoother as you go with your flow and grow from a healthy seed in a secure greenhouse.

Notes – Thoughts – Ideas – Affirmations – Dreams

Inner Child

"Never ever doubt in magic. The purest honest thoughts come from children, ask any child if they believe in magic and they will tell you the truth" ~ Scott Dixon

From the time we are children, it is a long, arduous journey to realizing that our true fulfillment only lies in constantly expressing who we really are. Once we know that, we are compelled to give forth what God has gifted us through our talents. It is in this state that the word 'being' takes on new meaning.

We are humans being what? Some of us are walking in a thick cloud, never really knowing ourselves. We fail to uncover our purposes, the things we have come here to accomplish. We fail to develop and utilize our gifts in a way that gives us inner satisfaction.

Others believe they know their purpose and are working to achieve it, yet keep running into problems finding something that works. This stems from not being aligned with our purpose because we are in conflict with our unused gifts. We keep driving up roads that seem like the right way on our path, only to find another dead end. Sometimes, we discover a brick wall. Some have reached what the consensus would say is the pinnacle of success, yet do not feel the fulfillment they hoped to realize.

People are born into this world with certain abilities. Even a child that has physical or mental challenges has many gifts to be expressed. I am a mother, grandmother, writer, speaker, etc. When I was born, I did not have a t-shirt on that said, "she is a communicator". Although, it may have made things easier at times in figuring out what to do with myself. Instead, we are born with a propensity toward certain things combined with a heightened ability to perform them. When we merge those abilities with our desire and put action behind it, it turns into an activity that is uniquely you expressing and sharing your gift with others.

As children, we gravitated toward playing with things that gave us the most fun and satisfaction. Hopefully, you had a childhood like that. Sadly, some did not. Nevertheless, a child can find the oddest things to have fun with and they will utilize those objects based upon their own predilections. Their imagination is active and they are able to work magic by turning their current existence into something else entirely just with the power of their minds. This is the magical aspect of being a child. And, it is this child we need to love and cultivate in order to soften the hard edges we have accumulated during our time "growing up".

Ideally, we should be able to drop our need for validation from others and do what we feel compelled to do in life. Releasing the need for approval from others brings out that magical child in us instead of the child suffering from too many "shoulds". In fact, the need of approval from others would be better if it were just blown up into shreds — obliterated.

Knowing who we are is critical. We discover that by doing the work that I speak of in these writings. Many of us do not take proud ownership of talents and skills we have. Instead, we always feel it is not good enough. This is a parental voice speaking inside that told us we need to try more, do better, cannot possibly accomplish this or that. Come to know and love your gifts. Cultivate them more. When you do, you can be more comfortable in your skin.

We must rediscover and ignite our inner fire. Be passionate. Children have an exuberance and experience elation in the smallest things. Is it too late for us to rekindle that? That feeling is closer to God Source than we realize. It is truly a way to step into the power of co-creating and being aligned with the divine. Passion — let's write about it, speak of it, feel it and cultivate it within ourselves. There is laughter contained within passion.

Be confident - treat yourself well. Push your shoulders back and proceed through life knowing that you are loved by the one infinite Creator. Children are confident until it is undermined by others. Don't be one of the "others" to yourself. It is time to congratulate that child within you. Look at what they have come through. Notice how incredible they are. They/You are a work of art in motion.

Be inspired - find things that make you sing inside. When you were a child, just swinging on a swing set could make you relax and smile. Perhaps you were like me and had to hang upside down on the bars as well. Maybe you cannot be that flexible now, but if you can, why not? There are so many things that make us feel better and raise our vibration. Often, we refuse to do them and make the excuse of not having enough time or just don't feel like it. Hey, I understand. I do it too. Yet I always find that if I push through and make myself engage, I have a great time and gain much inspiration from it. Visit that museum to peruse the art work. Go to an amusement park or a movie. Walk in the rain and purposely take note of every small sound or thing you see visually. Childlike inspiration can be found alone, with someone else or in a group.

We lose a good portion of our childlike magic due to the programming we receive growing up. Our parents repeat the words and actions taught to them by their parents, most of it is unconscious. It does not stop with our parents. There are many sources of programming that tell us what we can or cannot do or be.

Most of us grew up with television. There is a reason they call it television programming. That is what it is. From the shows that we watch that tell us how to be a family unit to the news that regurgitates mostly the negative, we were and are still being programmed. Commercials told us constant messages: you can never be perfect enough, strong enough, clean enough, rich enough, beautiful enough. You are not enough. I hardly know anyone who does not have bouts of feeling like they may not be enough. Guess what? I AM ENOUGH. And SO ARE YOU.

There are so many factors that tamped down our childlike spirit while we were growing up. For many, they included traumas that left wounds and internal or external scars. This can make it even more difficult to give up the voice of our internal critic we keep hearing inside each time we try to make goals or accomplish certain things. It is all those occasions you have been made to feel or even directly told that you do not measure up or count. It is what holds you back from feeling worthy of abundance in life or even life itself. I call it the negative ego and it is only through befriending this aspect of ourselves and retraining it that we stand a good chance of making major progress and growth in our lives.

It is difficult for the negative ego to be brought under control. One reason is because it loves poking its head out and voicing when we are under stress. We now live in a world where stressful situations are abundant … more numerous than the peace we would like to experience. This hypercritical ninny shows its ugly head just when the going gets tough, making it even more difficult for us to shut it up or even know if what it is saying is true or not. When we are stressed, we can easily slip into self-doubt.

Plus, if we are in a relationship of any kind with someone suffering from narcissistic personality disorder, those people are very adept at triggering our negative ego. They have studied and know our vulnerabilities. They then use this to try and manipulate us … if we allow it.

The negative ego operates like a little jack in the box that pops out at our lowest points or even high points if stress is involved. That critical side of us is very limited in knowledge.

Essentially, it only records certain things. It then proceeds to replay its limited one-liners each time you have doubt or are stressed. Because you are in a less desired state, you lose your focus to call it out for what it is. It is nothing more than a negative voice from past wounds.

It is sort of like a bully at school who keeps calling you names. If you had a child and they reported to you at the end of the school day that someone was treating them this way, how would you respond to them? And if this child began to believe what the bully was saying, what would you say to the child? The bully in you, your negative ego, is replaying the same stuff it has said to you for years. It is older now and such a part of you that you believe it at times.

You see, stress of some type was probably involved in training your negative ego. It recognizes that emotional state as its playing ground. When stress is induced, it comes out to play. Only problem, it is not a great friend for us to hang out with. If we let the judgmental negative ego stay around, we begin to believe the old programmed thoughts playing in our head to be real and true. When this happens, the inner critic can partially or even completely disable our higher reasoning centers.

The subject matter of the negative ego or internal critic could have a chapter to itself. However, I decided to blend it with the information on inner child work. This is due to the vast amount of negative programming we receive during childhood. I feel it is very beneficial to work with versions of yourself in the past, to erase the negative programming that the inner critic constantly offers.

When you feel stressed or upset, pause for a moment. Take note of what is going on inside. Make your inner analytical skills stronger each time by noticing what this false inner voice is trying to do. Each time it pops up, let it know its statement is based on old, outdated information or experiences. You live in the now — and what it is offers is an old story.

You may wonder how you can know for sure what voice is speaking. Just listen to its message or words in your mind. If it is telling you in so many words that you do not measure up or are not capable, this is your negative ego speaking against you.

If you are in a mental state of being a victim of anything or anyone, you have merged with your negative ego to now blame others. While difficult, try to understand this on a deep level. You are responsible for your world. This means you hold the ability to decide how you will respond to what is going on around you. You have the power. Change yourself, change your world. This is the way of the magical empath.

Unfortunately, we will never entirely remove this inner hypercritical voice. By shining a light on it constantly and paying attention to our thoughts, we can put it into a deep sleep. From thereon, it may only poke its angry head out when certain situations trigger it. Again, use your techniques you have learned and continue to find ways that subdue it so that you can have the magical life you deserve.

If you are able, eliminate the energy vampires around you. These individuals are very adept at triggering you. This would be those with personality disorders; people with lots of drama they want you to hear about; or just negative complaining types. If you have to be around them, strengthen yourself. Become aware of shifts in your feelings as they are around. Put on your mental or actual poncho to filter them a bit. Act disinterested instead of so compassionate or understanding of their dilemmas.

During and after the encounters, keep your self talk good. Have recordings available on your phone, in your car or home that uplift you. This could be inspiring music, visualizations or affirmations. Discharge negative energy and raise your vibration as quickly as you can with the techniques you have learned.

What do you deserve? The whole idea of deserving centered around childhood or adolescent experiences — even later in life. Words that people say to us — especially from our family of origin, All of these things can have an impact on our self worth because we don't understand these people are just showing their own programming or personal flaws contained within themselves. This is not a reflection of who or what we are.

When you mess up in one area or with one thing in your life, what is your initial reaction? How do you feel? Often, if we grew up in a very critical or even abusive household, we are never feeling good enough. Even though we may have several things we did well or even true accomplishments, those mean little. The thing we messed up on stands out to us. We need to realize this is just our own internal voice from our critical parent we are hearing.

Think about it. Who does not mess up? Who is perfect? Were your family of origin perfect? No, of course not. Love your inner child for trying and even forgetting or letting something slide they should have taken care of. Instead of beating up on ourselves, we must look at why the event happened and if course correction is desired, take it. Otherwise, forgive, forget and move on.

Reconnecting or getting to know your inner child is like breaking open the shell you've been contained in. There you were, a chick ready to emerge. You did so only to find a new shell built around you by those who knew better and were doing so for your own good. Once you go inside and figure out who you really are and your desires, you can emerge and break free from the childhood shell around you.

When we are children, our brains stay most of the time in a theta wave mode making us extremely receptive. If we experienced trauma during this time, it can greatly affect us. When we turn six or seven years old, our brains begin operating a little differently, but still anything that happens during childhood or adolescence impacts us greatly.

Children can carry emotional wounds from all kinds of thing. Neglect, as well as verbal, physical and emotional abuse is damaging. Being abandoned by a parent or caregiver is significant. It all affects our inner child.

When we were children and found ourselves in our unique situation growing up, we had to learn how to survive and be part of the family group we were in. You could have had the most wonderful parents, but they berated you when you did certain things. You quickly learned that was not acceptable and if you wanted to be part of the family, you had to conduct yourself in a certain manner. That would be a mild thing for inner child wounding, but could be carried over into someone's adult life by having a lack of confidence or feeling not accepted for your differences from others.

Some children learned to stay invisible. That meant not bothering their parents who may have been wrapped up in their own concerns and really not there for the kids. This made it hard for that child to speak up and ask for what they wanted. Feeling wanted was difficult. A child in this situation might even act out in some manner in order to gain attention. This also can carry over into adult lives.

Children need to be valued for who they are, given the right kinds of attention and help with learning new things. When parents cannot or will not be there for them, they begin to feel like they do not count or matter. This can be played out in a number of ways as they grow up and it can continue into adulthood all the way to old age.

With only those few examples, you can get an idea of how we, as adults, can still be acting out our inner child's wounds on a consistent basis. It might mean we lack confidence, hold certain fears, do things for attention, or just walk around not feeling good enough.

When we do not feel loved or safe as children, this carries over into adulthood. Some children were not believed about abuse they endured or were too frightened to talk about it. This can set up a dynamic in our adult lives that keeps us from having our needs met --- as if we do not count.

We carry that child with us all the time. And there is only one way to pacify it. It is for you to be the mother or father it deserves. To be the parent it never had – the parent who can give the inner child what it needs to heal from its trauma and wounds.

What happens if we do not heal our wounded inner child? Some people try to make the inner child feel better by overspending and buying lots of things. This sets up a vicious cycle with their budget and finances, often putting them into bankruptcy. Some acquire other addictions to calm their inner child. This could be alcohol, drugs, food, sex or any activity they engage in too much to where they know it is out of balance and hurting, not helping them. Most of the time, we see it in failed relationships with the wrong kinds of people. Inner child issues can show up in the confidence and creativity in which we approach our life.

So, it is worth trying to help this wounded child inside of ourselves. I would love for you to consider engaging in this activity. Find a photo of yourself as a child – a small picture is ideal. Put it in a location where you will see it often such as taped to a mirror, held by a magnet on your refrigerator, taped to the side of your computer screen – somewhere you will see it frequently. This is a technique used frequently in therapy.

Each day, look at the photo and say with meaning: "I love you." As days go on, say new things to your inner child. Tell them how beautiful or handsome they are, how smart, funny or any other thoughts that come to mind about this child. Become a champion for your inner child. Let it know that you, as the adult, will protect and keep it safe. Let your inner child know you hold no judgments about it and that you think they are wonderful. Because, they are!

Another idea shared by therapy is to allow your inner child to write a letter to you about their feelings and life. This can be very revealing and, for some, very emotional. Just like a child would write something, you will not need to worry about spelling, sentence structure or anything like that. Simply allow the inner child to share their thoughts with you on how they are hurting or feel they are missing.

This process can be very healing because your inner child has truths it wants to reveal to you. It wants to step out of the shadows and be heard without judgment or any fear involved. With that in mind, you want to hold a special place for this child part of you that they can rest assured is safe. Allow this child to reveal feelings – perhaps even images to you. You may want to gaze at your photo while connecting with your inner child like this. Working with your inner child is a very worthwhile endeavor and it can absolutely bring you considerable insights and speed your healing process.

Consider also – maybe a couple of times per month or once per week, doing something that is spontaneous, but safe, and childlike. Perhaps there was a sport, activity or something you wanted to do as a child or teen that you were blocked from doing. Now, might be a good time to consider something like this for you and your inner child. Perhaps you always wanted a certain item for your birthday that never came. You could gift it to yourself now. There is nothing wrong with that. Do something for your inner child in an area where they felt deprived.

You can experience beautiful transformations when doing the inner child work and it might be something that is ongoing for awhile. If you cannot allow your inner child to speak by writing to you, at least try posting a photo of yourself where you will see it often and remember to tell that child how much you love it.

Creativity

"Logic only gives man what he needs... Magic gives him what he wants." ~ Tom Robbins

Putting our fingers into clay, grasping a paintbrush and stroking it across a surface with colors frees us in a way that nothing else can. Either quickly or gradually, it opens up other vistas to us fueled by our imagination. Being creative and making things positions our head into a different space and clears away residue that has been building up. This opens an avenue for more imaginatively fueled conceptions. Of course, this is not limited to clay and paint.

I found myself going through an uncertain period in life which felt very stagnated, I felt unsure how to move forward. Truly, I was not sure what to pursue with my creative work. I had fooled around with various writing projects, but nothing was coming together into at least one finished project. I really like being a person that completes what they set out to do, even if I do not always follow that self imposed rule. I felt confused and fragmented.

Stored away in my home were many pieces of fabric and sewing materials. I had accumulated a ton of sewing patterns for things I wanted to make 'someday'. A few years prior, my husband had bought me a huge lot of rubber stamps, stamp pads and other items you would use in scrap booking or creation of things primarily from paper.

After looking through my sewing patterns and fabrics, I felt inspired to make some items as gifts for other people and did so. At some point, I switched to playing with the stamps. Soon, I was watching online videos showing how to make more elaborate things utilizing a lot of the items I had on hand.

Each week, I began to pick up a new paint, stamp, canvas or two at my local craft store.

During the time I spent doing these activities, I tried not to feel guilty. But sometimes I did. My little negative ninny in my brain would tell me I should probably be working toward making some money or even cleaning the house. My endeavors often felt illogical. It was like I got in a car with no destination in mind and was just driving. Traveling roads that were familiar and new ones I had never explored would be a good way to describe it. It felt indulgent as I drove with no destination in mind. But I began to feel that this time spent alone in my craft area was serving something my soul was crying out for. It was and is therapeutic.

Before I knew it, I was making things that followed themes I wanted to have fun with or express. Most would be given away as gifts. And it would also be during this time that I was unknowingly incubating larger creative projects that would lead me to my life's work.

Making things and playing with varied art media and crafts showed me many things too. It taught me follow through. In the beginning of an idea, you feel very excited to get it underway. Once you are about in the middle of it, it starts to look either ugly to you or feel so daunting and hard to finish. I realized I was the same way with my writing. This, more than any other excuse, was why I had so many books started and written at various stages, but not finished. I would reach a plateau with each where I was unsure of the next step. Or, I had reached a stage where I felt extreme doubt about the project in general. Yes, it had been a great idea in the beginning. Now, it seemed trivial or ridiculous. No one will be interested in reading it. Damn, I should delete it all. But, I did not do that. Too much work had gone into it. So, the words sat until I was ready later.

I learned that the act of creating can be an expression of love that can bring real inner joy. Making art can also be a release, allowing expression of ideas and emotions we want to share or discharge. Overall, I realized on a deeper level that it is truly a gift from the great Creator to receive inspiration (in spirit) and act on it by creating.

The creation process can show you how hard you may be on yourself. As empaths, I think some of us carry a level of perfectionism that is not only unachievable but a burden on our shoulders. I learned from my first book that no matter how many times it was edited, there was always a defect somewhere or something that could have been phrased better. If and when you decide to engage in any form of creative endeavors, let the perfect stuff go. Just create. In quilting , I believe a trend that began with the Amish was to deliberately put in a block that is sort of their messed up piece. This is to remind them of human imperfection and that only God is perfect. In a strange way, art that has accidental or deliberate pieces of imperfection seems more real and human. It blows away those ideas that we can be perfect, because we will never be that. Instead, it shows us that we are full of perfect imperfections and that is a part of our unique signature we give to anything we do.

At the end of a project, we should be able to say that we gave it our best and we enjoyed the process of creating it. We know it is not perfect and that some people will not like it. The important thing is that we made the effort to create and give in a way that was appropriate for us to do.

Over months, I refilled my well by making things. I came back into myself. I felt renewed and it turned out to be a more conducive time to work on my main artistic endeavor of writing. I learned that everything I make does not have to be perfect. I did not have to be the best at anything. I just needed to make things and share them how I saw fit.

Many of us have heard, follow your bliss. When it comes to carving out a creative life that brings your inner soul fulfillment, this is certainly true. For we all are creators and co-creators with God/Goddess/All That Is.

My favorite family physician, who has now passed on to the next realm, once looked at me during a check up and said, "You know, people who have addictions are very creative people." It took me a little time to really examine the depth of what he was telling me. On the surface, yes, many creative types have addictions. But it is more than that. The most creative people operate more off feelings than they do anything else. When they compose music, a painting, a book, or even the manner in which they decorate their home, they make a statement wherein their real attempt is to evoke a certain feeling.

Many artists are overwhelmed with feelings just like the empath. Many creative people, but not all, are empaths. I thought about what my doctor had told me. He was right. Creative people "feel" and they use their addictions to avoid the overwhelm of those feelings. I knew this all too well because of my smoking addiction. If I felt elated and super happy, there was such an overload of feelings, I needed to normalize by smoking. If I felt grumpy or negative, same thing. Whenever I felt anxious, I needed a smoke. And there is a dependence the brain relies on with smoking. It is looking constantly for you to upkeep the same level of dopamine from the nicotine. It is a vicious circle.

Many empaths use other substances whether they are legal or not to adjust their moods, avoid their feelings and move into a more dulled space where everything doesn't feel so intense for them. The problem is these same addictions are clouding their abilities to be the creative individuals they are. Because feelings fuel creativity. I also know of many situations where empaths can believe that psychoactive substances enhance not only their creative abilities, but their psi skills as well. You have to be the judge of that.

Addictions are vast. A test is to just ask: Do I need this substance or do I need to engage in this behavior in order to feel better on a regular, consistent basis? If so, it is probably an addiction which can eventually block creativity. Whether you are an entrepreneur or an engineer, creativity is important for solutions and problem solving. The more you have available, the better your life flows.

Notes – Thoughts – Ideas – Affirmations – Dreams

Fear of Conflict

"Words and magic were in the beginning one and the same thing, and even today words retain much of their magical power." ~ Sigmund Freud

For me, one of the most difficult things to learn was how to be inside my own power as a person and set appropriate preferences and boundaries with others. I am getting better at it. In fact, I plan on being an expert at declaring my preferences and drawing those lines in the sand. If you have read my memoir, you know that I grew up "walking on eggshells". Discounted, I often felt my emotions did not count. This carried over into my adult life in many ways.

Whenever conflict would present itself, I wanted to avoid it because I did not want to get "too upset" at the situation or persons involved. Additionally, I did not want them to not like me. I feared that if I expressed my needs and how they were not being met, I would be rejected. Often, I was put down and/or gaslighted by certain personalities such as the malignant narcissist.

Perhaps in your upbringing you encountered this also. I know my father often said for me to "ignore" such verbal and emotional abuse. When we allow people an inch, they will start taking a mile most of the time. It is important to put in place a line – a boundary that lets that person know their actions are unacceptable and we expect to be treated differently.

There is the temptation to think that if we can just avoid that person or situation in the future, the problem will disappear. It almost always comes back to you in a similar form but perhaps through a different delivery method. The reason is that your soul is yearning to correct things for your growth. Our circumstances, of course, show us what we do not want. Conflict is a feedback mechanism for learning and correction. It is hopefully moving us toward greater alignment with our purpose we incarnated with.

If you continue to tell yourself that if you just avoid those feelings that are producing your conflict, you will have knocked yourself down a few notches each time. To avoid learning a new way of handling difficult situations can keep you frustrated, unhappy and not feeling worthy. At the least, you may feel trapped in a job or relationship. You could eventually fall ill from holding all this inside and not feeling fulfilled. That is a huge price to pay for not being what you view as nice or trying to keep the peace.

In the past, I viewed the term power as a struggle – something that meant that one had dominion over another. In our present day reality, it can mean that. Yet, I learned that being in my own power was quite another thing. Not only did I need to redefine what "being in my power" was, it was necessary that I learned new language terms to bring it to fruition.

First, let us take a closer look at the definition of "being in our power" or "empowered". It means we carry with us an inner strength. In fact, each time we speak of the word power, try to visualize yourself standing tall as a being of light carrying a sword of truth. Not a sword of battle, but a sword that cuts through the bullshit to show you exactly what is true and what is not. As an empath, you instinctively know truth the majority of the time. Sometimes, your impressions are clouded by things collected in your brain and stored in filing cabinets there. Learning to sort those differences is also part of the process.

See yourself as kind, yet firm in your resolve of who and what you are. Allow others to be what they are, even if it is something that does not align with your being. There will be many people and situations that are not a match up to you.

They often exist to show you a contrasting aspect of what you need to take a firm, but thoughtful, stand against. They do not exist for you to fix them.

As we stand in our power (strength), we can begin to try and change our focus about the situation. Instead of seeing this as a problem, it is an opportunity to come up with a creative solution. As we do so, it becomes easier to handle this the next time it occurs, no matter how it is presented. We build our strength over time. The first few times are difficult. Each time, it is easier because we know our way around this. Soon, these conflicts no longer appear in our lives in the same way. There will be new ones that will present themselves so that we can stretch some more.

Part of your hesitancy to confront situations and people is that you don't want to be like them. Who wants to be someone who provokes anger in others, makes people feel bad? Not us, not as empaths. We know that to hurt others hurts us. Instead, look at this differently. You do not need to be like them to change the dynamics going on. You need a new creative solution to address the situation.

This is all about getting into a better feeling state. You don't have to let the other person make you feel bad. You must step up and let them know the situation is not working for you the way it currently is. It is the same with jobs. If you hate your job and you're staying there out of fear, the universe is urging you to make a plan and do something different. By not dealing with these things you are power less – weak and not full of your strength.

Boundaries and stating our preferences assists us in respecting our feeling states. This is our number one priority because when we are operating at higher states of love, contentment, peace and harmony, we are more fully able to manifest great things.

If we carry anxiety about expressing our feelings and needs, this is not being true to ourselves. When we do this, we can almost feel something stuck inside that needs to come out. Often, we are afraid of the reaction of others. Imagined or not, we carry angst that someone may criticize us, argue, or even become physical or violent if we express our needs. Afraid of being hurt and triggered more by confronting the situation, we stay powerless and the wheel keeps turning over and over. Each time, we find ourselves stuck in the same spoke wondering when will this stop? It stops when we take responsibility for being the half of it that is allowing it to occur.

Finding a way to express that the situation is not meeting your needs or even detrimental to you, is not being mean. Remember, you must treat yourself with lots of love and respect to receive that from others. When they realize you are not going to go along with what is not in your best interest, they will immediately or, more often gradually, change their approach with you. It may take time, especially if you have spent months or years of not expressing your preferences. Some may pull away from you entirely. If so, let it be.

Here is an example of setting a clear boundary: you could say to someone who has unfairly criticized you or been rude, "I felt disturbed by your statement to me. I'm sorry you feel that way, but I see things quite differently. If we are to remain seeing each other, you will need to do something more fair or positive. Otherwise, we will not be spending much time together."

If you are dealing with someone who just made a mistake and is otherwise a caring, rational being, they will probably apologize at this point. They may back step a little and say it was a joke. However, if you are dealing with someone afflicted with a personality disorder such as malignant narcissism, they will most likely tell you that you are being too sensitive. This is just a way of denying your feelings. They may completely lie and say they never said or did that.

You need to be prepared to act on the consequence of the boundary also. Parents often warn their children, if you do this, that will happen. If they don't follow through with the consequence, the child very quickly learns these are words that mean nothing.

The fact is there are many people in the world you have in your family, work life or come into contact with that act childish. Their emotional reactions to things are not mature and they will often strike out at others verbally, covertly and even physically. There are many books written on why they do such things, but for brevity, we will not go into all of those reasons.

You will never feel strength inside yourself until you can stand up in a mature, reasoned manner to these bullies. This is a most important lesson for the empath who wants everyone to be happy and feel good. Unfortunately, that does not happen most of the time. We cannot be responsible for everyone's feelings around us. What we can do is treat everyone fairly, with respect and expect the same treatment for ourselves.

Your focus as an empath needs to be on feeling good for a change. Bringing your consciousness down into your body and asking yourself, how do I feel? Is there something or someone making me uncomfortably stressed, depleted or hurt?

Have you ever been in a relationship with a person who seems to feel better once they have made you feel bad? It is like they gain some sort of satisfaction or sense of power from this. This is not the power you want to gain. This is a negative dominion over others type power. It fills an afflicted personality for a very short time until they can find the next person to pounce on and make feel that way. If you set a boundary with a person who regularly does that and they do not honor your request, it is highly suggested you end the relationship with them. At least take a vacation from each other until resolution can be achieved. And I know that is difficult. If it is a parent, child, life partner, husband, wife, co-worker, or boss, you have to figure out how to make that happen. But, you must find a way to do this or it will escalate inside of you until you burst and find yourself losing your cool.

To have a more magical life, the empowered empath grows tremendously strong in calling out poor treatment or behavior and setting a boundary. From experience, they have learned to recognize these personality types quickly and do not take up with them – avoiding them like the plague.

It seems as if there has been so much information in this first book of the series on boundaries. It really needs to be mastered as we move into the next book's information. Since boundary setting is a core foundational element of living the life of the magical empath, what are more ways we can do this? Let's begin by using our emotions and physical bodies as guides. And for those of you that are more psychic, you may even hear, see or have a certain intuitive knowing come to you. For now, let's just look at your physical body's response.

Your physical body is always connected to Source energy – that great force that knows all about everything. You may call on it anytime asking for guidance. You may call upon angels and guides to assist you. However, you must ask and be in a receptive mode. While you always are attached to non-physical through invisible lines, sometimes those pipes are clear – sometimes clogged. Our bodies can help us sort that out.

Let us trust our body's innate wisdom. It speaks to us in certain ways and it knows. Allow me to stress again that as empaths, we spend so much time in our heads and even in a strange hypnagogic state. It is vital that you first bring your awareness down into your body. Wiggle your toes, bend your knees slightly. Squeeze your butt muscles. Be in your body. Here are some ways your body may speak to you saying that you need to decline a situation or invitation:

The solar plexus area or upper stomach is very good at identifying when someone is not being honest or has an ulterior motive. This is our personal power center chakra. If you experience a slight discomfort ranging from a sharp or dull pain in this area, it could be indicating that you need to withdraw and say no.

The heart has more neurons than our brain. Our hearts are a second special type of brain. Increased heart rate not related to anything else obvious in the environment is something to pay attention to. This is not like being at the amusement park and standing in front of the newest roller coaster, experiencing an increased rate from anticipation. We are talking about noticing that you feel extremely nervous and your heart begins speeding up or racing without other stimuli.

Have you ever met someone new and all of a sudden you start getting some sort of involuntary muscle movement or pain in your body? This can be another indication to tread lightly and it is your body's warning signals. This could range from light eye twitches to muscular spasms.

The onset of sudden, unexplained fatigue and need to sleep can be an indicator of being around a toxic individual. If they are using up a lot of your energy, you may feel so drained during or right after being around this person.

If you suddenly experience severe pain that is sharp, stabbing or extreme anxiety, these are clear indicators to run away from the situation. Listen to your body. Do not worry what other people think. If you feel like you cannot get air or breathe and begin having a panic attack, listen to your body. Again, drop all worries about what people think about you. Remove yourself from the situation or person. You can always rejoin if and when you determine it is not toxic to you.

You may suddenly experience hives, low back or neck pain. Your body has its own wisdom and will give you signals when you approach a place, situation or person that may be toxic or harmful. Do not go where angels fear to tread. Get medical treatment also for any of these conditions that are more acute in nature.

Pushy people and even good friends may keep asking you to do something you do not want to. Remember that your body has already indicated your answer should be "no". Be brave and back up what your spirit is telling you through your physical body. If it is difficult for you to say no to others, this is a great time to break free from that. You can do this gently, but firmly. If someone asks you to do something and you are hearing a big no from your body, you could say, "No, I probably have several reasons why I don't want to, but the biggest is my body is telling me no right now."

Challenging connections exist for every empath. The most predominant one seems to be finding ourselves in relationships with people suffering from malignant narcissism. A little narcissism is good for everyone. You should feel delighted with yourself and who you are. The malignant narcissist has a real agenda and they gravitate toward empaths who they find easy to manipulate. They see power as dominion and control. Those with these personality disorders attempt to take away the strength of others for their own. This can be emotionally, financially, physically and even spiritually.

Why are light workers and empaths vulnerable to others with toxic personalities? What makes an empath engage in relationships with malignant narcissists? As said before, they can be tricksters and very charming. That is why your body can sometimes be a better source of whether to proceed or not. Second, there is the idea that you can help or lift them up. We often feel we can take away their pain, change them, or just navigate around the bad parts of their personalities. These people are charismatic and charming.

Those with malignant toxic personalities often engage in gaslighting. This means to make someone doubt their own conclusions, version of what happened, or even their sanity. Projection is another technique they often utilize. For instance, they may say during an argument:

"I'll tell you what's wrong with you. You don't care about anyone but yourself." This would be an example of projection (they are unable to care about anyone else) and trying to create doubt within you.

How can you shut a person like this down? There are actually several techniques. Some people use the gray rock method where they just totally ignore them. Sometimes, this may work. However, I believe in speaking directly and letting your position be known more of the time than not. You can simply say, "I'm sorry you feel that way." Then look for the right opportunity to escape their presence - exit stage one. You may be thinking that if you do not defend yourself with them, they will talk poorly about you to others. Don't waste your time and make things worse. They are going to talk bad about you. That is part of their method of operation. It brings us to the next thing they engage in which is called triangulation.

Triangulation is when those with disordered personalities begin speaking to many of the people you care about in an attempt to build a case against you. Because you dared to set a boundary or challenge them in any way, they are now out to get you. They will use all of their tactics to do this including making up complete lies. What should you do? The answer is nothing and it is one of the most difficult things to do. There is a part of you that wants the situation set straight. You desire to be treated fairly instead of unjustly. It is possible you will be treated as the scapegoat by others who will join in with the lies they have been fed.

I know how involved this gets and how it makes an empath feel because I have experienced it many times. You see, the people with disordered personalities are weak. They don't want to appear that way, however. They spend time deflecting attention away from their own pain, dysfunction and disorder. For them to be on top, no one shall challenge them, not even with a personal preference or slight difference of opinion. When they feel challenged, they feel attacked in some way. From that point on, they will throw all their venom at you to try and make you break down. Break away instead, temporarily or permanently ... whatever it takes for you to lead a peaceful life. And don't forget, you must give up worrying about what others think as you do this. There is no need for the empath to waste their energy and inner resources on trying to plead their side with other people. Just move on to things that will bring you closer to living more magically. There is no way you can accomplish that when embroiled in situations with these types of people.

All of this is especially painful when you are dealing with family. Many empaths were born into dysfunctional homes where a malignant narc is their parent. Often it will transfer to at least one sibling as well. It is a genetic trait, an actual brain difference that these people are suffering from. You cannot change or fix them. They have true deficiencies that cannot allow them to become genuinely loving, much less compassionate individuals. They will almost always not agree to counseling unless forced by a governmental or medical body. Some operate so covertly they can fool many therapists, at least for awhile. Steer clear of these individuals as much as you can so that you can walk in a world that is much different than the chaos they create around them.

The latest research shows through brain scans of those afflicted with malignant narcissistic personality disorder that they lack gray matter in areas of the brain associated with empathy (Altered brain structure in pathological narcissism, 2013).

All psychopaths also suffer from narcissistic personality disorder. However, not all narcs are psychopaths. Those who could be considered suffering from antisocial personality disorder, also show lack of empathy (Antisocial Personality Disorder, 2019).

No matter how much you love and give to these individuals, they will not return it close to the same level. They will drain you and when you are empty, leave you in a puddle of tears. So, stop fooling yourself that you can "make this work". You are hurting you instead of loving you. You are deceiving yourself with this blind spot.

Be kind and humble with yourself and realize that your love alone cannot make things right with this person. We do not have the ability to change anyone, only ourselves. It is so important to understand this for you to be an empowered, magical empath that is leading a fulfilled life going forward. It is not a failure this relationship cannot move forward any longer. It is a triumph that you have recognized this and are ready to move on, even if you will feel alone in that process. No relationship is better than a bad one.

What about just regular folk you have conflicts with? Learn the art of communicating your preferences. This can be said to others in a friendly manner, rather than accusatory. One of the best habits to cultivate is to let someone know how you feel, rather than blaming.

Blaming examples:

The reason you did that is because you don't really like me. You obviously want to make me upset.

Non-Blaming Examples:

You probably did not mean to upset me, but when you said that to me, I felt really hurt and angry. When you did that, it made me feel like my preferences do not matter.

Just by taking blame off the other person, you can see how it gives them a chance not to feel attacked. By framing it more on how you have interpreted what happened, it gives the other person some wiggle room. This allows both of you to come to some resolution. You will encounter conflict, as surely as you will have some rainy days. Have your umbrella and raincoat ready for every storm that will present itself. Stand in your personal power!

Alone or Lonely?

"We are master alchemists: We may not have discovered how to make gold out of lead, but we are able to make heaven out of hell, hell out of heaven, and purgatory out of nothing."
~ Khang Kijarro Nguyen

Modern society is not the most conducive environment for empathic individuals. Unless you are the more extroverted type of empath, you will often struggle with feelings of stress and anxiety especially in larger metropolitan areas. Even the most extroverted empath will find they need a great amount of alone and regeneration time after a night out on the town with friends. If their professional life has them speaking or showing their art, they too will need a hideaway from the world on a regular basis. This downtime is critical to recharge batteries and maintain equilibrium.

While empaths seek communion with nature and a peaceful solace within, they still often feel lonely. This is especially true if they had to end relationships that were toxic. The empath can easily slip into thoughts of what if they had done this or that, could that have changed the outcome and made the relationship work? It is not uncommon for the empath to feel a certain sense of failure at the relationship ending in a way they considered less than desirable.

If the other person they were in the relationship with is affected by personality disorders, there could be a push-pull going on where they still find ways to either try and talk you back into the relationship or are out to punish you in some way. This could be under the guise of love. It could be performed overtly or covertly. If you experience this, it is really important that you stick to those boundaries you drew in the first place. And, it's hard. Because many times you do feel lonely. Even though that person was not really the best for you, the familiarity of that relationship can entice you back. You at least know this person instead of striking out into something new or feeling lonely. Plus, they did say they would change, right?

You must look at the core problem you are experiencing with yourself. Ideally, you can experience more success being with someone you truly deserve vs. the old familiar one that tears your heart apart. Your core problem is being alone for awhile and not able to distinguish between aloneness and loneliness. When you feel lonely, first try to change that up by using the term alone. There is a huge difference between being alone and being lonely.

So often now, we reach for social media to fill this void inside us. The problem is that it often leaves us feeling worse than when we picked up our phone or logged on. For the most part, people are posting about new possessions they have, vocation advancements, educational achievements, family events, nights out, what they're eating for dinner, and vacations. It seems like everyone is busy with others and having fun and that is the illusion social media provides much of the time. This can be quite depressing and lead you into the false belief that you are just going to be lonely.

What are things you can do when you are alone? How could you do some of those things with another person? Let's explore that a bit.

Any artful creative expression is a wonderful outlet for empaths and you are master creators. There may be hobbies you have ignored and not participated in for awhile that will give you pleasure and fill this alone space.

Painting (walls or canvas)
Sew, Knit, Embroidery or Crochet
Redecorating a room
Scrap booking
Coloring or Drawing

Writing or Journaling

Designing something new

Gardening (indoors or out)

Experimenting with teas and herbs

Trying new recipes

Making a gift for the next birthday coming up

Play or learn to play an instrument

Repurpose items or give them away

Plan a perfect vacation just for you. Make a vision board of it

Plan something else you want and vision board it

Read a new book

Reorganize a drawer or closet

Have a pampering day at a spa or at home

If desired, play music that relaxes and inspires you during some of these activities. You can even post photos if you like on your social media so you do not feel like you're not participating.

Now, what could you join and do with others? Many of the same activities above. If you play an instrument or sing, you could join other musicians. You could create your own knitting circle, attend a gourmet cooking class, start a Tuesday night acrylic or oil painting group that meets at a local coffee or bar establishment. Some may want to join a writer's group or attend a live poetry reading. You could begin a monthly book club in your area or take a class in something you have always wanted to learn, like French. Learn Tai Chi, Yoga or Martial Arts. Volunteer at an animal shelter or in another capacity close to your heart.

Still not feeling inspired? Jump on Pinterest or browse magazines for more ideas. It should be something you want to do that will fill your time with more people and opportunities to create something meaningful at the same time.

It is critical that we deal up front with our feelings of loneliness. If you are on a healing path where you have ousted all the toxic people in your life, you may find yourself all alone for awhile. This is temporary but can seem like a stark desert, a lonely eternity. It would be unwise to immediately get into another love relationship at this time. You are still vulnerable and in need of a little transformation time before you hook up romantically again. Likewise, pick your friends carefully using the methods you have learned for discernment such as listening to your body's signals while communicating with that person.

You need a discovery period — a love bombing period just with you. Once you do the inner work, you will resonate differently, making for better future connections with others. This gives you a way forward to attract a loving, healthy connection. If you do not do the work, you will find yourself lonely, craving an interaction with another. Who will that most likely be? It could be a relationship that you will have some regrets about.

Have you done considerable inner work? I know some guru's tell you to ignore the subconscious thoughts you are generating and just get into the right frame of thoughts and mind. This may work for some. For me, I literally needed to travel back to those incidents and speak my truth about them, even if it was only to me I was conversing. As I saw the patterns so clearly, I could see why I hooked up with this person or did that action. I could see clearly everything was a reflection of how I was operating at a base level in life.

The point here is to be wise and cautious with your need for companionship. By falling into another relationship within weeks or a few months, you will most likely be jumping into the same soup. You have to change you inside to change your outside in order to attract the right partners, friends and people. It is a process, not an overnight thing.

And the journey is rewarding if you choose to see all the good that is going to come out of it. Does that mean you have to live some dismal life in the meantime? No, of course not. Get busy on the list above of possible fun things to do or come up with your own. Where you can, join in with groups that are doing the same so that you can have a chance to meet new people. Remember the techniques you have now learned so that you may be more selective on who is your friend or lover.

Empath and Friendships

Empaths make the best of friends. They are understanding of the needs of others and a true shoulder to lean on in times of trouble. Yet, they need to make sure they choose people as friends that reciprocate and are not just takers. Two empaths as bff's are going to get along well. The only thing they have to watch for is giving too much advice to each other. They both instinctively know what the other needs to do. Sometimes, they need to step back and let their friend experience things on their own terms without too much advice.

As you have progressed on your empathic journey, you realize that a lot of the friends you had do not connect up with you now. This is very predictable. As you have begun to change and resonate differently in a vibrational way, the attraction factor between you and that person has vanished or is waning. This can be a really difficult time for empaths. Suddenly, you find yourself friendless. At a time like this, you must look at some other ideas about being alone or lonely.

I want to share Thomas' dilemma. He stated he feels very lonely and has tried to reach out to people who say they are his friends to get together. Something always comes up for them. Plans fall through the cracks. However, these same people find a way to communicate with him when they need advice or encouragement. Those friends will even ask him to help move their belongings into their new apartment or house.

Thomas is not into partying or drinking alcohol very much at all. Occasionally, he will smoke pot but even that can sometimes leave him feeling a bit paranoid instead of expanding his awareness. Since this is what a lot of his old friends do recreationally, he has felt like the fifth wheel at times when he was with them. His interests have taken him not just into spiritual teachings, but he likes to study philosophy as well. He recently inherited his grandfather's woodworking tools and equipment and has begun to make a wide variety of items. This gives him much pleasure. When the weather is decent, he would much rather be outdoors doing something active. It's just a bummer to do it all alone.

Sometimes, Thomas feels there is something wrong with him. Perhaps it is his personality. Because of these feelings, he did not reach out to any of his old gang for quite awhile. He entered a few months of depression. This made a larger gap between him and his friends since they did not hear from him for awhile. Perhaps this spiritual growth and awakening has made him into someone that his friends laugh about behind his back. Whatever it is, he would love to have at least one good friend that he could trust and talk to.

There are several clues above in Thomas' situation of why he is having a difficult time maintaining a friendship with someone. First, we learn that his current or former friends will make time for him when they need something. This tells us that Thomas could really benefit from developing better boundaries. Second, Thomas does not enjoy a lot of the same activities that held those friendships together, namely partying and altering consciousness with substances such as alcohol or marijuana. Thomas has moved past those things and is developing a keener interest in other ways to raise or alter his consciousness. Third, Thomas spent time really down and out over the changes in him and his lack of friends. This time away from the individuals or group he was involved with furthered the divide between them. He carries fears of what they may really say behind his back.

Just as there are clues to Thomas' reasons why he does not have friends, there are also several clues on how he can make new ones. First, the woodworking he has taken up as a hobby. Even though it is something people generally do alone, they don't have to. There are many opportunities from that one activity to meet people in person and on the Internet. A simple search returned several ways he can join and meet others. Every state in the USA has a fine woodworking club. They have open sessions or meetings for making things together, plus classes and holiday celebrations. This would be a great chance to meet others and build new friendships. There are woodworking groups on social media sites to join and possibly find other people close to you in your area. Once he has produced several items, Thomas may want to sell them at local art fairs or shows. Additionally, many of those same woodworking clubs have special opportunities for showcasing or selling the art. Besides the other woodworkers, look at the exposure to the public this would now give Thomas. You have to get out of your cozy place at times to open up opportunities.

Thomas' love for the outdoors is another opportunity. He could join a local group of bicycle enthusiasts or hikers. The possibilities are endless. Once Thomas finds himself within any of these groups, he should just allow things to take their course. He will naturally attract those he needs to have a friendship with. With his willingness to follow his bliss toward the things he loves and forget about his old friends, he will magically make new ones.

The Empath and Lovers

Some people believe that opposites attract. I believed that for a long time and was surprised to find it really was not always true. In fact, common traits between us and our amour are more conducive to a longer lasting relationship. The best relationships for long term success combine the following elements:

1) Respect
2) Tolerance
3) Teamwork
4) Physical Attraction
5) Mental Attraction
6) Similar Goals/Wants/Needs

When you begin to engage in another love relationship, keep these significant six elements in mind and look for them in your potential partner. Remember, try to slow down and become friends first.

Struggles

Many empaths want to be around others like them. This is not always possible because we find ourselves in jobs and families where there are others that are not the same. They may not be awake consciously or have a completely different set of values than we do. This also means their problems are quite different. We want to help them at times but can also see that many of them like staying stuck where they are no matter how much they complain about it. It is at times like these that we often have a hard time being around these people for extended periods of time. It makes us want to curl up in our cozy room and be alone.

When you are ready, challenge yourself to grow beyond this. Empaths can sometimes put limitations on the good they have to offer if they only hang with other empaths or stay alone. Let me be very clear: I am not suggesting you should hang with those toxic people you just tossed out of your life or are in the process of getting rid of. No, that's too challenging for even the most adept empath. I am speaking of just people you see on an everyday basis that may grate on your nerves a bit. While I covered many things for managing energies, here are some additional techniques:

The Naked Experiment

Imagine those around you in their poor moods with no clothing on. It does not matter whether they are 25 or 85 years old. Just imagine this in your mind and you will find yourself smiling, almost laughing out loud. This is also a concept to use when you attend a party or event where an introverted empath may initially feel uncomfortable. Many speakers and performers have used this technique to gain more confidence by simply imagining their audience in the nude.

Sending Technique

Put your invisible or real poncho over your body and imagine the feelings of the negatively oriented people around you bouncing off of you today. Instead, send out positive, loving vibes to everyone, no matter how screwed up you previously thought they were. Just a little light, my fellow empath, just a little love can help. Visualize this as you desire. Sometimes, I imagine dark pink and emerald green heart shaped clouds coming out of my aura, floating in the air toward anyone who wants to step into one, like bubbles floating. They have the free will to decide if they want to be in your energy field or not. Keep this in mind as you watch some retreat.

When you perform any of these techniques or those you devise on your own, you are strengthening your empathic abilities. Perhaps one of the reasons these people are on your path is to assist you in reaching out to build stronger skills so that you may spread your light and love easier, even in the most difficult of situations.

Ultimately, I know this about you. As an empath, starseed, lightworker, indigo or crystal soul, you have already endured lots of alone time. You know what being separated and feeling lonely is. Begin to try some of the suggestions in this chapter to cure that situation for yourself. Keep discernment levels high as you meet new people. Look at the remedies offered to Thomas to meet others that are more like him. Most of all, know that you are never really completely alone. You are a loved child and spark of divine light from the almighty Creator!

Victim or Victor

"There is an alchemy in sorrow. It can be transmuted into wisdom, which, if it does not bring joy, can yet bring happiness." ~ Pearl S. Buck, *The Child Who Never Grew*

Almost all empaths have had trauma inflicted upon them. Most humans of any sort have experienced being a victim of some type. But the empath does seem to receive more of this, especially in their younger years. It is almost like a pre-written part of our life script. There is something carving us with these experiences into the magnificent people we will later be. However, these happenings often leave deep grooves in our psyche. Removal can seem daunting at times. In fact, depending on your dedication to having a better life and the weight of the trauma you endured, it can take a lifetime. Perhaps a better description would be to revise those files in your subconscious — to write over them — rather than remove them.

In order to transform from victim to victor, we must take some sort of action. Waiting until something pinches us and makes us move is the slow route. If we take active responsibility in our circumstances, we can progress on our path to victorious wholeness much faster.

Part of being a victim is feeling out of control and that things are not working for you. Yet, if you look at things more closely, you will see that there are many things working in your favor.

Begin with what feels easy and add more ideas or affirming thoughts each day. Exploring that, what could you begin with that you know you can believe? Let's start with your physical body. Right now, there are a million processes or more going on to keep you in homeostasis. You are not aware of them. You don't even think about them. Can you see how there is something greater than yourself taking care of you all the time. Even if you are ill, injured, paralyzed, think of the parts that are working correctly right now. If you have cancer in one or two parts of your body, think about all the healthy cells that make up every area of your body except those one or two. What a miraculous thing the human body is. On autopilot, it is constantly guided to heal and find homeostasis.

Look at your environment. Have you ever thought deeply about an element like water. Water gives life and is essential to it. Water can become so extreme it can take life. Yet always, if you tried to pick this liquid up in your hand, some would slip through your fingers. Water is so soft, yet the constant movement of it can cut through rock. Water can become hard when exposed to the right temperature. Likewise, it can evaporate right before your eyes when exposed to enough heat. You cannot be water but it is a good portion of what forms you. It is beyond a chemical. It is a compound element that forms the basis of life. How miraculous is that? Who or what makes water happen? Think deeply on this to feel the depth of miracles in your environment and in yourself.

What if you just decided to go through an entire day feeling lucky and driving that with the thought "I always have good luck." Everything I need comes to me easily because I am so lucky. Repeating that little mantra to yourself over and over like a needle stuck on an old record. If you do this, first you will notice that your feelings begin to change. Putting emotion behind it makes this happen. If you're driving to work, yell out "I am so darn lucky!" If you hit a traffic jam due to a wreck ahead, say to yourself "I am so lucky that I am here and not in that wreck." So, you can turn anything you need to into your good fortune. It does not have to be something where you believe, oh no, now I'm going to be late. Maybe you are lucky to be late, maybe you avoided something by being where you are at. You are lucky – think it – say it with emotion – feel it and you'll find yourself in a lucky mood all day.

These simple ways are the beginning of the better you and a new enriched life. These are the start of silencing the victim memories and reaching out toward something greater that is already inside you, just buried and in need of retrieval. You were born for your own greatness and it is there. Begin anew each day now and practice these types of thoughts you can believe over and over. Through rote and repetition, you will become so different than you were before. You will heal that part of you that has been retaining its hurt for too long.

During this time of reinventing yourself and filling your mind with healthier thoughts and feelings fueled by intense emotion, give up that which is not serving you. Give up watching the negative things on television that are not propelling you forward to the new you. Fill your time with thoughts of the future – hopefully very near future. Look up places you would love to travel to. If possible, collect photos of these places and start a vision board for your new adventures.

Imagine people in your new life who are supportive, loving and healthy in their responses to you. Daydream about this each day and you will attract those people to you at the perfect, right time. Affirm "I attract people to me that are loving, healthy and supportive of each other."

See yourself handling your finances with a new finesse you did not have before. You deftly take care of balancing accounts and keeping track of things responsibly and with care.

What do you fantasize doing that you haven't done? Make a bucket list of items you want to accomplish. See yourself doing them.

Try changing some of the music you listen to. Ever notice how many songs sing of lovers done wrong and victimhood? It is so pervasive and much has been said about people wanting to wallow in their misery. Yet, realize you are cutting a groove in the LP of your mind each time you engage in this. Now, there is something to be said of sorrow, grief and loss, but we don't want to stay there in it. What if you listened to something that evoked different feelings in you? You could try and change things up with sounds that give you feelings of triumph, power, true love, positive beliefs, or calm instrumentals. Some people listen to mantras spoken by monks, religious or new age music. There are so many options now.

So, for your new life ahead, remember this. Daydream and see yourself fully functional with opportunities constantly for you to grow. See yourself ready more than ever to handle whatever situation you find yourself in. See yourself surrounded by relationships and people who are understanding and loving. Light an inner fire inside to tell yourself affirmations you can believe in. Trust that if you hear doubts arise in the beginning, these are just memory reflections stored in your subconscious. They will finally subside and be written over with more life affirming beliefs.

The simple act of not being able to speak our mind or express how we are feeling puts us in victim mentality. Additionally, when people are not allowed, even encouraged, to express anger in a healthy way, it results in stuffing feelings that come out as passive-aggressive behavior. It can also lead to the inability to draw boundaries which means we are not stating our own needs and requirements.

There are some people in our lives that it is near impossible to get them to respect our boundaries. These people generally have agendas in which they see the world as existing to fit their desires only. Some are quite cunning and you don't see it coming. Others are very forceful and blatant. Many are extremely charming, but still ignore your rules of engagement. Ideally, all humans should respect the feelings of others. They should try to make sure they do not force their way or wishes on another. Too often, the opposite can occur. To make sure you do not fall into victim role in those relationship dynamics, you must stay watchful and aware. You also must accept the fact that as an empath you unknowingly attract these types of people into your life by your very essence. You can avoid them, but more will find you and this will continue UNTIL you change internally into an empowered empath who has clear set rules of engagement and consequences when those rules are not honored. Because the individuals with hard core personality disorders will trespass all over your desires and preferences again and again. You must make a decision about this. Speak up and make your preferences known, preferably from the beginning of a relationship or encounter.

The cost to yourself in deciding to just acquiesce and go along with these individuals for the sake of keeping the peace is too high. It takes you away from who you are — a human with your own beliefs, thoughts and desires that are not being met.

Remember: Boundaries are simply you being able to tell people what is acceptable to you and what is not. To have clarity around everyone's boundaries is a kind and loving thing to do. It shows you care about yourself and the furtherance of the relationship. Boundaries are what help you keep your own inner power intact. Instituting them will level out wildly conflicting feelings you are experiencing and shield you from being overwhelmed by others or living in a victim state.

Always respect the boundaries of others. This goes along with treating others the way we want to be treated. If needed, you can always say to another that you respect their boundaries, and ask them to respect yours.

This is a core concept of increasing your empathic abilities. Many times, people want to increase their skills but they feel overloaded by their senses. Everything we are talking about in this book is designed to allow you to move forward with doing so. If you have appropriate boundaries, are not living in victim mode, and feeling more of your own inner power and creativity because of it, this is the cure.

Notes – Thoughts – Ideas – Affirmations – Dreams

Anxiety & Depression

"An entire sea of water can't sink a ship unless it gets inside the ship. Similarly, the negativity of the world can't put you down unless you allow it to get inside you." ~ Goi Nasu

Dear Fellow Empath,

As I write this chapter, I am dealing with heavy feelings of anxiety and since it has lasted for more than a day now, it is time to do something. When you cannot pinpoint the root cause of your anxiety and you keep feeling it intensely, you soon feel perturbed it is there. And because you have no rational reason to feel anxious, you try to stuff it away. This is a tight circle that you keep spinning around in. It takes something else – or even several things to break out of it. I felt that this chapter could not be written at a better time than now.

I have not written this book to fool you into thinking I am always an empowered empath. I flounder and flip around at times just like you do. And perhaps it is fortunate that I do so. That way, we can identify with each other.

So what is the anxiety about? The same feelings I woke up with – the same feelings I went to sleep with – the same feelings I had yesterday. I don't know precisely. Some of it revolves around other people close to me and needless stress they are creating. Some of it could be coming from world conditions in general. It is difficult to know what I am picking up on but I don't think these feelings are coming from me personally. It would be so easy to end them if that were the case.

I find myself constantly covering up my third eye area with my hand. While unconsciously doing this, I often find myself sitting with this area of my forehead covered and that is why I believe these feelings are being transported from somewhere else. I also notice that I am crossing my arms over my solar plexus area when around others – a posture I rarely use.

Therefore, it is important that I ground today. The weather has turned warmer and I will go outside shortly. There are many leaves that need to be raked and if I could just plant one thing – even a seed and discharge my feelings into the soil, I know I will feel better.

Also, I am focusing on my root chakra and being in the present moment. Even though I feel on edge, I know it is temporary and will pass. I don't want to stay in this mood any longer. It is cutting into my productivity and keeping me from my joy.

Once I have finished touching the earth and raking leaves outside, I will indulge in a pampering self-care exercise in the bathroom. I will make some tea. One of the ways I distress is by utilizing herbal teas that I have come across that truly change me internally and how I feel. *Tulsi Sweet Rose* is one of my favorites for times like this. It is described as stress relieving and magical and I have found it to be so for me. With its heavy rose scent and holy basil ingredients, this is one of my favorites.

I plan on drawing a warm bath with Epsom salts and a few drops of an uplifting essential oil. I will listen to a guided meditation while totally relaxed in the tub. I could meditate on my own, but I am afraid my anxious feelings would get in the way and I will be better served at this time by being guided on an audio experience instead.

Once out of the tub, I will continue to do self-care as I see fit. Things I have put off such as a facial masque and slather my body in nicely scented moisturizer. I will then get dressed and see if my mood is gone.

If I have forgotten my vitamins – which is likely – I'll make sure to take those now and also drink extra water today and stay hydrated. If I need to make another herbal tea, I'll switch it up to *Yogi Tea's Positive Energy*, which has lovely orange scents and truly does make me feel perkier and happier. Herbs are magic!

So that is my plan for relieving the anxiety today. I'll let you know how it works out on the other side.

Namaste, Lyra

The Other Side

Tempted to take a nap instead of trying to keep my plan to relieve the anxiety, I resisted doing the very things my mind and body told me I needed to do to feel better. I failed myself on this day.

Why do we do that? Why stay in such an awful state? It felt like trying to move lead to go toward something healthier. Instead, I got in bed and drifted off for a nap. But, I could have changed everything quite dramatically by sticking to the plan I had. I am not beating up on myself, but I need to know why so that I can head this off in the future. Do you ever do this? I am really thinking I was just too physically exhausted. "The spirit was willing, but the flesh was weak" scenario.

I am human and struggle with issues too. Like you, I often know what is good for me — what will change things up. So, why did I resist going toward something that would help? Honestly, it could have just been emotional exhaustion. Plus, sometimes a nap does help to change things for us. Still, I have had times when I stayed in a bad mood too long and I would imagine you have as well.

Something impressed upon me by the teachings of Dr. Joe Dispenza is that, if we do not regulate and cultivate better attitudes, our moods can become our outer personalities that we project into the world. Sometimes we feel so stuck in the mud, or sinking in quicksand, that we cannot see how to pull ourselves up and out.

Utilizing substances like drugs or alcohol to cover or uplift our moods is not a tangible answer either. Often, we need to get by ourselves and do something that gives us pleasure. Make ourselves have a little fun to break the mood. When an empath is burned out, we just become our own worst enemy and this is definitely the time to take a break — just for yourself.

Many things can be utilized to break the spell of our moods:

Yoga
Dance
Tai Chi
Qi Gong
Music
Herbal teas
Clean your physical space
Reiki
Massage
Pottery
Scrapbooking
Art Journaling
Painting
Coloring
Gardening
Walking
Writing

Indulging in a novel

In other words, you find a way to release these negative emotions and transform them into something else. This is alchemy. You must find a way out of the funk. Let me address the fact that performing any of these acts suggested above may not cure or solve the original source of anxiety or depression you are experiencing. However, it will make you feel better. It will assist you in bringing in more light to yourself which will transform your current vibration. You will feel increased energy along with a more positive mood.

Ultimately, you must find the root cause if it persists so that you can pluck it out and send it on with love and light. This often means visiting what Dr. Carl Jung referred to as our shadow side. The easiest way to begin doing that is to make mental and sometimes literal notes of what your self talk is saying to you.

If you need a fast transformation, try the music suggested as it brings the most immediate results. Move your body, even if you are just swaying back and forth, to the music.

All of this is part of releasing your own baggage and changing things up to clear your energy. Even if you have picked up energy from another, this still works well to release. Basically, there is a bit of them in you or it would not be something you have attracted into your life. Their vibes or behavior have something to teach you — even if it is just setting boundaries or standing up for yourself which could involve conflict — the same thing you are trying to avoid. Here are more ideas to help:

1) Remove clutter in your personal spaces. Even if your space is not overly filled with objects you are not using or need, try reorganizing a drawer, closet or cabinet. Look for those cobwebs hiding in high or low corners and ceilings. All of this activity will make your space feel brighter and more under

your control. Light some incense or sage the area to clear the air. Purify your environment. Recharge any crystals or minerals you own. Rededicate sacred objects, spaces and yourself to the highest good of all.

2) Indulge in some me time. Carve out and schedule alone time. You need this solitude to manage your energy. You will have more to bring back to the world when you consciously monitor and correct your energy on a regular basis. Spend time doing something you love whether it is a money making endeavor or not. Art is a wonderful way to express so much and put your brain into a different, slower wave state. Explore any form of creation you desire with no payoff required at the end. Approach it as a fun activity that does not have requirements.

3) Improve Health - Be more fit. Strengthening your physical body results in you feeling more in control of your energy field. Stress is your demise and it weakens you on all levels. Begin small with exercise if you are in a weakened state. Over time, this will increase your ability to cope and deal with situations, feelings and other people. Nutrition is very important in that it has the capacity to supply us with chemicals critical to all of our body processes — including mental. Often, lack of certain nutrients can create or exacerbate depression and anxiety.

4) Many empaths feel crushed in crowded places. You can still go to concerts, fairs, amusement parks and other places where you will encounter many people. Adopting a mind set prior to arriving is the trick. The key is to not let everyone's energy stick to you by allowing things to go around you instead of through you. At times, you may attend an event where the group energy is very positive and uplifting. It's okay to let your guard down here and revel in the group's emotional dynamics.

You are far enough along to know the difference in what feels good and what does not.

5) Consciously and deliberately radiate love. Your first love must be for yourself. This is not a selfish act, but a self-preservation act. If you love your home, you will take the best care of it you can physically and financially. The same is true of the body/mind/spirit complex you inhabit.

Finding Root Causes & Triggers

In an effort to find what is triggering depression or anxiety, let's look first at our physiology and then the other 'stuff'.

To calm your delicate nervous system, make sure you are getting enough B vitamins including B12. These essential nutrients assist your entire nervous system in running smoothly. Reduce caffeine so you are not pumping out so much adrenaline and reducing magnesium. Enjoy protein rich foods and drinking lots of good quality water. How are you sleeping? Enact methods for better rest time as this is when your system heals the most.

Do not forget your grounding techniques! Connect to the earth by visualizing roots coming from the bottom of your feet down into the ground. Walk barefoot on sand, soil, grass. Utilize some nature time for yourself every week if you can. State and National parks can be a place of refuge and recharge. Do not over exercise, but engage in things that raise your vibration and make you feel energized instead of depleted.

Consider what products you use for house cleaning, laundry or other chemicals in your environment. One or more could stress your nervous system. Look at your personal care products in this way too.

Internal & External Housecleaning

Clean the temple! Sweep the debris from your inner and outer environment. If you are experiencing depression or negativity, this is the time to engage in working with yourself on the inside to clean things up in your thought and behavior patterns. Often, these are deeply ingrained beliefs from the past. This is the perfect time to work with guided visualizations or meditations because they lay down new beliefs in your brain. Using them with regularity will increase their effects.

As you do this, begin to freshen up your outer environment. While I do not recommend creating anxiety for yourself, start simply. Perhaps just getting the laundry caught up, folded, hung put away. Vacuuming and cleaning the floors. Dusting cobwebs in corners. Putting on positive music while you do this. Organize a closet or a couple of drawers.

Stagnation can build up in your physical environment. Keep the chi moving in your home with music, sounds of waterfall or any other things that assist.

Disengage from your phone, tablet, computer and social media for awhile. Very healthy thing to do! And if it is difficult for you to do, determine if you have allowed it to develop into an addiction. You cannot be a magical empath and have this going on. You are receiving too many thoughts and energies digitally to stay in touch with your own sense of self and Source. Limit these things greatly for internal happiness.

What about the feelings that seem to pile up that we are not expressing? Do they contribute to anxiety? I believe they do. Many things can cause this to happen including caretaking of others, financial burdens, worries, health challenges, geo-political circumstances, too much social media or news, broken or toxic relationships, and more. Which of these can you limit your exposure to? Which of these could you begin to affect by paying more attention to what is manifesting before you?

If you are in a toxic relationship, you have the power to change that. Even as you shake your head from side to side saying "no, I can't", you really can. Except within the concept of being someone's shackled slave, no one can force you into staying in a relationship. While some may choose to stay because of the kids or financial reasons, this is a choice. Another choice really can be made.

Financial burdens are within your control as well. There are many ways in today's world to make extra money. With so many people now able to work at home utilizing technology, this could be an option for you to earn some extra cash. You may want to pick up two evenings a week at a second job for awhile. The point here is not to keep you working yourself to death though. You just want to bring your head up out of the debt you may be drowning in. You need a plan that you can make work for you.

If you do not have a budget, write one out. Many people want to avoid doing this. They confidently will tell others that they already know their bills. By writing down everything — absolutely everything you spend money on each month, you can see where the holes are. You can look at certain bills and begin to think how you could shop around and save a little here. When you do this, you may free up quite a bit of money each month you did not have before. I now do this yearly. Even if I stay with the companies I currently use, I still look for better rates and service. If the switch seems like a good fit, I make it.

Are you engaged in extreme care taking of others? If so, get a handle on it so you can find more balance in your life. Bring others in to share the burden if the person you are helping cannot do so on their own. Often, this happens with children and perhaps elderly parents. Whatever the situation is, exhaust as many situations and people as you can to assist you so you are not the only one. Share the load with others and insist upon it. Stay in your personal power and let others know you want to help and here are the exact times you are available and what you are able to do.

Another contributor to anxiety is worry. Always when we worry, we are not staying in the now. We are projecting worst case scenarios of the future. While it is always good to have thoughts of the future, allow yourself to make them great ones and vibrate at that level. Remember, we are constantly manifesting our experience. Make it a happy one that has minimal challenges.

If you are experiencing an illness or health challenge that is creating anxiety for you — or if someone close to you is, get proactive with it. Subscribe to the latest research updates with reliable online medical sites. Learn all you can about the condition. Listen to your intuition about what your body needs to feel better or heal. In conjunction with traditional western medicine, look into alternative therapies too. Find what feels good for you. Keep a diary of what worked and what does not make you better. Allow your fears, thoughts and worries to fill the journal as well. They already exist, might as well get them out on paper. Pray, meditate and surrender things to God Source when it is too overwhelming. Ask what you should do next.

When it comes to the daily round the clock news, turn it off if it begins to affect your mood. Be cognizant of how much time you spend on social media as it can really drain you emotionally as an empath. Sometimes, it feels like there is something invisible coming from the screen, sucking the life out of you. Set time limits for these things and stick to them. Engage in other activities that bring out your creative side.

Part of being a magical empath is a constant inventory taking of our inner selves. We grow on our path, moving always toward exemplary empowerment. Even on our worst days, we must try to remember that "this too shall pass". Abundance and beauty are much more prolific in our world than we realize. If we unplug from the negative and focus on what is working; what is good; what is peaceful; what is abundant; what is gorgeous and breathtaking, things around us change. When we change ourselves, we change the world.

Breaking Ties

There are times in life when we must rid ourselves of relationships that are producing fear, anxiety and depression. It is important to know how much of it is them and how much is us. This requires spending time analyzing the dynamics of the relationship and the personalities involved. It can be tough when we are one of the personalities. Many times, we may need to speak with an objective third party to be sure. However, it has become evident from a stack of stories that are taller than the mattresses in the fairytale, *Princess and the Pea*, that empaths attract those with certain personality disorders.

In the beginning, the relationship was magical, meant to be and very lovely. But, little invisible monsters began rearing up and making themselves known. Little bastards! Why did they have to come along and ruin everything. Here honey, we can fix that. All you need to do is _____ (fill in the blank).

Yes. The solution to the other person's little monster dilemma may seem quite simple to us. The only problem is: they cannot see it. They may think it is us. Guess what, in a way, it is us.

When we expect other people to change their behavior to make us feel alright, loved, appreciated or any other emotion, we are giving them our power. We are powerless at that point. We are saying, if you will just do this, I will be alright.

Tigers really do not change their stripes. Sometimes, we continue having conflict of some sort with persons we hoped would change. We all know about love relationships where we begin to see flaws in our partner that we did not notice before.

If we move into a phase where we hope our partner will grow and change, we often use covert or overt ways of trying to make that come about. This is the root of codependency.

The magical empath does not wait for others to change so they can feel better. If conditions are not acceptable, they let that be known and make a change. In the alternative, an empath can decide to stay in the situation knowing they will have to supply their own good feelings and not be dependent in any way upon the other for same. While the latter choice may build inner fortitude, it can be a lonely point to operate from in the relationship.

We all carry some sort of little monsters. The difference is that an empath is much more likely to have been on a path of eliminating the ones they carry. At the least, the empath is actively working on this at least part of the time. But many other humans are not working on it. And here is how you can tell:

- Would the person you are having trouble with ever go to therapy voluntarily? Would they even consider the idea?
- Do they read self-help material? Would they seek out a book about such topics on their own?
- Are their words or actions truly hurtful? If you imagined them behaving this way with another person, would it be alright? How would the other person be likely to feel or react?
- Are secrets involved such as not telling you the whole story about a situation; keeping something hidden?
- Do their words betray the feelings you get from them?
- Do they make blanket excuses for behavior such as "all families are dysfunctional"?

We cannot change other humans, especially when they do not see anything they are doing as being causative to a situation. We can only decide how we are going to react to this person and whether we want to have limited or no contact with them.

They have no interest in changing. Worse, there are those that really know they need to change and promise they will do so to retain the relationship. They do so for a short while ... maybe even up to three or four months ... and then they are back to their old self. Those stripes never changed color on a real, internal level. They were simply putting on a mask or facade to keep things on an even keel. True change and internal growth never happened. Sad for them.

Be strong in yourself and forgiving of them. Let what they have done or not done go so that it does not eat at you mentally and emotionally. Decide the best course of action to protect yourself in the future. Depending upon who this person is in your life, you may need to institute a no contact policy or a very limited contact.

As an empath, you have to come to the realization that you are not just different in the way you process things. You are different because your path here is something else entirely from those who will not change their stripes during their lifetime here. You may be working constantly on improving yourself, but those people will not. Life's challenges will carve them to a degree, but they will not actively seek change as you do.

Here is the real question you must ask: why am I in this predicament? What is the nature of this relationship showing me as I look into the mirror at myself. Is it teaching me that I must learn to stick up for myself? Or, that I have a tendency to try and fix others in an attempt to elevate my own ego? What is the pay off if I stay in this situation? What could my life be if I choose to remove myself from this relationship or situation?

The scenario I give above assumes that the empath is in a relationship with just a fairly normal human being. Perhaps this is someone who is a bit set in their ways and unwilling to make any changes to please their partner. It could have been a situation where the two were really not that suited mentally to begin with. If there was a strong, purely physical, attraction with not many things in common, this is often the case.

Surrender

There may be a time in your life when you find yourself backed into such a corner that you do not know what to do or how to get out of your situation or turmoil. I have been there more than once. Each time, it has brought me to a point where I could do nothing but surrender. Waving the white flag. This is not a flag of defeat, but of knowing you cannot sail your ship alone right now. You need help to get to safer, sunnier shores. The only solution for me during those rare times has been to give it totally to God/Goddess/All That Is.

Perhaps you have two or three things you need to do now and only the money for one. These are survival things, not something frivilous. It could be a health crisis situation and you are not sure what to do. Even in death, there comes a time when we must surrender to a higher power. But that death should come at the right time, not at our own hands because we are backed into a corner.

Trust me when I tell you that almost everyone gets backed into a corner at some point and this is where you just need to ask for help from your guides, angels, your God. Then, take refuge the best way you can and wait for divine intervention. Follow the intuitive clues that come to you. Meditate and pray. "This too shall pass." Surrender is a powerful tool!

Control vs. Allowing

"It's still magic even if you know how it's done."

~ Terry Pratchett, *A Hat Full of Sky*

The best way the magical empath resonates in their world is through thoughtful anticipation of the things they want to create combined with utilizing their intuition to discern which way they should move in order to flow with the current. When they fall away from that, the culprits are usually fear and unconscious replay of the past. When the magical empath holds knowledge of these pitfalls, they can watch for them in their external environment as things manifest that they do not want. Ultimately, the magical empath can make corrections because they realize they have the power to change how they experience what is around them simply by shifting their focus. This can simply be instituted by thought alone.

There are many ways we use our human mind to trick ourselves. If we are using the concept of control of others in any situation, this is often rooted in fear. At times, a belief is constructed that we are controlling out of "love". This is one way we can fool ourselves. Every situation is different, so the empath must take a candid look at their motives. The place to begin is with base fears. An empath could ask of their self the reasons they are afraid of just allowing and letting go of control. Many fears involve:

Vulnerability — It can be very difficult to be authentic and true in our presentation of our personality in the world and in relationships where we may have experienced betrayal, bullying or mistreatment of any kind. As we attempt to control the responses of others by not letting our guard down and being ourselves, we miss out on expressing our true nature. This all goes back to conflict. Yet, it also involves discernment. There are some people you can be vulnerable with where you can enjoy an open conversation or relationship. There are some you cannot. You have to use your intuition and know the difference. Just remember it is important to not shut out all closeness with others due to the actions of some.

Abandonment — Control issues can exist around those leaving or deserting you. Slyly checking the email, social media or texts of your lover means you have abandonment and trust issues. There may be a very good reason you feel this way, but you are engaging in a form of control and not being honest when you do this. This hurts you more than them. Especially with the way it can begin to consume your thoughts.

Validation — This type of control falls more into the codependency category. People use control to help others to a degree that they should not. By doing so, they avoid the real issues of their own self they need to work on. Instead, their time, energy or money is tied up with the other person or people. They feel if they just keep giving or doing, this person or situation will fall into place the way they need it to. At that point, they will feel validated.

Trust — This can involve trusting others to be able to learn and take care of situations on their own. Again, this follows codependency issues. It can also be an overall lack of trust in the Tao. It is the opposite of going with the flow or allowing space for things to emerge. When we hold fears regarding trusting life and its processes, we are basically experiencing a loss of faith that everything will work out.

Another clue that we are low on trust is the lack of spontaneity in our lives. By having preordained conclusions and expectations of others, we shut down the possibility for better outcomes — ones we did not even think of. We lay down what we think should happen which equals our expectations on people and situations. Then, reality happens. We compare this reality with our expectations and when it does not measure up, we are condemning our experience. The play never ends exactly the way we planned it. It could be better. It could hold very humorous or wondrous moments if we trust and let go.

We must surrender to the flow or we will continue to be engaged in a fight for things to be the way we thought they should be. We will miss opportunities to learn, grow, have joy and discover. It is important to think about the control factors we may be holding in our mind. We cannot expect our outer world to be a certain way in order for us to feel good. We must work with our inner selves, clear that and then the outer manifests in a much more desirable way.

Leave room for creativity and spontaneity as you allow the above fears to die a silent death each time you recognize you are engaged in them. Regarding unconscious fears of the past, we usually see some sort of attachment involved. Often, we do not know we are participating in this at and it can be hard to discover. Rooted in the unconscious, the easiest way to recognize is by looking at patterns that keep repeating in our lives.

In the attachment phase, we are insisting that our old story is the only, or at least the primary, way things are. We allow that story to affect our approach to life, our overall mood and expectations for what will occur for us. By not letting go of the old stories of the past, we are latched on vibrationally to the things around us we may not truly want on a higher level. However, we feel stymied or completely lost about how to change things and move toward something different and better.

Staying attached to the past means we keep experiencing the same situations repeatedly in our life. It might be with a different person, job or living situation, but the basic story and end of the play are the same.

In this out of sync state of living, we are not in the present moment. We are not aware this is where we are vibrating — the signature we are sending out. Of course, the universe follows orders to send more of the same because of where we are resonating. This is in accordance with the Law of Correspondence (Initiate, T., 2012).

Imagine guides and angels viewing this from the spiritual realm. I can see them stomping their ethereal foot each time we again take the wrong turn or make a decision based upon our unconscious story we are still telling our self. "Damn, I thought they would get it this time. Everything could be beautiful if they would just follow the bread crumbs I am putting in front of them."

Until we look at our patterns through examination of self and the situations we have encountered during our life, we remain clueless. Once our eyes are opened and we see the pattern, we can work on changing our old story into a new one that we tell ourselves consistently.

Wealth

"Whatever you think you can do or believe you can do, begin it. Action has magic, grace and power in it."
~ Johann Wolfgang von Goethe

The feelings you carry about yourself combine with your subconscious beliefs you hold about your money situation. What are your real underlying expectations about how you see yourself with money now and in the future? This is not the same as your goals or things you want to achieve. But what are the true hidden thoughts that come up from time to time? For people who are experiencing lack, it might be something like: "I will never really have what I want because of _____." There are a million things to fill in that blank. So, this is what we are looking for in our exploration about wealth. We have to discover, then deeply transform, the thoughts and expectations you have around the idea of your personal worth and what you deserve.

Empaths are notoriously difficult at receiving. They are such givers that receiving is almost completely foreign to them. Becoming adept at receiving is a noble goal to have as you level up and change your wealth status. If you are a giver, you need to be open to receiving as much as possible. This way, you can keep some and give some to others of your choice. This also keeps the current (and currency) moving.

It can be difficult for empaths to ask for what they want or even feel they deserve. They do not want to anger anyone or appear greedy. We must feel more comfortable asking for a fair monetary exchange. This undervaluing of self is something that we must not let persist. Too often, empaths minimize or negate their worth. They will price their services or products too low. Some are guilty of giving away too much.

Empaths have a lot of worth. Worth is value that can be exchanged for money. Money is nothing more than something we have come up with in our world to exchange with each other as a trade. You give me this and I give you money. Some people receive a lot of money and they cannot tell you exactly why. But, I know they must be much more open to asking and receiving.

The more money you have, the more money you can give. Whether you help people you know, donate on a crowd funding site, or play Santa anonymously, you do no one any favors when you don't have more than enough money. You need money. You are worthy of it and you can then do anything you want with it including giving to yourself, which I highly encourage you do as well.

The entire concept with money and wealth abundance in any form - even an abundance of time to have fun or explore what you want to do with your life — has to do with self-worth and your actual expectations. What do you think you are worth? Can you actually put a price on it? What do you really expect to have happen for you?

It is easy to answer that you are worth this amount or that. This is usually proclaimed right before a chuckle. When we speak of worth, we are speaking of what you really feel on a deep level you deserve. Without knowing it, we are often operating in a cloud of thoughts that promote lack instead of abundance. We must be brave explorers who are willing to part the mists on this elusive concept called lack thinking. We have heard many speak of it, but what does it really mean and how in the world can we stop doing it so we may experience the bounty we deserve?

As an experiment, I began tracking my lack thoughts for a few days. I was amazed at what I found. Too often, I captured thoughts occurring in my head that are not the abundant thinking I need to be engaged in. For instance, in response to working on this book, these thoughts occurred:

"It's going to be hard to sell."
"The market is over saturated."
"I'm afraid the cover won't attract the readers."

Just during one doubtful moment, I had so many lack thoughts occur. Obviously, I do not think that way all the time or I would not finish this book. I would engage in something else that I like to do. To turn this around, I decided to take the whole idea of the book selling strategies away from my beliefs. Instead, I replaced my thoughts with:

"I want to make this book exactly what my fellow empaths need."
"This book will be evergreen and classic in nature. The information it provides is timeless."
"Every empath that wants this information will find it easily."
"I write this book because I want to further the cause and help."

Having this shift allowed me to move in a more seamless way toward completion and feel more elation about my creation. It also took a huge burden off my shoulders.

What happens when we do not know we have beliefs that are holding us back? Usually, these are tied up with expectations we possess inside. Located deep in the cloud of lack and almost invisible, it takes some looking to find them. Without being conscious of it, we are projecting to the universe exactly what we expect. Guess what, the universe usually delivers according to your feelings and expectations. Not only do we need to work on our self-talk going on in our heads, we have to look deeply at what our authentic expectations are.

Each Christmas, for the past few years, I somehow lose at least one gift that my parents give me. I do not consciously think about this at all. But, it happens with regularity each December 25th. I end up calling my parents and siblings saying, "if you see such and such gift, let me know. I can't find it. It's gone." I do always end up finding my gift. This is a strange situation because I have no conscious idea about it. I only know that it is too frequent to be coincidental and I do not lose gifts from anyone other than my parents. Could it be that I have difficulty of some sort receiving gifts from my parents? This is the place to begin to explore.

Do I hold an inner expectation that I don't deserve gifts from my parents? We have a rocky past. Now, I might be getting closer. Perhaps I need to institute a mantra of being so excited about being gifted by my parents and that I deserve their gifts. But, would this really represent what I feel?

Here is what I know about the lack paradigm. Whenever we are in this mode, we are expecting on some level that our needs are not going to be met. Once we part the mists on the big cloud of lack, it begins to dissipate and the skies clear. Sometimes, it can be murky and hard to see what we are doing or not doing that is causing the same things to come around for us time and again. So, the big questions we have to explore are varied. Here are some to begin with:

Are my needs being met?

Do I deserve to have my needs met?

How important are my desires?

Am I worth all that I want?

Do I feel guilty if I receive what I desire and someone else does not?

Do I believe people with wealth are evil?

Do I believe I will leave less for others if I have what I desire?

Do I believe I will work hard, but others will get the credit?

Do I believe I will be cheated somehow?

Do I believe that even if I achieve the goal I desire, something will happen to negate it or bring it down?

Do I feel comfortable writing down a money goal I want to achieve by a certain date?

How hard is it for me to ascertain what my net worth and salary should be?

Now, I will assume this next question does not represent you because you are here reading this book. Still, I have to ask. Do you feel you do not have time to monitor your thoughts for a week and pay attention to what your deep beliefs are that you hold about personal worth? If you feel you cannot take the time, this is also how you are stuck in the lack paradigm of thinking. You deserve to take the time to sort this out. Time is actually more valuable than money. We can always get more money, but not more time. Are you worth the time it will take to sort this out? If not, it is likely you will continue racing around on your hamster wheel your entire life until you drop dead wondering why other people have it easier and you do not. Making time to do the exercises and self examination needed shows you know you deserve to do so. It demonstrates that you care about yourself and want to live better.

How do you guard your time? Do you make time for yourself and the endeavors that will move you toward more wealth? How do you manage your personal energy and power? Do you give it up too easily to others when you need to conserve more for you? Wealth can only come to you when you respect your personal energy and make realistic allotments with your time. We all only have so many hours and days within a week. If we spend it constantly working hard for something that does not really suit us, it is not likely to bring us true satisfaction.

Ultimately, it is not entirely about money. The most important energy you have is that which is within yourself. When you make peace with that fact and the time you have allotted, you will find things opening up for you to work toward a greater, fulfilling purpose that also brings you the wealth you seek.

Now, get to work on those thoughts and hidden expectations. When you win big at your endeavors, let me know your success story. I can't wait to celebrate with you!

Attracting Synchronicity

"I want to be magic. I want to touch the heart of the world and make it smile. I want to be a friend of elves and live in a tree. Or under a hill. I want to marry a moonbeam and hear the stars sing. I don't want to pretend at magic anymore.
I want to be magic." ~ Charles de Lint

Occasionally, someone will tell me they never have synchronicity occur in their life. I am always astonished when I hear this. Really? Are you sure? Synchronicity has been a part of my life for a long time. To me, it is like an old familiar friend. I do not know when we will run into each other, but I know it will happen. My synchronicities are small, medium and large. They are all unmistakable to me and beyond mere coincidence.

Synchronicity is a friend and guide to help us out of this heavy mist that surrounds our memories of who we really are beyond this physical realm and dimension. There is so much I would like to impart to you and give you as a blueprint for moving more gracefully in life. To experience the best version of you, attracting synchronicities along the way that serve as 'aha' moments and guideposts on your path. I only feel qualified to give you part – the bits and pieces I have figured out about synchronicity that have worked for me. I also assume that if they work for me, they will also work for you

How do we attract synchronicity? Carl Jung is one of the early pioneers of this concept which he used to describe events that were happening that did not seem driven by the laws of cause and effect. Further, they were exceptional in their occurrence in that the odds of them having happened by chance were phenomenally high. A third requirement of calling something a synchronicity is that it holds a significant meaning to everyone involved. Here is a fictitious example:

Perhaps you are working on a drawing or plan of your dream home. You are stuck on some area regarding the roofline design. You feel you will need an architect to help you pull it all together. You set your drawing aside and wonder who to hire and what the cost would be.

It has stopped raining outside and you take your dog for a walk at the park nearby. You pause near a park bench during the walk to adjust your dog's collar. The bench is glistening with raindrops in the light that is now peeking through clouds. You notice a wet piece of paper lying on the park bench and can see writing on the other side of it. You pick it up to dispose of it in the trash can to the left of the bench. As you look at the advertisement, it is someone who freelances drawing house plans. Do you consider this a synchronicity or coincidence? You just had the thought that you need to get help. You set your drawings aside. You take your dog for a walk and find this lone piece of wet paper advertisement. I would call this a synchronicity.

In the scenario above, what part of the synchronicity is forced? Remember, synchronicity is acausal, meaning it comes out of nowhere; it cannot be created on demand. Instead, we see the observer in the example above in a flow that progresses toward his or her desire. Their thoughts and feelings are one of submission to the idea they may not be able to do this alone. They put a question out by thought alone of needing help, but wondering the cost. Lastly, they release the idea and take their dog for a walk, free of worry. Suddenly, a potential and viable answer appears for them from an unlikely place.

When a woman is nurturing an unborn child, we can use scientific means to measure the child's health, sex and even their future personality characteristics through identifying and classifying patterns of DNA. Yet, we do not know the full mystery. We do not know all the twists and turns this child's life will hold. Will they grow up to be a leader in their field or a person who never reaches their full fruition?

Synchronicity is the same way as this unborn child. We do not know what outcome it holds for us. We only recognize that it is there and it has certain attributes. We follow those clues like we are on the yellow brick road, looking for someone or something to show us, tell us what to do next, where to go next.

Sometimes, we realize in the end that there is no place like home. We realize that we had the answers all along deep within ourselves. Synchronicity is a teacher and a catalyst that urges us to follow its clues. It helps us make the connections, showing us the way down our path.

There are several synchronicities chronicled in my book *Dreaming Synchronicity - Journey of an Empath.* In my life experience, synchronicity has been a guidance system. Often, it has provided urgings or warnings, especially through dreams. While my dream may have been precognitive in nature, certain things would occur that day after awakening that correlated ... or more like collided with the dream to produce a synchronicity.

Often on a regular basis, synchronicity allows me to know if I am on track with how I am progressing forward. For each of us to enhance our ability to experience this enigmatic force, I believe the following attributes attract it more often.

Surrender Under Duress — When I have experienced an extreme situation in my life that found me under great personal stress, I have often been driven to the point of surrendering the problem to God/Goddess/All That Is. In that state, I feel I opened a door by asking for help from this higher Source that loves us so much. This has never been for anything that was not profoundly significant to me. Each time I have surrendered and asked for help, I had things happen that were at the least very coincidental to what one could easily call a miracle. In fact, I attribute the fact that I lived and became the person I am now due to divine intervention. I was rescued from sex trafficking as a teen and one man who had participated actually went to my home and admitted to my mother and the police that he had taken me, letting them know the city I could be found in. Surrendering our troubles that we cannot humanly fix to our higher Source opens the desire dialogue with that higher power. Do not forget to ask for help ... to be shown what you need to do next. This often leads to miracles.

Anticipate Guidance — While synchronicities that may occur in my daily life are not nearly as dire or dramatic, they always make me smile as they further solidify my belief in this feedback system. I keep an eye out for synchronicity in my life, I also write down these happenings so that I have a record. I hold a feeling inside me that when I need to know something, an occurence will happen that will reveal things to me. I have an overall trust that I am really not walking blindly in life. Nor do I walk my life path solely with an analytical, scheduled plan. While that can be important for time management and self accountability, I give more weight to flashes of intuition and synchronistic moments that occur. Again, I know I am being guided for my highest good on what to move toward or what to move away from. This is because synchronicity can often warn us about events also.

Respect The Feedback System — Synchronicity provides clues to us that something is working or not. In that way, it is helping to guide via a system that is striving to give confirmation or warning. I believe when we respect the fact we are gifted with this feedback, we ultimately receive more of it. I try to constantly be mindful and anticipate that coincidences will reveal to me when something is a yes or a no. While I have discernment and strong intuition, I can be wrong or blinded by other things. Synchronicity is a trusted feedback for me to know with certainty.

Let Synchronicity Be — Do not try to over analyze and break down what makes synchronicity occur or actually work. This is like trying to dissect a fantastic sexual experience with your partner. There are so many dynamics working underneath and behind the scenes to make it what it is. Why ruin the feeling? Just bask in the sun and feel blessed to have this amazing feedback system. When it comes to synchronicity, you have to decide if you are going to be the dancer or the choreographer. The dancer has more fun and can add steps the choreographer never thought of. The choreographer is focused on the steps.

Feel Gratitude — Synchronicity seems circular or spiral like in nature much of the time. There could be some sort of sacred geometry behind it. Just feel tremendous gratitude that you are a loved soul in this huge experience and you have synchronicity as a system of guidance. When we look back in time and appreciate the synchronicities of the past, we are able to see that without certain things happening, we would not be where, who or what we are now.

Living with and experiencing synchronicity is our natural state. We think or ask and it occurs. We are in our flow and synchronicity is a teacher of sorts. It is showing us that something was meant to happen in the pattern or fashion it occurred or not. We may not understand all of the reasons. Yet, always synchronicity serves as that guidepost to let you know that you needed to connect with that person who you thought of just moments before and who called you out of the blue.

Honor your own coincidences that you know have meaning to your situation and are indeed what can be termed a synchronicity. While skeptics may not respect your view, you do not live your life for them, do you? Some people feel more comfortable having some sort of overwhelming scientific proof for everything. I doubt you are one of those people or you would not be reading this.

We know that some things happen that are way, way beyond coincidence. I see synchronicity as elusive. If you tried to reach out and grab it, you cannot. It has to come to you. Yet, you set up the conditions to be an attractor of it. You need to be a lightening rod for synchronicity. You have a magnetic pole into the earth and where electricity strikes — where they meet — that's where the synchronicity happens.

The most natural way I know of to attract it is just a real belief and trust in it coupled with an anticipation that it will happen for you when you need it. Hold a trust in your background programming that says the right thing is coming to me. I will meet the right people at the right time. Everything will work out. This mental framework that you can program into your brain is very conducive to attracting synchronicity. Affirmations work extremely well for this type of reprogramming of thoughts. Use recorded affirmations liberally when you are doing mundane tasks with earbuds.

Steps to Embracing Synchronicity

Clarification

We need to know what it is that we want. Some people are driven and already know their purpose. Many are still searching, wondering what they can do that will give them a sense of fulfillment. Still others are on a wheel like a hamster moving through the same motions each day in a repetitive state of motion and never question there is anything more. In some cases, they feel afraid to have these deep questions as they may lead to them leaving their safe way they have been conducting themselves in the world.

A very specific clarification is ideal, yet you may find that you need to leave room, even within this wanting, for better things to arise for yourself. Often, there are surprises in our future that we did not anticipate. Almost always, our higher self has something for us greater than we expected.

If you are still searching for your purpose, do not feel there is anything wrong with you. You have grown up in a society where you are encouraged to be something other than what you really are. From a young age, the messages we receive are that the world knows who we should be and how we should act, even what we should feel. These messages are subtle and more powerful because they are subdued and registering at a certain level within our brains.

Tell yourself: Each day, I am moving toward my true higher purpose in this life. I recognize the signs along the way and my intuition assists me constantly as I stop and listen to it. My good can never be kept from me and I see the value of all situations I encounter.

Keep your notebook handy and spend as many hours or days as needed in getting clear about what you do want in your life. Remember to leave what you want open ended. In other words, if you want a relationship with a certain person, this would be closed ended. Instead, keep it open to having the best, highest relationship you could have happen in your life. After you have a written idea of what you want, go to the next step which is:

Ask

Some say that help is there just for the asking. I believe this also. There are many ways to ask. You can begin with an inquiry to yourself. Many people have questions they are unsure of or have no solution for. Try writing your question on a piece of paper and placing it under your pillow at night. Then, mentally ask for a dream that will show you the answer to your question. Repeat each night until something significant happens either in a dream or your waking life that points you in the direction you need for your answer.

Begin a meditation with your question and go forward with your practice. In the silence, you may hear a clear answer. Pray to be shown a clear answer to your question and then let it go with a sense of assurance and faith that you will be led to the right answer. If this is something you are very emotionally attached to, it could make things more difficult. By letting the outcome or answer go out of your mind and focusing on other things, you open the door for your answer to appear.

Become The Receiver

Now that you have asked to be shown, open yourself to receiving the answers. Notice intuitive thoughts instead of ignoring that voice within you. Notice the smaller synchronicities such as contact from someone you have not heard from for many years, but had just thought of within the past few hours. Perhaps, you will receive an email with just the right information you were looking for. Follow all of those bread crumbs. When your intuition tells you to take a different route home, go ahead and do that. You may miss a traffic jam or see something along the road that sparks you into another action.

Feed your right brain. Be consciously aware that you need to get out of busy mode at various times and do a little daydreaming or put yourself into a creative project of some sort. What about your visualization process? Can you practice that for five minutes as you take some time for you?

Utilize Intention

Turn the high beams on your headlights toward your goals as you write down your desires as if they have already happened. Recite them to yourself, putting a lot of emotion behind each desire. See yourself getting that job or raise, making your next physical or spiritual goal with ease. Feel how happy you will be with this accomplishment.

Entering the secret chamber of true contentment and fulfillment is as easy as dropping your perceptions of "what is" currently. Conjure the feelings you will experience when you have received what you want. These emotions are the food, the fuel that drives intention to fruition. Ignore the current reality momentarily as you daydream and focus on the feelings you want to experience when you have your wishes fulfilled.

Gratitude

For awhile, many people were posting something each day they were grateful for on social media. Holding feelings of gratitude raises your vibration significantly because it changes your attitude. By posting in a journal or even online, you can chronicle over a year or more everything you have to feel grateful about. Gratitude is a powerful igniter for change. You are changing your focus with it and allowing better things into your life. Gratitude can be an attractor of synchronicities so try to be in that state often. Bless your circumstances as wondrous or chances for growth.

Number Sequences

Often, we wonder if number sequences experienced have real meaning. Are they just another set of digits on a license plate, sign or clock or do they mean more? I would guess that much of this depends upon frequency and what is going on around you just prior or during the event of viewing the numbers. Because you can just happen to look at the clock and it says 12:12, but you also saw it at 11:49 and 12:04 because you are a clock watcher.

However, I know in my own case, I am not one who watches the clock. The fact that when I do look at it, I often see a set of repetitive digits is somehow significant to me. I also explore this idea by asking what I was doing or thinking just prior to seeing the number sequence. To be fair, we must also ask how many other numbers we saw that have no relation to this, as in people who watch the clock.

I noticed around 2008 or 2009 that people on social media were reporting the number phenomenon frequently, especially 11:11. We were coming up on the Mayan calendar year when something significant was supposed to happen. If we go back to the definition of a synchronicity, we see that the event must have real significance to the observer of that event. And, should be astronomically high for it to occur randomly.

As far as meaning goes, this is where you create your own interpretation of what repetitive numbers mean or adopt the meaning others have brought forth. But an overall reaching theme of these numbers would be that they are showing a certain alignment of something as they are all identical and equal. It is a tuning into something greater than human self.

Further, this definitely reaches beyond numbers. Let's say you are deeply aligned with a particular flower. Perhaps it is your favorite or was loved by someone close to you. If it is a lily, each time you see that flower or hear the name or word lily, you may find this is a way the universe is speaking to you or giving you feedback. You can program your higher self to provide you clues by making certain names, objects, symbols or shapes relevant to you. Then, when you experience them, you do the same exercise of stopping and identifying what is going on with you at that moment. What were you thinking of or doing just prior to hearing the name Lily?

There are also number patterns that are not identical that hold meaning for some also. Over time, I came up with the meaning of these numbers with help from others and also meditating on each set in some form. I have included that in the

Appendix. By all means, assign meanings that resonate with you.

Notes – Thoughts – Ideas – Affirmations – Dreams

Where Are Our Shamans?

"The great leaders are like the best conductors - they reach beyond the notes to reach the magic in the players."
~ Blaine Lee

One early morning in January of 2019, I saw the relationship between our increasing dependency on the Internet and codependency. It is a trap whereby we are giving up our power for something we perceive is giving to us, but ultimately is seeking to absorb us into itself. Like falling into a giant black hole, it consumes our creativity and relationships with one another. Most of us do not see it happening. At times, we may have a glimpse of this complex situation we find ourselves in now. It has become a situation where the Internet is a necessity, not an extra tool or frill.

If the world ends up utilizing free energy, it will probably occur by having one huge netted source running it. We need to be co-creating with the true God Source of this entire uni or multiverse — not just an artificial system that purports to control by knowing what is best for us. We need to be co-creating with each other via our powerful thoughts and not allowing an oligarchy system to police our thoughts. We need to put our hands together and get greasy in the engine of life. How different would life be if we notice the flecks of paint on our fingernails from our last personal masterpiece we created, instead of something that popped out of a simulator? Can artificial intelligence create the sea? Can it create a mountain or the stars? Only in a digital format that can easily fall away if the grid goes down. We are giving up our human sovereignty to our handlers. The Internet is the initial net we have been captured in.

We are often so infected by this codependency that we cannot pick it apart — fail to see it. Unknowingly, we fool ourselves that we are the victor having the power of the Internet at our fingertips or voice command. This is truer for our millennial born generation, but all of us have fallen under the spell of this technology. This piece of writing will have touched the Internet numerous times before you read it. Newspapers and bookstores are struggling to stay open or have closed up shop. It is ironic that I now have to criticize the very source I will use to share these words with you.

How do we utilize the vast resources of the Internet and keep it from swallowing us whole? Ultimately, I do not know for sure that we can. But if I had to take a stab at where to start, it would follow the same sequence people follow to eliminate codependency. We must be the master of it and not allow it to make us its slave. We need to speak up, speak out and decide what is helpful to us and what is not. We must look at this not out of helpful conveniences only, because within those confines, it can be harmful over time.

First, we need to set some boundaries. Boundaries with data collection procedures, data mining, spying, etc. If those boundaries are breached, what are the consequences to those who have done so? There must be stiff penalties for digital aggression, not just offering free credit monitoring.

Second, we need to learn to detach in a huge way. How often do we touch and read a real physical book? Do we really need a refrigerator that keeps track of what we purchase and digitally sends out our grocery order? How dependent are we on technology? A good test is to see what happens when the electricity is out for a time period — even three hours. It is then that we realize how incredibly wrapped up we are in the matrix that has been created here.

As I remind my daughter, in my human voice, to put a hat on the baby as she leaves, I wonder if we are not replacing our own parents with Suri and Cortana. Will we eventually reach a stage where we don't need each other? Will we live where we simply perform our tasks robotically as we are reminded by our speech assistant? How will we have empaths working with the super fine energy of the cosmos when they are bombarded with the static of a denser digital signature? Who will be our future shamans? This is all something to think about and make a plan for. Because advanced technology continues to arrive, entrenching us deeper into learned thoughtlessness. Hopefully, we will not allow it to take our children into helpless states of a human being overly influenced by a consensus of programming in this matrix. In other words, we cannot let this digital force steal our free will, free thought and creativity. Once that happens, we lose our magic.

Notes – Thoughts – Ideas – Affirmations – Dreams

Geo-Politics

"Courage and perseverance have a magical talisman, before which difficulties disappear and obstacles vanish into air."
~ John Quincy Adams

Releasing heaviness we take on from geopolitical situations is paramount to staying in our role and position as magical empaths. Each day, points of view that are highly polarized are happening in our world. These opinions are constantly pumped out by the media. Much of it falls into a category of propaganda that serves an overall purpose to control the story of our lives. That is why we often hear politicians and media use the word 'narrative'. It is a euphemism for the story they want us to repeat and believe. They know if it is repeated enough, we will believe it. It is like a spell they cast upon our minds.

In today's world, humans are constantly bombarded with information and programming. This is taking place by other humans who control the consensus version of reality. When we consider that all major media for television, Internet, newspapers and radio are owned by a few small corporations, it is easy to see why they are all saying the same things each day. Pay attention – or you may already know since you are very intuitive. Each day, there are two to three main news stories that are continually repeated. Flip stations and you will hear the same buzz words repeatedly. There is little to no variation on this with major media. It is as if someone is controlling what they should focus and talk about each day.

For many people, if they did not read it in an academic textbook, peer reviewed article, government document or on a major news source, it's not real. You, as an empath, are blessed as you develop your discernment and do not fall under the spell of the mass manipulation that is occurring.

If we can detach and see it as such, we have a much better chance of retaining our personal power and goals. It is necessary to pull the plug on much of what goes on around us, but is actually far away from our physical location.

As I finish up Book I and bring it to you, fires have consumed a great deal of Australia. Certainly, for the people there, the situation is real. Several earthquakes have caused damage and havoc in the Carribean.

There are numerous political situations going on in a power struggle that seems never ending in many countries across the world. The current President of the United States is hated by many and this has become a rotting emotional situation that I have seen affect even those in the spiritual community.

I have lived through many presidents I did not care for. In the United States and many other countries, we have elections. Leadership and things change according to the majority and the rules in place. I noticed that Baba Ram Dass had a ritual table in his home in Hawaii that held photographs of President Obama and President Trump. While he said he did not vote for Trump, he said he loves both of them daily.

Love, my fellow empaths, is something we must have for all, not just those we find palatable. It is all about how we focus so that we can achieve more balance and continue what we came here to do. If we are focused on disdain and hate of an individual while on our spiritual path, we are going to clog our engines. Yes, we may still have opinions, positions and stand in our own power. There is nothing wrong with peaceful demonstrations. However, we must not seek to control others or spew hatred as this hurts everyone, most of all those who engage in it.

Earth is going through a turbulent time with the shift from third to fourth density. To make the jump, we are needed now more than ever to hold and project a loving energy from our hearts. The coming years will reveal a new renaissance when we see science and spiritual proofs of connection. I know they are coming soon. Yet, we could also see fanaticism, hatred, dis-ease, war and destruction. Let us hold regular daily or weekly meditations to heal the intense emotions circling the planet. Let us see the earth healing herself and celebrate as creative entrepreneurs find new ways to clean our oceans, waterways, land and air. Let us manifest a beautiful, loving environment around each other. This is the way that is needed.

We are here to be healers, thought leaders, positive influences, teachers, students, truth seekers and magic makers. If we allow ourselves to take on the emotions of the entire world, we will fail. We are human and cannot handle that type of response to all the turmoil presented. With so much darkness, we must take care to make sure our own lights burn bright. With self-regulation of our own circumstances, we stand the highest chance of being magical empaths that have something of real value to lend to those in need. That can come in many different forms from creative endeavors like speaking, writing, leading and teaching. Problems can often be repaired or eased with money, so let's make sure we totally embrace our own worth so that we accumulate wealth to share as we see fit.

This first book has been focused upon performing the final clearing and healing we need to move forward. In the second book, we will work toward a complete rebirthing process toward master manifesting and magical living. One empath cannot take on all the ills of the world. However, one empath can take on their own ills, heal them and then be able to help others. Collectively as a group, we have more positive power than we can imagine.

With love, light and gratitude to you,

Lyra

Thank you for reading this first book in *The Magical Empath* series. I wish you much success as you move magically along your path!

Yes, please leave a review of this work ☺

♥ ♥ ♥

Book II of The Magical Empath is available now

Visit Your Favorite Retailer or

Magicalempath.com
Lyraadams.com

Appendix

Fishing For Energy Technique

Stand with your feet about six inches apart and posture fairly straight. It does not have to be perfect .... That's not the point. Just stand straight with a little space between your feet. Or, if you are physically challenged, sit or lie as straight as you can comfortably. You should be relaxed and not strained. Take a few deep breaths.

Place your hand palms facing your chest, but not touching. Close your eyes and feel the energy from your body. Hold this position with eyes closed for about twenty seconds or whatever feels right to you. This can also be done with one hand instead of two. But, if you have two, use them until you feel more adept at this.

Next, quickly turn your palms outward and push. Simultaneously, imagine yourself pushing your own energy out into the world. As you do so, tell it to bring back what is out there so you can scan it. Take your hands from the push position and turn your fingers up in a receiving position. I want you to imagine that this fishing expedition is bringing you a ball of energy that you can roll around in your hands and decide what to do with it.

Visualize you are holding those emotions out from you. This little energy fishing method works very well but may take time for you to feel smooth with it. You may latch onto this immediately.

If you practice this, you will learn to move about in the world not taking the problems of others inside you so much. Of course, you may not want to do the actual physical movements around others. Again, if you practice this, you will find that you can do it all through your mind. And, it works just as well.

The physical movements are only to lay down memory lanes for you to accomplish this mentally. Practice!

The next time you walk into a room or situation where things feel stressful or uneasy to you, visualize catching that energy in your hand and dispensing of it how you see fit. Here are some ideas:

- Mentally toss the energy out of a window or door
- Mentally toss it back where it came from
- Mentally transform the energy with white hot light and watch it begin to melt and then turn into butterflies

Aura and Space Clearing/Cleansing Shamanic Smudging of Body

For this technique, a bundle of specific herbs are used. Basically, you light one end of the bundle or stick, holding the safe opposite unlit end. Allow it to burn momentarily, and then blow it out releasing smoke. This is the same as lighting an incense stick — which can also be used in a pinch. It is advised and helpful to have a separate vessel that you can place the hot smoldering end of the stick or bundle into. Many people use an abalone shell with a little sand inside to absorb the heat. Smudge bowls can be made from many items you have on hand or a special one purchased just for this use.

Hold the smoking bundle or stick and twirl it around your body. Begin at the feet, perhaps sitting down so that you can pass it around the area in a circular way. Twirl and travel up the body swirling the smoke around you. Imagine it dissolving all stress and negative patterns. Allow the smoke to chase away that which is unnecessary in your auric field. As it rises into the air, see your positive dreams and desires making their way upward. Make your wishes known!

Suggested herb bundles could contain: palo santo, sage, sweet grass, or cedar. You can also burn, in a separate vessel, a few sprigs of lavender or rosemary. Resins from frankincense or myrrh are also utilized in this way.

Practicing Psychometry or Building Skills in Clairtangency

You may use any object to practice this skill. I often use geodes, but you could also try it with pre-owned objects from auctions or thrift stores. Plants and even animals can whisper their secrets to you as well. Do this at a time when you feel balanced and with a clear mind. Purposefully, clear yourself with a few deep breaths, taking yourself into a more relaxed state.

Close your eyes softly while you hold or touch your object, animal or plant. Mentally, ask its purpose. Keep your mind still and be patient waiting for mental images, sounds, feelings or word thoughts.

This is a rewarding exercise that helps you build your intuitive skills. It may also bring you closer with the energy of the object, animal or plant. There seems to be an understanding that takes place. Have fun with it. Perhaps, take photos of the object to add to a journal you keep on this and other energy activities.

Ball of Light Technique

When you enter any situation, workplace, room or meet someone at the grocery or mall, instead of being "so nice" as you usually are, place your feet one step back from where you would normally stand. Always when we come face to face with another person that were are meeting or greeting, we tend to go a certain distance into their space ... or they into ours. Deliberately stay one or two steps back from what you would normally do. As they look at you and/or speak, imagine holding their energy just outside of yourself. See it as a ball of light or a cloud, whatever you want to imagine it as. What color is it? Does it provoke any thoughts in you? Most importantly, what are the feelings you get? Does this person's energy remind you of anyone else's energy you've ever known? That is a very important question. Remember, those that have lessons for us come around and around with different faces until we master the lesson.

Another advantage of learning to use this method is that it will make you feel a little more secure and in control of situations. Instead of you being a sponge absorbing every incoming energy, you are holding it a bay, examining it and letting it tell you more about it before you get closer. So, basically all you are doing is holding that energy that is coming toward you outside of your auric field so that you are not absorbing it so easily. If you get an icky feeling from the energy that has presented itself, make your excuses to the other person and send that light ball or cloud away. Send it back with love and compassion to the other person. Smile, say excuse me, and exit stage right to another person or situation. This may sound odd, but you have to decide if you are going to be more mindful and watchful of your own energies. You also must determine if it is more important for the other person to have their needs met or for you to have yours tended to. As empaths, we are often nice to a fault and it ends up affecting us.

Your journey to becoming the magical empath involves a shift in perception. It requires clearing away all the old patterns you have been operating under. A warrior mindset is needed in the sense that you see the way forward as something that may have a few interruptions, but ultimately results in victory. When the empath finds they are slipping back into an old way of thinking or being, they utilize course correction to get back on the road toward finding and owning their own magic.

The Poncho Experiment

Imagine a poncho that you wear covering your arms and torso. Instead of it being constructed by a thick blanket like material, see it made from a light, sheer fabric. If you are good at imagining things, pretend this poncho covers you when you are in your next situation with other people. Imagine this is your filter that nothing can pass through unless you allow it.

You may even want to wear a poncho in your home environment to practice this technique. Ponchos are easy to construct if you would like to make your own from sheer fabric. By wearing it often, it will be much easier to imagine having it on at your next meeting or gathering with others.

Creating Sacred Space

You may find it necessary and very beneficial to have a sacred space where you live to recharge and connect with Source. It does not need to be large or elaborate. Make it yours – anything you want to do. Let me give you some examples of what this space should do for you or how it can make you feel.

This is an area that is just your spot on the planet – your safe spot. The size can be tiny, small or large. It can be something in a corner, on a large table or desk, or take up quite a bit of a room. Make it the size that fits your desire and space available.

Transform your chosen area into a shrine of all you love, find comfort in and brings you joy. You may want to begin with a piece of cloth as a table cover in a color or design that pleases you. Place items in this area that make you feel happy or joyful. Items to consider are a photo of someone you really enjoy and love. It could even be a picture of you – perhaps as a child, teen or later in life.

Place a vase with your favorite flower. This could be a fresh flower that you replace every so often or a silk one you can easily obtain at so many different stores. Add something that smells good, whether it be your favorite cologne, perfume, incense, scented candle or other aromatherapy products. Place something that connects you with your spiritual or religious faith, if any. This could be images of the Buddha, Jesus Christ, Mother Mary, an angel, Goddess archetypes -- whatever is appropriate for you. If you do not subscribe to anything like this, consider a beautiful landscape photo from a place you have visited or would like to visit. You might place a picture of your favorite super hero – one that you feel closely identified with and would be if you could. Any archetype you feel drawn to.

How about adding a physical book --- one that you know you can open anywhere within it and read something valuable. I would have a notebook and pen available too. Add something soft you can hold if you want, or just stroke with your hand if you are feeling anxious. This could be a small stuffed animal, a folded baby blanket you have kept since childhood, a beanie baby that calls to your heart. And speaking of hearts, place an image of that on your table as well. How about a favorite rock, crystal, gemstone, sea shell or even a piece of jewelry that brings you joy?

These are just some ideas and I know you are going to come up with better ones, especially those that are closer to what pleases you. This sacred area must be about you and what brings you feelings of contentment.

You might want to place a soft rug in front of this area for your comfort when sitting. If you prefer sitting in a chair, maybe you have room to place it beside your special area.

Now, what is the point of this little shrine? It represents all that you love, trust and find joy in. It is also a physical place that you can touch and go to when you need to transcend what you are feeling and be in the now. This is your sacred space. It is an area that holds special meaning just for you and you only.

When you feel fearful or are experiencing any distressed feelings, go to your shrine. If possible, sit cross legged on the floor in front of your joy area. Touch and hold your items. Journal any thoughts you have at this time or speak them into a recorder on your phone.

Breathe! Through your nose, take deep, but comfortable, breaths that expand your belly. Then allow the air to blow out your mouth. In through the nose – out through the mouth. As you exhale, see all negativity in your mind's eye leaving your body. Do this several times.

If possible, play soft relaxing music that assists you in calming your inner self. Repeat in your mind. "All is well. Everything will work out for me. I may not have all the answers now, but they are coming. All is well with me."

Did you play hide and seek or chase as a child? Remember, there was always one place that was base? This is your base – your safe spot where nothing can touch you. This is your go to spot during times you need it for renewal.

The Naked Experiment

Imagine those around you in their poor moods with no clothing on. It does not matter if they are 25 or 85 years old. Just imagine this in your mind and you will find yourself smiling, almost laughing out loud. This is also a concept to use when you attend a party or event where an introverted empath may initially feel uncomfortable. Many speakers and performers have used this technique to gain more confidence by simply imagining their audience in the nude.

Sending Technique

Put your invisible or real poncho over your body and imagine the feelings of the negatively oriented people around you bouncing off of you today. Instead, send out positive, loving vibes to everyone, no matter how screwed up you previously thought they were. Just a little light, my fellow empath, just a little love can help. Visualize this as you desire. Sometimes, I imagine dark pink and emerald green heart shaped clouds coming out of my aura, floating in the air toward anyone who wants to step into one, like bubbles floating. They have the free will to decide if they want to be in your energy field or not. Keep this in mind as you watch some retreat.

Synchronicity Number Sequences

As the frequency increased and people began seeing consecutive numbers in the early twenty-first century, I compiled this list of possible meanings. This was based upon impressions during meditation and also cross checking with numerology definitions. Please utilize your own meanings as well. They always override the impressions of others as they hold significance for you.

000 – Be still and listen. Receptive Yin Energy
111 – Yes, go ahead. Active Yang Energy
222 – Balance & Partnership
333 – Balance Mind-Body-Spirit
444 – Angels Watching Over Me
555 – Beneficial Change – Drop resistance and go with flow
666 – Progress upward on the spiral of life
777 – Believe – You are co-creating with the Divine
888 – Abundance and Mastery
999 – Completion – Ready to Jump To Next Level

11:11 – Cosmic Confirmations – A Big Yes from the Universe. Can also be seen frequently by those who are awakening on their spiritual path

1234 – Everything is working out as planned

Notes – Thoughts – Ideas – Affirmations – Dreams

Bibliography

(Screenplay), N. P. (Writer), & Ruben, J. (Director). (1991). *Sleeping With The Enemy* [Motion Picture].

Abdul Saad, B. (. (n.d.). Retrieved from Vital Mind Psychology: https://vitalmind.com.au

Bekkali, S. Y.-U. (2019, March 20). Is the Putative Mirror Neuron System Associated with Empathy? A Systematic Review and Meta-Analysis. *PsyArXiv*, 1-87. Retrieved from https://psyarxiv.com/6bu4p/

Buck, C., Lee, J., Morris, S. (Writers), Buck, C., & Lee, J. (Directors). (2013). *Frozen* [Motion Picture]. Retrieved from https://www.imdb.com/title/tt2294629/?ref_=ttco_co_tt

David R. Hawkins, M. P. (2014). *Power vs. Force*. Hay House Inc.

Dean Radin, P. (2018). *Real Magic: Ancient Wisdom, Modern Science, and a Guide to the Secret Power of the Universe* (1st ed.). Harmony Div. Penguin Random House.

Dr. Stefan Röpke, e. a. (2013, June 19). *Altered brain structure in pathological narcissism*. Retrieved from ScienceDaily.com: https://www.sciencedaily.com/releases/2013/06/130619101434.htm

Gawain, S. (1978). *Creative Visualization* (1 ed.). New World Library.

Initiates, T. (2012). *The Kybalion: A Study of The Hermetic Philosophy of Ancient Egypt and Greece*. Rough Draft Printing.

Judith, A. (1987). *Wheels of Life: A User's Guide To The Chakra System* (1 ed.). Llewellyn Publications; 1st edition.

Lucas, G., Johnson, R. (Writers), & Johnson, R. (Director). (2017). *Star Wars: Episode VIII - The Last Jedi*

[Motion Picture]. Retrieved from https://www.imdb.com/title/tt2527336/?ref_=fn_al_tt_1

Psychology Today. (2019, February 26). *Antisocial Personality Disorder.* Retrieved from Psychology Today: https://www.psychologytoday.com/us/conditions/antisocial-personality-disorder

Schmitt, K., Grimm, A., Dallmann, R., Oettinghaus, B., Restelli, L. M., Witzig, M., . . . Eckert, A. (2018, March 6). Circadian Control of DRP1 Activity Regulates Mitochondrial Dynamics and Bioenergetics. *Cell Metabolism, 27*(3), 657-666. doi:https://doi.org/10.1016/j.cmet.2018.01.011

Tolkien (Author), J. R., Walsh (Screenplay), F., Boyens (Screenplay), P., Jackson (Screenplay), P. (Writers), & Jackson, P. (Director). (2001). *The Lord of the Rings: The Fellowship of the Ring* [Motion Picture]. Retrieved from https://www.imdb.com/title/tt0120737/?ref_=ttls_li_tt

What is Cortisol? (2018, Nov.). Retrieved from Hormone Health Network: https://www.hormone.org/your-health-and-hormones/glands-and-hormones-a-to-z/hormones/cortisol

www.ingramcontent.com/pod-product-compliance
Lightning Source LLC
Chambersburg PA
CBHW071955290426
44109CB00018B/2024